JUNIOR COURSE
OF
ENGLISH COMPOSITION

JUNIOR COURSE
OF
ENGLISH COMPOSITION

BY

J. C. NESFIELD, M. A.

GYAN

Published by

Gyan Publishing House
5, Ansari Road
Daryaganj, New Delhi-110002
Phone: 011-47034999, 9811692060
E-mail: books@gyanbooks.com

Distribution Network
gyanbooks.com
India, USA, Canada, UK, Australia

ISBN: 978-93-6208-789-8 (HB)
First Published, 1901

2nd Impression 2024

Printed at: Gyan Press, Delhi.

JUNIOR COURSE OF ENGLISH COMPOSITION
Author: J. C. NESFIELD

JUNIOR COURSE

OF

ENGLISH COMPOSITION

BY

J. C. NESFIELD, M.A.

AUTHOR OF 'ENGLISH GRAMMAR, PAST AND PRESENT,' 'MANUAL OF ENGLISH GRAMMAR AND COMPOSITION,' ETC.

MACMILLAN & CO., LIMITED

ST. MARTIN'S STREET, LONDON

NEW YORK: THE MACMILLAN COMPANY

1901

PREFACE

THE purpose or purposes for which this "Junior Course of English Composition" has been prepared can be seen partly from the title and partly from the table of contents.

In Chapter I., headed the Reproduction of Extracts, we give examples of the kind of composition prescribed for the upper classes at Board Schools, for the Local Examinations held by Oxford and Cambridge respectively in their "Preliminary" standard, and for the Government Examinations of Pupil-teachers at Training Schools.[1] These exercises all consist in requiring the student to reproduce, from memory, but in his own words, the substance of extracts, which he has either studied in class, or has heard read out to him without any such previous study, immediately before he begins to write.

Such exercises presuppose, as we need scarcely add, that he has been already grounded in the main principles and inflections of English Grammar, and has gone through an earlier course of composition,—especially of that

[1] If this book should at all come into use in India, we take this opportunity of saying that the method which has been found most suitable in England for examining candidates in English composition up to the "Preliminary" standard prescribed by Oxford and Cambridge, would be found equally suitable for the "Middle Class Examinations" in the different provinces of India. Perhaps, however, this method has been adopted already in some of them.

elementary kind which consists in the forming of Simple sentences and the combining of them into longer sentences either Compound or Complex.[1]

Before introducing the student to the more difficult subjects of essay-writing and letter-writing, we have in Chapter II. attempted to show him by a few cardinal rules and examples how to write clearly and effectively, what errors are most common and therefore most to be guarded against in the use of common words and constructions, and what is the proper structure of sentences and paragraphs. In Chapter III. we have gone rather fully into the subject of punctuation, to which a great deal of importance is attached in the Local Examinations held by Oxford and Cambridge, in the examinations held by the College of Preceptors, and in the matriculation examinations of some Indian Universities. A large number of examples to be worked out by the student is attached to both chapters.

In Chapter IV., which is headed "Expansion of Outlines," we introduce the student for the first time to the subject of Essay-writing. As the first attempts in essay-writing are very difficult to a beginner, we have in all cases given him an outline to be expanded. The outlines have been arranged in the order of increasing difficulty,—the first set consisting of outlines of Æsop's Fables, the second of object-lessons taught in class (for it is assumed that object-lessons form part of the curriculum),

[1] A great deal of practice in the composition of Simple, Compound, and Complex sentences, and in applying the grammatical rules that bear upon it, has been provided in Chapters I.-IV. of a book by the same author, called *Oral Exercises in English Composition*. *Oral* practice, as distinct from written, is there recommended—(1) because it effects a very great saving in time, enabling the student to get more than four times as much practice as he could get by putting all the exercises into writing; and (2) because it stimulates quickness on the part of the student, a ready use of words, and a facility in saying what he has to say impromptu.

and the third of miscellaneous subjects descriptive or reflective. To this chapter we have appended a valuable note by Mr. Battersby on the teaching of essay-writing, which appeared in the *School World* in September 1899, and a list of subjects for composition set by Cambridge for the "Junior" Local Examination, and by Indian Universities for matriculation.

In Chapter V., the last, we have dealt with the subject of Letter-writing,—private, official, and commercial: and to the kind of letter last named we have appended a list of trade terms in common use. We have given this list, partly because we thought it might be useful to lads who are leaving school and about to take up employment in some business office, and partly because "Letter-writing and Use of Commercial Terms" is prescribed in the Oxford Syllabus for the Junior Examination as an alternative to the composition of an essay.

J. C. NESFIELD.

CONTENTS

CHAP.			PAGE
1.	REPRODUCTION OF EXTRACTS		1
	Section 1.	Prose Extracts read and studied in Class	1
	,, 2.	Prose Extracts not read or studied in Class	19
		Examples from Cambridge Preliminary Examinations	19
		Examples from Government Examinations of Pupil-teachers	23
	,, 3.	Poetry read and studied in Class	27
		Specimens of Poetry reproduced in Substance	28
		Examples for Practice	34
2.	GENERAL HINTS ON WRITTEN COMPOSITION		43
	Section 1.	How to Write Clearly and Effectively	43
		Four sets of Exercises on Section 1	53
	,, 2.	Common Errors in Common Words and Constructions	59
		Exercise on Section 2	69
	,, 3.	Sentence and Paragraph	74
		Exercise on Section 3	81
3.	PUNCTUATION, CAPITALS, SYLLABIC DIVISION, UNDERLINING		83
	Section 1.	Punctuation, or the Use of Stops	83
		Three sets of Exercises on Punctuation	90, 97
	,, 2.	The Use of Capital Letters	103
	,, 3.	How to divide Words into Syllables	105
	,, 4.	When to Underline a Word	106
		Examples from Preceptors' Third Class Examination	107
		Examples from Calcutta Matriculation Papers	109

CHAP.		PAGE
4. EXPANSION OF OUTLINES: ESSAY-WRITING		110
Section 1.	Outlines of Æsop's Fables to be expanded	111
,, 2.	Outlines of Object-lessons to be expanded	117
,, 3.	Outlines of Short Essays to be expanded	130
	Note on Essay-writing from *School World*	151
	Subjects set for Essays in Cambridge Local Examinations	154
	Subjects set for Essays in Indian Matriculation Examinations	156
5. LETTER-WRITING,—PRIVATE, COMMERCIAL, AND OFFICIAL		159
Section 1.	Preliminary Remarks	159
,, 2.	Private Correspondence	166
	Specimens of Private Letters	173
	Outlines of Private Letters to be expanded	183
,, 3.	Business Correspondence	189
	Specimens of Business Letters, Notices, etc.	193
	Outlines of Business Letters to be expanded	208
	Advertisements to be answered	209
APPENDIX.—TRADE TERMS IN MORE OR LESS COMMON USE		212

CHAPTER I.—REPRODUCTION OF EXTRACTS.

SECTION 1.—PROSE EXTRACTS READ AND STUDIED IN CLASS.

1. **Method of this Section.**—For the working of the method described in the above heading it is recommended that every student in the class should have his book before him. While one student reads the selected extract aloud before the teacher, every other student should follow him with his eyes on the book. When the reading is finished, the teacher, if he thinks fit, can draw the attention of the class to one or two salient points. The extract might then be read aloud to the class a second time by another student; after which all books should be closed, and the students asked to reproduce as fully as they can the **substance** of the extract, each student doing so *in his own words.*

Note.—We lay especial stress upon the word "substance," because any attempt to reproduce the *exact* words of the original must be discouraged, or rather strictly forbidden. The lesson is intended to be an exercise in composition, not an exercise in memory.

Let the student feel assured that if the drift of the extract is mastered, the words will come. Let him know clearly what he has to say, and he is not likely to find much difficulty in saying it. If some difficulty is felt at first, it is certain that by practice it will become less and less. But if he trusts to remembering the exact words of the extract that he has heard or read, he is wasting his time and making no progress in composition.

The following rules which appeared in a recent Review are worthy of attention :—

(1) Know what you have to say.
(2) Say it.
(3) Use your own language.
(4) Leave out all fine passages.
(5) A short word is better than a long one.
(6) The fewer words, other things being equal, the better.

The time by which all papers are to be given up should be fixed by the teacher and announced beforehand. The student should have time enough allowed him not only for reproducing the substance of the extract, but for revising what he has written and putting in the necessary stops.

2. Punctuation.—The subject of punctuation will be discussed in full hereafter (see chap. iii.). Meanwhile, we give a few main rules, which the student should observe at once in all written exercises.

I. The longest division between one statement and another is called a full stop (.); and the first letter of the next sentence must be written as a capital. The full stop (or period, as it is also called) indicates that the assertion has been made in as complete a form as the writer intended to make it, and that the assertion so made is entirely distinct from any other sentence or sentences that may follow.

II. The shortest division between one part of a sentence and another is marked by a comma (,).

III. A division intermediate in length between a full stop and a comma is marked by a colon (:) or by a semi-colon (;), *i.e.* a half-colon. The latter name implies, what is the fact, that the colon marks the longer pause of the two. Where a colon is used, it indicates that the construction is complete, but that something has still to be said, without which the full force of the foregoing remark will not be felt. A semi-colon indicates a closer connection either of construction or of meaning between two clauses than that indicated by a colon.

IV. A sentence which asks a question ends with a note of interrogation (?). The first letter of the next sentence must be written as a capital.

V. A sentence which is so constructed as to express some strong feeling of the mind ends with a note of admiration (!). The first letter of the next sentence must be written as a capital.

VI. A sentence which consists of words spoken by some one or quoted from what some one has written must be enclosed in commas ("———").

Exercises on Section 1.—*Specimens of Extracts to be reproduced in Substance.*[1]

1. *A Child rescued by a Pony.*

A little girl, playing one day in her father's grounds, fell into a stream that flowed through the estate. The part of the brook into which she had fallen was deep enough to drown her, and there was no one near to pull her out or give her a helping hand. But a small pony, which the children of the house were especially fond of riding, and which had become a great pet amongst them, happened to be grazing on the rich grass that grew on the bank. The cries of its little mistress fell on its ears. Plunging into the stream, it seized her frock between its teeth, and drew her ashore with such gentleness that she was not hurt by anything worse than the fright, from which she soon recovered.

2. *A Cat routed by a Bird.*

A fledgeling, that had just left its mother's nest, and could not fly more than a few yards, was standing on the ground motionless, fixed to the spot by the fierce eyes of a cat that was crouching under a bush, ready to spring upon it at any moment. The mother-bird was watching the cat from a tree close by. Suddenly the cat sprang upon the young bird and held it down with one of her front paws without killing it, as a cat often holds down a mouse before devouring it. At the same instant the mother-bird swooped down on the cat's head. There was a

[1] The following extract from "Instructions to H.M. Inspectors of Schools" may perhaps be generally useful. "In Standard V. the passage selected for writing from memory should be an anecdote occupying from ten to fifteen lines of ordinary length, and containing some sufficiently obvious *point* or simple moral. Neither accuracy in spelling nor excellence in writing should secure a pass, unless the exercise is an intelligent reproduction of the story."

struggle for a moment or two, the old bird flapping its wings violently in the cat's face and threatening to peck her eyes out. The cat was so startled that she jumped back into the bush. The fledgeling, being released, hopped off as fast as it could, while several other birds who had watched this event fluttered around it with so much noise and excitement, that it had time to escape before the cat was able to recover her courage and pounce upon it again.

3. *A Dog baffled by a Fox.*

A fox pursued by a dog took its course along the channel of an ice-bound river, hoping to find on the bank some hole into which it could flee for refuge. Instead of finding a hole in the bank, it came suddenly upon a large hole in the ice, and any one looking on would have thought that the fox would run into it and be drowned. But the fox saw the danger in the nick of time, and turning suddenly round the edge of the hole, reached the further side and continued its flight on the solid ice as fast as it could. Meanwhile the dog was on its track and was rapidly gaining ground. Trusting as dogs do to scent rather than to sight, it kept its nose an inch or two above the snow-covered ice, without looking where it was going or caring what might lie in front of it, so long as it followed the scent. Darting along at full speed, it fell straight into the hole, before it had time to pull itself up and take a turn round, as the fox had done. It was borne along under the ice by the current of the river, and was never seen again.

4. *A Boy asking to be Shaved.*

A boy of Corinth, named Glaucus, was fond of assuming the airs of a grown-up man: he wore a man's dress in public, and was in the habit of shaving, or pretending to shave, his downy cheeks. One day, with an air of great importance, he strode into the shop of a well-known barber, and with a loud voice ordered the barber to shave his beard. The barber was fond of a joke, but appeared to take the order quite seriously. He got the hot water ready, seated the boy on a chair, lathered his chin, and sharpened the razor. Having made all these preparations, he quietly walked away to the door of his shop, and stood there chatting with a friend. The boy bore this behaviour patiently for a while; then, losing all control of himself, he turned angrily to the barber and asked him in a loud voice what he was waiting for. The barber, with the utmost gravity and composure, replied, "I am waiting for your beard."

5. *How a Fox caught a Wild Duck.*

A fox had made its home among some rocks near the bank of a lake. One evening, seeing a number of wild ducks in the middle of the lake, and being very hungry, he said to himself, "There's my dinner, if I could only get hold of one of them." Creeping up to the water's edge, he noticed that the wind carried bits of moss and heather towards the middle of the lake where the ducks were feeding, bobbing their heads in the water. Tearing off bigger and bigger pieces of moss and dropping them on the surface of the lake, he saw them float among the ducks without causing any alarm. Then tearing off a much larger piece, and finding that this too floated in the same direction, he entered the water and followed it, concealing his head and body behind it as well as he could. When the moss reached one of the birds, the fox dived, seized the bird from below, and swam with it ashore.—*Little Folks*, 1892, p. 277.

6. *The Brahman who distrusted his own Eyes.*

A Brahman had bought a goat, and was carrying it away on his shoulder, when he was met by a man, who came up to him and said, "Sir, how is it that you, being a Brahman and a priest, carry such an impure animal as a dog on your shoulder? This is not becoming. I beg of you to put it down." The Brahman took no notice, and continued his way; but he had not gone much further before he was met by two other men, who rebuked him in similar terms for carrying a dog. At this the Brahman was much astonished, but went on as before, carrying the goat on his shoulder. Presently, three more men came up and said, "How is it that you carry that dog? Surely you must be a hunter and not a Brahman, and that is the dog with which you hunt your game." The Brahman by this time was so astounded that he threw the goat down, saying to himself, "Surely some demon has smitten my sight and made me see things wrongly." The men, who had planned this trick, took up the goat and made their supper off it.—*Indian Story.*

7. *An Elephant's Revenge.*

An Indian tailor, whose small shop opened on the street, and, like most Indian shops, had no glass window to protect it, was squatting on a small wooden dais, making some very fine clothes. An elephant, that happened to be passing along towards a river, put in its trunk, not meaning to do any harm, but begging apparently for a biscuit. The tailor, from the mere love of mischief, pricked the end of the trunk with a needle, which gave the poor animal a good deal of pain; for the trunk is the most sensitive part of an elephant's body. The elephant hastily withdrew, and jogged along toward the river to take a drink of water. Having satisfied its thirst, it took up a large quantity of water into its trunk and mouth, and reappeared at the tailor's window, where, holding its trunk well inside the shop, it discharged all the water over the tailor, spoiled the fine clothes he was working at, and made him the laughing-stock of his neighbours.—*Indian Story.*

8. *A Stag caught by his own Horns.*

A stag, while quenching his thirst in a clear lake, was struck with the beauty of his horns, the shadow of which he saw in the water. Observing at the same time how slender his legs were, he said to himself, "What a fine creature I should be, if only my legs were as grand as my horns!" In the midst of these thoughts he was suddenly disturbed by the barking of hounds and by the shouts of huntsmen. Seeing his danger, he ran off at full speed, bounding over the plain, and left the dogs and huntsmen so far behind, that he would have escaped, if he had kept to the open country. But, instead of doing this, he rushed into a thick wood, where his horns were caught in the branch of a tree. Here he was held fast, till the hounds came up and seized him. The legs which he despised would have saved him; the horns of which he was so proud brought him to destruction.

9. *The Loss of the "Royal George."*

The loss of the *Royal George*, a fine ship mounted with a hundred guns, occurred at Spithead, near Portsmouth. Everything had been put on board, and she was about to start, when it was discovered that the water-pipes were out of order. To repair the pipes, the commander did not take the ship into dock, but made her heel over to one side by moving the guns, till that part of the hull where the pipes were placed was raised high enough above water. The repairs had been completed, and the guns were about to be replaced, when a large open boat, containing many casks of rum, came alongside to deliver the cargo. The port-holes were already nearly touching the water; but when the men began to take the casks of rum on board, depositing them on that side of the ship which was nearest the water, the vessel heeled over more and more. A breeze suddenly sprang up, and the waves caused by the breeze began to rush into the port-holes. An order was then given by the officer in charge to put the guns back in their right places. The men scrambled down through the hatchway to carry out the order. But it was too late. The vessel filled rapidly and went down, carrying with her the admiral, Kempenfeldt (who was at that time writing in his cabin), all the officers, all the crew, and a large company of visitors, making in all nearly a thousand souls.

10. *An Elephant's Patience.*

An elephant at Calcutta had a disease in its eyes, and for three days it was completely blind. The mahout or driver asked an English doctor if he could do anything to restore the elephant's sight, and relieve the animal of pain. The doctor said he would try the same remedy as that commonly applied to similar diseases in the human eye. The huge animal was made to lie down; and at first, on the application of the remedy, it raised an extraordinary roar at the acute pain which it felt. The effect, however, was wonderful. The eye was in a manner restored, and the animal could partially see. Next day, when it was brought again and heard the doctor's voice, it lay down of itself, placed its enormous head on one side, curled up its trunk, drew in its breath just like a man about to endure a surgical operation, gave a sigh of relief when it was over, and then, by trunk and gesture, evidently wished to show its gratitude. What sagacity! What a lesson to us in patience!—*Bishop Wilson's Journal.*

11. *Personal Influence.*

When Mr. Stopford Brooke was collecting materials for his *Life of Robertson*, a curious little incident occurred which enabled him to realise how much Robertson was respected by those amongst whom he had lived. To collect information he had gone to Bristol, the city in which Mr. Robertson had ministered for the few years of his adult life. In the course of his inquiries he called on a tradesman, who had known Mr. Robertson and was fond of hearing his sermons and addresses.

The tradesman took Mr. Brooke into the parlour at the back of the shop and showed him a portrait of the preacher, which he kept hung over his mantelpiece. "There," said he, "whenever I am tempted to do anything that is not fair or right in the little business which I carry on in the shop, I step into this parlour and look at that picture; and the memory of his words and looks makes me for his sake scorn to do anything mean."—*Little Folks*, 1892, p. 278.

12. *The Bear and the two Travellers.*

Two men set out together on a journey; and as they were travelling on foot and without any protection, they agreed that if any danger occurred on the road, each would stand by the other. As they were going along, they saw a bear coming towards them. One of them ran off, climbed up a tree, and hid himself in the branches. The other threw himself flat on the ground and pretended to be dead; for he had heard that bears would not touch a dead body. The bear came up, felt him all over with his snout, and seeing no signs of life (for the man held his breath while the bear was snuffling at him), passed on and left him. The other traveller, when he saw that all danger was over, came down from the tree, and congratulated his friend on his cleverness. "But tell me," said he in joke, "what did the bear whisper in your ear? for he held his snout so close to your face that he seemed to be telling you some secret." "He cautioned me," said the other, "never again to travel with a friend who, after promising to stand by me in time of danger, leaves me in the lurch when danger comes, thinking of no one's safety but his own."

13. *A Man caught by his own Sharpness.*

A distinguished lawyer, named Roscius, was watching the performance of some public games in Rome, when a rustic—who, however, was anything but a rustic in sharpness—came up to him and said: "Give me your advice, O most distinguished Roscius, on the following point. A dog belonging to a wealthy neighbour of mine entered my field and carried off three of my fowls. What fine do you think I should impose on the owner of that dog?" "Fine him four silver pieces," answered Roscius. "I will do so," said the rustic: "give me therefore the four silver pieces; for yours was the dog that killed my fowls." "It is most equitable," answered Roscius, "I will gladly pay you the four coins: but you must first pay me five; for lawyers do not give advice without being paid for it."

14. *The Last Words of William Pitt.*

We are always interested to know what were the last words spoken by eminent men and women. Perhaps we attach an undue importance to them; for the last words are not always the most weighty, and they are not always correctly recorded; for when the voice of the patient is failing, his words may be misunderstood. A curious example of this is given by Lord Rosebery in his *Life of William Pitt*, the illustrious statesman who was Prime Minister of England during the greater part of the long struggle between England and Napoleon Bonaparte. He died in 1806, about seven weeks after the battle of Austerlitz, in which Napoleon had crushed the armies of Austria and Russia. The news of the battle was a very great shock to him. The last words usually ascribed to him are—"Oh, my country! How I *love* my country!" Lord Rosebery, however, has shown that the words were misreported, and that the last words really were—"Oh, my country! How I *leave* my country!" He was thinking of the terrible struggle that lay before England, engaged as she was almost single-handed against the overwhelming power of Napoleon, who, by the victory of Austerlitz, had reached the very height of his power and made himself master of the best part of Europe.

15. *Truth spoken in Jest.*

An amusing example of truth spoken in jest occurs in the following story relating to the late Lord Hertford, who lived in Paris during the last twenty years of his life. This nobleman was in the habit of going to bed very late: his page was under the strictest orders not to disturb him, or allow any one else to disturb him, in the morning. One evening he said to his page, "I shall require an unusually long sleep to-morrow morning: nothing but an earthquake or a revolution will get me out of bed to-morrow." The page promised to attend to the order; and attend to it he did, but not in the way that either he or his master contemplated. The morrow morning, as it turned out, was the 24th February, when Louis-Philippe, the Citizen King, had to flee from Paris and take refuge in England. The page knocked at his master's door at eight o'clock, and awakened him with a great deal of excitement. "What is the matter?" said the nobleman. "A revolution, sir; I have obeyed the order you gave me. We must leave Paris as fast as we can."

16. *Requital—I. The Talkative Wife.*

The man to whom this story relates was married to a wife, who was too much inclined to leave her own house and gossip amongst her neighbours. One evening she had gone out to sup with one of her friends, and he sat up a long time waiting for her in vain. At last he gave up expecting her, locked the door, and went to bed. In the night he heard a loud thumping at the door, and a voice calling to him and saying, "Open the door; do you not hear the voice of your wife?" "Not at all," said he, "you are not my wife, nor do I know your voice; my wife is with me here in bed." She continued her entreaties for some time, but in vain. At last she said, "If you do not open the door, I will throw myself into this river." Having so said, she threw a heavy stone into the river, and stepped aside to keep out of his sight. The man, alarmed at the sound of a heavy body falling into the water, rushed out of bed and ran to the bank of the river to rescue his wife. While his back was turned, she ran into the house and locked the door. Finding that his wife had been playing him a trick, he returned to the house and demanded admission. "Begone," said she; "for you have just told me that you are not my husband."

17. *Requital—II. The Scorpion and the Tortoise.*

A tortoise had formed a strange friendship with a scorpion. As each wished to find a new home in some other place, they started on their journey together. After going some distance, they came to the bank of a stream. The scorpion now became much alarmed, since he could not swim, nor did he wish the tortoise to leave him. "Never fear," said the tortoise, "I can swim, and I will take you over on my back." The scorpion, thus reassured, placed himself on the tortoise's back, and the two entered the river together. In the middle of the river the tortoise felt a sharp pain in his neck, as if he was being pinched, and asked the scorpion if he knew what it was. "It is I who am pinching you," said the scorpion; "I was obliged to hold your neck to avoid slipping off your back. I held it lightly at first; but it is my nature, when I get anything within my claw, to give it a sharp pinch." "It is my nature," said the tortoise, "to dive down sometimes into deep water, and not to be always swimming on the top." Having so said, he dived down into the water and drowned the scorpion.—*Indian Fable.*

18. *Hasty Anger—I. Story of Beth-gelert.*

A Welsh prince, named Llewellyn, had a faithful hound named Gelert, which was fond of accompanying its master to the chase. One day, however, the dog remained behind, and took charge of its master's son, a child in the cradle. As Llewellyn returned from hunting, his favourite hound ran to meet him. The dog showed more than usual eagerness and delight at seeing its master again; and what was still more extraordinary, its mouth and neck were covered with blood. The prince, being alarmed at the sight of these blood-clots, ran into the house to see if any harm had been done to his infant son. On entering the room he called to the child, but got no answer; and instead of finding his child, he found the cradle overturned and the bed-clothes sprinkled with gore. Thinking that the dog had killed him, in a fit of blind fury he stabbed it to the heart. The dying yelp of the dog awakened the child, who was still slumbering under the bed-clothes. Not far from the upturned cradle lay the mangled body of a huge wolf, which Gelert had fought and killed in order to save the child. If dogs could learn our speech, as they learn our ways, how many things they could tell us! A stately tomb, called Beth-gelert, "the grave of Gelert," was put up in memory of the faithful hound. But Llewellyn never ceased to reproach himself for having slain so true a friend in a moment of hasty anger.—*Welsh Tradition.*

19. *Hasty Anger—II. Story of a Mongoose* (a kind of weasel, domesticated for killing snakes, rats, etc.).

In an Indian village there was a Brahman, who made his living, as many Brahmans do, by the performance of priestly rites for those amongst whom he lived. His wife, on going out to have a bathe in the neighbouring river, asked him to remain in the hut till she returned and take charge of their infant son during her absence. While the wife was still absent, a messenger came from the lord of the village, summoning the Brahman to a ceremony, at which he was to act the principal part. The prospect of receiving a liberal fee was too tempting to be resisted. So he set off at once with the messenger, leaving the child in charge of a mongoose, which he had brought up from its birth. On his return to the hut, the mongoose, stained with blood, went out to meet him. The Brahman felt certain that the mongoose had killed his child, and in a fit of anger took up a stone and crushed it to death. But when he had gone inside the hut, he found his child sleeping soundly as he had left him, and by the side of him a dead snake, which the mongoose had slain to save the child. The Brahman reproached himself bitterly for having acted so thoughtlessly. There was indeed no excuse to be made for him; for snakes often crawl into Indian huts, and a mongoose is almost the only animal that knows how to kill them.—*Hindoo Tradition.*

20. *The Effect of Trifles—I.*

Jenner was a youth pursuing his studies like any ordinary student at a medical school, when his attention was arrested by a milkmaid, who had come to a chemist's shop to buy some medicine. Smallpox, which was then raging in the neighbourhood, was mentioned. The girl said, "I can't take that disease; for I have had the cowpox." This casual remark, thrown out by a country-girl whose opinion no one would have taken, was not lost upon Jenner. A man of genius will take note of incidents, which have no effect on the ordinary observer. But Jenner was not an ordinary observer, and he left the shop with a determination to find out how cowpox could be a preventive of smallpox,—a malady which had destroyed many lives and for which no remedy had yet been found. After completing his medical studies, he returned to his native village to practise his profession and make experiments, in which he occupied himself for a period of twenty years. The result of these experiments was the discovery of vaccination. His faith in this discovery was so implicit, that he vaccinated his own son on three several occasions. The discovery was received by the public, and even by his own profession, with much disfavour at first. But vaccination was a truth, and because it was a truth, it prevailed, and has prevailed ever since. It has been the means of rescuing countries, and even continents, from the scourge of smallpox.

21. *The Effect of Trifles—II.*

Mahomed, when pursued by his enemies, before his religion had gained a footing in the world, took refuge in a certain cave some miles outside of Mecca. To the neighbourhood of this retreat his pursuers traced him. When they were standing at the very mouth of the cave, and were on the point of entering, their attention was arrested by a little bird darting from an adjoining thicket. Had it not been for this trivial circumstance, which convinced them that here the fugitive could not be concealed, Mahomed would have been discovered, taken back to Mecca, and probably put to death. As it was, he made his escape and fled to Medina, where he gained the protection of his friends, and by slow degrees succeeded in laying the foundation of a religion which now prevails over a large portion of the world.

22. *How a Wizard redeemed his Credit.*

Off the Malabar coast, Southern India, the sea abounds in pearls. But it also abounds in sharks, and these voracious animals sometimes make a meal off the men, who, naked and unprotected, risk their lives in diving for pearls. There is a class of magicians, however, who are supposed to control the movements of sharks by their spells. No diver will go out without first consulting one of these men and going through the ceremonies which he directs. In spite of all the spells and ceremonies a diver one year lost his leg, and for this loss the magician was called to account. The answer he gave showed how well he understood the childishness of the men he had to deal with: it is even possible that he was superstitious enough to believe his own tale. He gravely told them that an old witch who owed him a grudge had just come from a place on the Malabar coast and performed a piece of counter-magic, which rendered his spells fruitless; that this had come to his knowledge too late to prevent the accident which had happened; but that he would now show his superiority over his antagonist by enchanting the sharks and binding up their mouths, so that no more accidents should happen that season. Fortunately for his credit, no further injury was done by the sharks for the remainder of that season; and the simple divers believed that this was owing to the charms of the wizard.

23. *Greediness—I. The Jackal.*

In a certain village in India there lived a hunter, who was celebrated for the strength of his bow and the skill with which he used it. One day, going out for sport, he came across a herd of wild deer, and taking a good aim brought one of them.

to the ground. As he was carrying the body of the deer home, he came across a herd of wild boars. Laying the deer upon the ground, and fixing an arrow to his bow, he shot one of them. But the boar, though badly wounded, was not killed. Rushing upon the hunter with an angry grunt, it ripped him open with its tusk, and then dropped down dead at his feet. The hunter fell like a tree cut down with an axe, and lay dead on the ground alongside of the boar. A snake happened to be on the spot where this took place; and it was killed by the boar trampling on its skull and crushing its brains out.

Not long afterwards there came that way a jackal; and its eyes fell on the hunter, the deer, the boar, and the snake all lying dead together. "Ha!" thought the jackal, "what luck! Here's a feast! The man will be fine picking for a month; the deer for another; and the boar for a third. The snake will be quite enough for me to-morrow. To-day I am not hungry, as I have had enough to eat already. But I might as well have a nibble at this bit of sinew on the bow-horn." As it began to nibble, the bow-string snapped, and the bow sprang back with such violence that it killed the jackal.—*Eastern Story.*

24. *Greediness—II. The Porter or Gate-keeper.*

A man was giving a great feast after the celebration of a marriage. He had obtained every kind of food that he required except fish. Fish of the kind that was wanted for such a banquet could not be got; for the weather had of late been too stormy for fishermen to go out to sea in boats. On the very morning of the feast, however, a fisherman appeared at the rich man's house with a fine turbot and offered it for sale. The fish was gladly accepted, and the fisherman was asked to name his price. "One hundred lashes, sir, and nothing less," was the strange answer; "and these lashes must be laid on my bare back." As the fisherman could not be persuaded to take money instead of lashes, the lashes were administered. After he had received fifty strokes out of the hundred, he cried out, "Hold! I have had my share. I have a partner in this business, and it is right that the remaining fifty should be given to him." "What!" said the rich man, "is there another such madman in the world? Call him in, and let us see him." "You need not go far, sir," said the fisherman; "he is your own porter. He would not let me pass until I had promised that he should have half of the price to be paid for my fish." "Call him in," said the rich man angrily; "he shall have his fifty lashes with the strictest justice." The fifty lashes having been given, the porter was dismissed, and the fisherman received in money the full value of his fish.

25. *How a Man was cured of Sobbing on board a Ship.*

A king of Persia was safely seated in a ship with the slave who accompanied him on the voyage. The slave, who had never been on the sea before, began to moan and sob, as if he were in terror of being drowned; and nothing could keep him quiet. The king was a good deal disturbed by these moanings; but as slaves are very kindly treated in Persia, he left the man alone, and suffered the inconvenience. Presently a fellow-passenger came up and offered to silence the slave, but stipulated that he should be allowed a free hand to treat the slave as he thought fit, so long as he did him no harm. To this the king gladly consented. The man then took the slave, tied a rope securely round his waist, and had him flung into the sea, one of the sailors keeping a tight hold of the other end of the rope. The slave, as soon as he was pulled up into the ship, was flung back again into the water; and this process was repeated several times. When they thought he had had enough, he was pulled up for the last time and taken to a corner of the ship, where he sat down, not moaning or sobbing as before, but keeping perfectly silent. "Now tell me," said the king, turning to the man who had wrought such a complete change in the behaviour of the slave, "what is the secret of the remedy that has succeeded so well?" The man replied: "Until he had been flung into the sea, he had not tasted the pain of drowning, and did not know how to value the safety of a ship. Now he has learnt a lesson. He will not sob or moan again this voyage."—*Eastern Story.*

26. *How a Cat's Paw was used by a Monkey.*

The merchant Apicius, who lived at Capua, took home with him in his ship a kitten from Egypt and a very young monkey from the country below Egypt. As the two animals were both of a tender age, and were fed and brought up together, they became attached, and showed no signs of the antipathy that ordinarily exists between animals of such different natures. Yet friendship could not destroy the differences of disposition that showed themselves more and more, as the two animals grew older. The cat was lively during the night, but disliked the bright sunshine, and was inclined to sleep during the day. The monkey, being more like a man in his habits, slept during the night, and used to tease the cat during the day for being so fond of sleep. One day Apicius was having some chestnuts roasted on the fire. The cat was asleep, as usual, lying with its paws stretched out towards the fire. But the monkey was wide awake, casting wistful eyes towards the chestnuts, and wondering how he could get them out of the fire without burning himself. Suddenly a thought struck him. Seizing the paws of the cat and thrusting them into the fire one after another, as if he was using his own arms, he drew out as many chestnuts as he wanted, and left the cat smarting with pain. Hence "to make a cat's paw" of any one (that is, to use him for one's own purposes, whatever harm it may do him) has become a proverb; but many who use the phrase have never heard the story which gave rise to it.

27. *How a Beetle helped a Prisoner to escape.*

A prime minister, who had incurred the displeasure of his master, an eastern king, was placed as prisoner in the top storey of a very high tower. As escape seemed impossible from such a height, the base of the tower was left unguarded at night, and the iron bars of the top window had not been kept in good repair. In the silence of the night the prisoner heard the lamentations of his wife at the foot of the tower. He spoke cheerfully to her from above, and told her to come again next night and bring with her a live black-beetle, a little rancid butter, a skein of the finest silk, a ball of linen thread, a ball of string, and a coil of rope. She brought all these things with her next night, not at all knowing what use her husband was going to make of them. Speaking to her from the top of the tower, he said, "Tie one end of the silk thread round the beetle's body, touch its head with the butter, and place the insect on the wall with its head turned upwards directly towards this window." Now it is the habit of a beetle to move straight in the direction of any strong scent. Smelling the rancid butter on its head, and thinking it came from a point above it, the beetle crawled on, dragging the silk thread after it, till it reached the window. The prisoner then took hold of the end of the silk thread and let the beetle go. "Now," said the prisoner to his wife below, "tie the end of the silk thread to one end of the linen thread." She did so. Having drawn up one end of the linen thread, he told her to fasten the other end to one end of the string. Having drawn up one end of the string, he told her to fasten the other end to one end of the rope. Having drawn up one end of the rope, he fastened it round one of the iron bars of the window, and having managed to remove another bar, which had become rusty and brittle, he let himself out through the aperture, slided gently down the rope with his hands, and escaped.

28. *The Blind Old Horse.*

In a famous city of olden times, says an ancient chronicle, they had a belfry, and in the centre of the belfry there hung a rope which, by passing through a door that was never shut day or night, any one could pull who had a grievance. There was an old horse which, having grown blind and useless in its master's service, was turned out and left to starve. Straying blindly about the town, it chanced presently to go through the open belfry door, and in its blind search for food the poor creature caught hold of the end of the rope. It happened to be night-time, and peal upon peal broke out upon the still hours, straightway bringing the magistrates to the spot, only to find a blind old horse chewing away at the rope-end. But they understood. Its cruel master was found and fined, and that horse never again had cause to ring up the city for its relief.

29. *How Water-fowls are caught alive in India.*

The winter months of Northern India are warm enough to attract large flocks of water-fowls, which settle for a time near the swamps and river-banks, and when the hot weather sets in fly off to some cooler latitude. The way in which they are caught alive by certain fishing tribes is very ingenious. A man takes an earthenware jar, and makes two eyeholes in it at the same distance apart as his own eyes are. He puts his head into the jar, taking care to fix it in such a way that he can see through the eyeholes. He then ties to his back a basket that has no lid, but is covered with a network of string which he can open or close whenever he likes. That the birds may become accustomed to the sight of such jars, he sets two or three of them floating on the water among the birds. He then enters the water himself, wades towards the birds so cautiously, that they perceive nothing new there except the jar, which, though it contains his head, appears to be floating empty like the other jars. In this way he comes amongst them, and there he stands waiting his opportunities. Passing his hand slowly and noiselessly through the water, he seizes one fowl after another by its legs from below, and drawing it under water deposits it in the basket, from which there is no escape, since the top of the basket is covered with a net. The disappearance of a fowl excites no alarm among the other birds, and is not even noticed. In this way he fills his basket, and then leaves the marsh or river. The Indian fisherman is in one respect more successful with his ingenuity than he would be if he were armed with a gun; for he catches the birds alive and can keep them without risk, until he has found a purchaser. Moreover, his silent method does not frighten them, or render them more difficult to manage for another day's sport.

30. *Capturing a Male Elephant.*

For catching a solitary male elephant the hunters in Ceylon are assisted by trained female elephants, without whom they could do nothing. When the females see a male grazing about alone, they come gradually towards him, plucking leaves and grass as they advance, and with as little appearance of purpose, as if they were in the habit of being his constant companions. When they close round him, he feels flattered with their attentions and forgets his usual caution. They so entirely take possession of his thoughts, that he does not perceive what danger he is in, or notice that the hunters are silently creeping up towards him. These men, when they see that their intended victim has been entirely thrown off his guard by the wiles of the females, creep silently along the ground, and tie nooses of strong rope to his ankles. They then silently retire and fasten the ends of the cords to some tree near at hand. If there is no tree within reach of the rope, the females know what to do. They draw the elephant on till they bring him near some tree, which will be strong enough to bear his struggles and contortions, after his legs have been tied to it. As soon as the ropes have been securely fastened to the tree, the hunters give the signal, and the females go away, leaving their dupe to his fate. The elephant then becomes mad with rage, and struggles with all his force to get free, rolling on the ground, and rending the air with his cries. But all his struggles are in vain. After a while, being exhausted with his efforts to escape, and finding that all such efforts are useless, he permits himself to be led away by his masters. By degrees he is tamed and broken into work. Nor do we ever hear of his taking vengeance on the females, by whose wiles he was captured and whose captivity he now shares.

SECTION 2.—PROSE EXTRACTS NOT READ OR STUDIED IN CLASS.

3. **Method of this Section.**—In this, as in the preceding exercise, the student is required to reproduce the substance, not the exact words of the original. But the method is rather more difficult. In this exercise the extract is not to be read or studied in class. The student is to sit with pen and paper before him, and listen attentively while the teacher twice reads out the extracts slowly to the class. He must ask no questions during the reading, but must do his best to catch and retain the drift, while he hears it read, and then at once reproduce the drift or substance in his own words.

(*a*) *Cambridge Preliminary Examinations.*—This method is peculiarly well suited to a public examination; and it is the method adopted by Oxford and Cambridge in their "**Preliminary** Local Examination." To exemplify its working we herewith quote the "Instructions to the Presiding Examiner" issued by Cambridge in 1900.

INSTRUCTIONS TO THE PRESIDING EXAMINER.

1. *Let the Candidates be told that they are to reproduce from memory the substance of a passage which will be read to them. Let them further be informed that the passage will be read twice, and that they must listen attentively both times, but* **without taking notes.**

2. *Let the passage then be read out* **distinctly** *and* **rather slowly**. (*This will take a little more than 2 minutes.*)

3. *Before any Candidate is allowed to begin writing, let the passage be read a second time—not slowly, but at an ordinary pace.* (*This will take a little less than* 1½ *minute.*)

N.B.—*If the time occupied in carrying out the above instructions exceeds* 8 *minutes, a corresponding allowance of time must be made to the Candidates, so that they may not have less than 37 minutes* **net** *for writing their composition.*

(1) Extract read out in Preliminary Exam. held in December 1896. (In reproducing the substance of this and the following extracts, the student may of course use the Indirect form of speech as freely as he likes.)

The following anecdote of General Napier's interview with an Indian juggler strikingly illustrates his cool courage as well as the honesty of his character. On one occasion a famous juggler visited the camp and performed his feats before the General, his family, and staff. Among other performances, this man cut in two, by a downward stroke of his sword, a lemon placed on the outstretched hand of his assistant. Napier thought there must be some trick or deception in this. To divide by a sweep of the sword so small an object, without wounding the hand, he believed to be impossible. To determine the point, the General offered his own hand for the experiment, and stretched out his right arm. The juggler looked attentively at the hand, and said he would not make the trial. "I thought I should find you out!" exclaimed Napier. "But stop," added the other, "let me see your left hand." The left hand was submitted, and the man then said, "If you will hold your arm steady, I will perform the feat." "But why the left hand and not the right?" "Because the right hand is hollow in the centre, and there is a risk of cutting off the thumb; but the left is high, and the danger will be less." Napier was startled. "I now saw," he said, "that it was a genuine feat of delicate swordsmanship, and, if I had not abused the man as I did before my staff, and challenged him to the trial, I honestly acknowledge that I would have retired from the encounter. However, I set the lemon on my hand and held out my arm steadily. The juggler balanced himself, and, with a swift stroke, cut the lemon into two pieces. I felt the edge of the sword on my hand, as if a cold thread had been drawn across it, and was quite satisfied without desiring any repetition of the experiment."

(2) Extract read out in the Prelim. Exam. of December 1897:—

A curious custom is observed in the German city of Hamburg. It is a festival for the children, who march in procession through the streets waving branches of cherry-tree, laden with fruit. This festival has been held for more than 400 years, and serves to remind the people of a grand victory that was won by none but little children over an army of fierce men.

In the year 1432 Hamburg was besieged by a great army. The war had been raging for many years, and on both sides it had become very bitter and cruel; and so the people of Hamburg were terribly afraid; for they could not hope to hold out long against superior numbers. A council of the chief citizens was held to consider what should be done; and after much discussion some one suggested that they should send out the little children; for, when the soldiers saw them, the sight, it was thought, would melt their hearts and they would do no harm to the town.

Then all the children were gathered together from their homes, and they were put in order in the streets, and the city gate was opened, and they were told to march out to the army. The soldiers lying outside, who had come to destroy the city and murder all who were in it, were surprised to see the gate swing open, and greater still grew their amazement when they saw the little children, clad all in pure white robes, come forth; and when they heard, quite close, the pattering on the road of little feet, and when the little ones drew timidly up to their tents, the eyes of the rough soldiers began to fill with tears, and (as there were cherry orchards all about) they threw down their arms, and gathered beautiful branches off the cherry trees full of fruit, and sent back the children to their parents with answers of peace.

(3) Extract read out in the Prelim. Exam. of December 1898:—

A poor Turkish slater in Constantinople was at work upon the roof of a house, when he lost his footing and fell down into the narrow street upon a man who was passing. The passenger was killed on the spot, while the slater himself escaped without receiving any serious injury. The son of the man who was killed considered it to be his duty to bring the slater before the Judge and to demand that he should be punished or else forced to give liberal compensation. The accused did not attempt to deny what had happened, but he said that it was a pure accident, and expressed his sorrow for it. Besides, he was only a poor working-man, and it was quite impossible for him to pay anything in compensation. The son would not give way, but insisted on his right either to receive compensation or to see the slater severely punished. The Judge considered the case for some moments, and then gave the following decision. The slater, he said, must take his stand in the street in the same spot where the man had been killed; the son of the deceased could then, if he pleased, go up to the roof and fall down upon the slater. In this way punishment would be strictly visited upon the offender by the person who considered himself entitled to demand it. But this was a sentence which the son neither expected nor desired, and he left the court without pressing his claim any farther.

(4) Extract read out in the Prelim. Exam. of December 1899:—

In the days of old there lived a wealthy English Baron who owned broad lands in England and Wales, and who often considered anxiously how his possessions should be divided after his death among his three sons. When at length he lay on his death-bed, he called them to him and said: "If you were compelled to become birds, tell me, each of you, what bird you would choose to resemble?" The eldest said: "I would be a hawk, because it is a warlike bird, and lives by plunder." The second said: "I would be a starling, because it is a social bird, and flies in coveys, and never seeks to rob or grieve its neighbour." The youngest said: "I would be a swan, because it has a long neck, so that if I had anything in my heart to say, I should have plenty of time for reflection before it came to my mouth." When the father had heard them, he said to the first: "Thou, my son, as I perceive, desirest to live by plunder; I will therefore leave to thee my possessions in England, because it is a land of peace and justice, and thou canst not rob in it without the certainty of punishment." To the second he said: "Because thou lovest society, I will leave to thee my lands in Wales, which is a land of discord and war, in order that thy courtesy may soften the fierceness of the natives." And then turning to the youngest, he said: "To thee I bequeath no land at all, because thou art wise and wilt gain wealth by thy wisdom." It happened to the youngest son as the father foretold: he prospered by his wisdom, and was advanced in the king's service until he became the greatest statesman in the realm.

(5) Extract read out in the Prelim. Exam. of December 1900:—

A traveller, having arrived at a certain town in Tartary, went into the king's palace by mistake, thinking it to be a public inn. Having looked about him for some time, he entered into a long gallery, where he laid down his knapsack, and spread his carpet, in order to take his repose upon it after the manner of the eastern nations. He had not been long in this posture before he was discovered by some of the guards, who asked him what was his business in that place. The traveller told them he intended to take up his night's lodging in that inn. The guards let him know in a very angry manner that the house was not an inn, but the king's palace. It happened that the king himself passed through the gallery during this debate, and smiling at the mistake of the traveller asked him how he could possibly be so dull as not to distinguish a palace from an inn. "Sir," said the traveller, "give me leave to ask your Majesty a question or two. Who were the persons that lodged in this house when it was first built?" The king replied, "My ancestors." "And who," said the traveller, "was the last person who lodged here?" The king replied, "My father." "And who is it," said the traveller, "that lodges here at present?" The king replied that it was himself. "And who," said the traveller, "will be here after you?" The king answered, "The young prince, my son." "Ah, sir," said the traveller, "a house that changes its inhabitants so often, and receives such a continual succession of guests, is not a palace, but an inn."

(b) *Government Examinations of Pupil-teachers.*—In these examinations a similar system is followed as a test in composition. But the passage is read out once, not twice. The instructions given in the code are as follows:—

The passage should be read out once *distinctly, and then the substance of it is to be written down from memory by the pupil-teacher.*

The following extracts have been given at different times in the Government examinations [1]:—

[1] The following examples have been selected from those given in pp. 90-105 of the *Stories and Fables for Composition*, published by Messrs.

1. The leader of a gang of banditti in Corsica, who had been famous for his exploits, was at length taken and committed to the care of a soldier, from whom he contrived to escape. The soldier was condemned to death. At the place of execution a man, coming up to the commanding officer, said: "Sir, I am a stranger to you, but you shall soon know who I am. I have heard that one of your soldiers is to die for having suffered a prisoner to escape. He was not at all to blame; besides, the prisoner shall be restored to you. Behold him here! I am the man. I cannot bear that an innocent man should be punished for me, and have come to die myself: lead me to execution." "No!" exclaimed the French officer, who felt the sublimity of the action as he ought, "thou shalt not die; and the soldier shall be set at liberty. Endeavour to reap the fruits of thy generosity. Thou deservest to be henceforth an honest man."

2. At the court of Francis I., king of France, a fight of lions was one day exhibited. A lady of the court threw her glove among the lions, and called upon her lover, one of the bravest and most gallant captains of France, to recover it for her. He wrapped his cloak round his left arm, sprang into the arena, and with drawn sword advanced boldly upon the lions. They were awed by his intrepidity, and did not touch him. So he picked up the glove, and returned safely to the place where he had been sitting with the lady. But when he came there, he threw the glove in her face, and said that he renounced the love of one who, out of vanity, would expose her lover to such useless peril.

3. A noble Venetian, whose son was plunged in drunkenness and vice, finding the young man's expenses grow very high and extravagant, ordered his cashier to let him have for the future no more money than what he could count, when he received it. This, one would think, could be no great restraint to the expenses of a young gentleman, who could freely have as much money as he could count. But yet this to one, who was used to nothing but the pursuit of his pleasures, proved a very great trouble. At last the young fellow reflected: "If it be so much pains to me barely to count the money I would spend,

---

Blackwood and Sons, who took the trouble to collect them from examinations held by Government Inspectors. They have been transcribed with the consent of the publishers named.

what labour and pains did it cost my ancestors not only to count, but to get it?" This rational thought, suggested by that little effort imposed upon him, wrought so effectually upon his mind, that it made him wake up, and from that time forward he proved himself a good and careful manager of his money.

4. Lamartine, the French poet and statesman, was never rich. He had a great desire to possess a carriage of his own, and for this purpose he saved money, which he put by in a box. He had saved about a thousand francs, when one day a humble neighbour, a poor widow woman with several children, came into his room, threw herself at his knees, and told him with tears that she had no bread to eat, that her furniture was seized, and that she and her children had been turned into the street. "How much do you require?" said Lamartine, going quickly to his box. "A thousand francs," replied the poor woman. "Come, here they are," said the generous poet, and he emptied his savings into her hands. The next day a friend asked him what he would do about his carriage. "Oh, my friend," said he, "I shall continue to go on foot; it is better for my health."

5. On one occasion an officer was sent by the Sultan of Morocco to reduce some provinces to submission. When he arrived, a grand entertainment was given to him by the rebel chiefs, and immense quantities of provisions were sent in to furnish his table. Among the provisions there was a large supply of a particular dish, of which the officer was known to be very fond, and this was all poisoned. The officer, suspecting that it was poisoned, ordered his soldiers to guard the doors and let no one escape. He then called upon the chiefs one by one to partake of the dish. Most of the chiefs refused to eat, but some few came cheerfully forward at the officer's call. Those who were willing to eat of the particular dish, however, were not allowed to do so, while those who refused were compelled. Thus the officer in one day got rid of his enemies and saved his friends, whom he rewarded by putting the management of the rebel provinces into their hands.

6. Camillus, the Roman general who took Veii, beholding the sack of that powerful city, the rival of Rome, by his soldiers, exclaimed, "What man's fortune was ever so great as mine?" But then in a moment he bethought him how little a thing and how short a time can bring the greatest fortune

down to the lowest, and he prayed that if some evil must befall him in return for such great glory, it might be light and reasonable. Whilst he prayed, he veiled his head, as was the custom of the Romans in prayer, and turned round towards the right. But as he turned, his foot slipped, and he fell on his back upon the ground. Yet he was comforted rather than dismayed by his fall; for he said, "The gods have heard my prayer; and for the great fortune of my victory over Veii, they have sent me only this little evil."

7. A Swiss militiaman, on his way to be present at a muster, lost his way on the mountains and rolled over a precipice. He clung to a bush, which had struck its roots into the face of the precipice, and which broke his fall. Two schoolmasters on an excursion heard his cries; but as the man was some twelve feet below the top of the cliff, and the bottom was quite as far below him, they found it impossible to give any help. They hurried off to the nearest village, and a dozen mountaineers equipped with ropes started forthwith for the precipice. The man was still holding on to the bush, to which he had been clinging a day and a night between life and death. Besides suffering from hunger and cold, he had been hurt in the fall. Hoisting him to the top was a perilous undertaking, but it was safely accomplished. None of his hurts were dangerous; and after a long rest and hearty meal, he was able to continue his journey.

8. A sudden storm drove several ships from their anchors, and it being low water one of them struck the ground at a considerable distance from the shore, when the sea made a clean breach over her. There was not a vestige of hope for the vessel; such was the fury of the wind and the violence of the waves. There was nothing to tempt the boatmen on shore to risk their lives in saving either ship or crew; for not a farthing of salvage was to be looked for. But the daring intrepidity of the boatmen was not wanting at this critical moment. No sooner had the brig grounded than Simon Pritchard, one of the many persons assembled along the beach, threw off his coat and called out, "Who will come with me and try to save that crew?" Instantly twenty men sprang forward with "I will" and "I." But seven only were wanted. Running a boat down into the breakers, they leaped in and dashed through the dangerous surf, amidst the cheers of those on shore. How this boat lived in such a sea seemed a miracle.

But in a few minutes, impelled by the strong arms of these gallant men, she flew on and reached the stranded ship, catching her on the top of a wave; and in less than a quarter of an hour from the time when the boat left the shore, the six men who composed the crew of the collier were landed safe on Walmer beach.

9. When the ship *Leander* was brought into harbour after her voyage, she was so infested with rats that a wholesale destruction of these four-footed pests was rendered absolutely necessary, not only for the comfort of the crew, but for the very safety of the vessel. The entire contents of the ship were therefore landed on the wharf, a number of pans filled with lighted brimstone were placed between decks, and the hatches being battened down, the animals were soon stifled by the suffocating vapours. As soon as the preparation for this wholesale destruction commenced, the rats took alarm, and endeavoured to make their way on shore by traversing the ropes by which the vessel was made fast to the shore. Sentinels were accordingly placed by the ropes, and furnished with sticks, so that as soon as a rat came running along the ropes it was speedily checked by a sharp blow, which struck it from its foothold, and knocked it dead or dying into the water, where it soon perished. It is a curious fact that the rats were all found lying dead in circles round the pans, heaped thickly upon each other's bodies. They had instinctively run towards the spots which were comparatively free from vapour, as the heat of the burning coals forced the suffocating smoke to rise from the spot where it was generated.

Section 3.—Poetry Read in Class.

4. **Reproduction, not Paraphrase.**—To reproduce, in the form of simple and ordinary prose, the substance of a short tale or narrative told in verse is a more difficult task than either of the two already described, and for this reason we have placed it last in this chapter.

The kind of exercise to which we now refer must not be confounded with paraphrasing from poetry to prose. Paraphrasing is not a reproduction of the contents of a poem, but a translation from poetry to prose, a rendering of each phrase and each line from one form of speech to another, similar in principle to translating from English to French or *vice versa.* Poetry and prose are distinct forms of composition, as distinct in their own way as French and English are in theirs. Each has peculiar merits and beauties of its own, and each gives a distinct kind of pleasure. The higher the poetry, the worse the prose that will come out of it by means of paraphrase. Paraphrasing, if it is done successfully, may be useful in its way: if it does nothing else, it will give the student an opportunity of showing that he has not missed the sense of the original nor failed to grasp the syntactical construction. But the rendering of poetry into prose will not help him to form an easy, natural, and idiomatic style of prose-composition; and this is what we are now trying to help him to acquire.

What we ask the student to do in this form of exercise is to put the poetry aside altogether,—to think only of the drift or substance, and reproduce this in plain and ordinary prose, as if no such poem had ever been written.

(*a*) We take as our first example a short and easy poem describing the well-known anecdote in which King Canute rebukes his courtiers for flattery:—

1. The Danish king upon his throne
   Is sitting on the sand,
   The sea is foaming on the beach,
   His courtiers round him stand.

2. They praise his power and majesty;
   "O mighty king," they say,
   "How great thou art! the sea itself
   Will thy command obey."

3. He answered nought, but to the waves
   He turned: "O roaring sea,
   I charge thee, keep thy waters back,
   And come not nigh to me."

4. But forward still the waters rush,
   And on the shore they beat,
   Foaming and splashing as they roll,
   And overflow his feet.

5. Then to those courtiers turned the king:
"Let this a lesson teach,
And warn you not to tempt my ears
Again with flattering speech.

6. "For God Most High is King of kings;
Him all the world obeys;
Lord of all power and might is He;
To Him alone give praise.

7. "By Him were earth's foundations laid;
He rules the roaring sea,
And fixed a bound it should not pass
By His divine decree."

8. 'Tis said that from that day Canute
His diadem laid down;
"For God alone in Heaven," said he,
"Is worthy of a crown."

E. WORDSWORTH.

The Substance reproduced in Prose.

A great king like Canute, whose dominion extended over England, Denmark, and Norway, was sure to be exposed to flatterers. The following story shows how well he silenced his courtiers on one occasion and put them to open shame. His chair of state had been placed on a beach facing the sea, and his courtiers were standing around him. "How great a king art thou!" said they; "thou art lord of many lands, and the sea itself, on which thy navies ride, will obey thee." The king took note of what they said, but made no answer. It happened that the tide at that time was coming in, and was already approaching the chair on which he sat. Turning to the sea he said, "I command thee, O sea, to keep back thy waters, and come no nearer." But the tide moved on as before, rising higher and higher, till it dashed against his feet and threatened to overwhelm both him and his courtiers. Then turning round to them, he said, "Let this be a warning to you not again to tempt my ears with your foolish flatteries. There is no being really great and powerful but God. He alone, who made the sea, can tell it when and where to stop." There is a legend that from that day Canute resigned his kingly office, declaring that God alone was worthy to wear a crown.

(*b*) The next example is much more difficult. In this poem there is less story and more sentiment; the language too is much more unlike that of prose, and there is a refrain at the end of each stanza which, though suitable in poetry, must not be imitated in the reproduction.

1. Three fishers went sailing away to the West,
 Away to the West as the sun went down;
Each thought of the woman who loved him the best,
 And the children stood watching them out of the town;
  For men must work, and women must weep,
  And there's little to earn, and many to keep,
   Though the harbour bar be moaning.

2. Three wives sat up in the lighthouse tower,
 And they trimmed the lamps as the sun went down;
They looked at the squall, and they looked at the shower,
 And the night-rack came rolling up ragged and brown.
  But men must work, and women must weep,
  Though storms be sudden, and waters deep,
   And the harbour bar be moaning.

3. Three corpses lay out on the shining sands
 In the morning gleam, as the tide went down,
And the women are weeping and wringing their hands
 For those who will never come home to the town;
  For men must work, and women must weep,
  And the sooner it's over, the sooner to sleep;
   And good-bye to the bar and its moaning.

KINGSLEY.

The Substance reproduced in Prose.

As the sun went down, three fishermen entered their boat and set sail towards the west. Their children had followed them out of the town and were watching them from the shore. It was a cheerless night, and the moaning of the sea from the outer side of the harbour-bar betokened a rising storm. Nevertheless, each of them went out with a stout heart, thinking of the loving wife who would welcome him back and of the children who depended on him for support. Seeing that the storm increased in violence, the wives of the three fishermen could not go to their beds that night, but sat up in the lighthouse tower and trimmed the lamps, so that their mates might at least have some light to guide them homewards and not be lost in the darkness. But all their care was in vain. By the morning, when the storm had abated, the sun shone upon a painful sight,—three corpses thrown up by the tide, lying on the glistening beach,—three women wringing their hands over the bodies of the loved ones they had lost. A sad example this of the darker side of human life! At whatever risk, a man must earn a living for himself and family; and when the bread-winner is cut off, the woman is left to weep, until death comes to her release.

(*c*) We give one more example. In the following poem the story and the language are as simple as in the first example. But the poem is twice as long, and the story is told with a greater amount of detail. The difficulty therefore lies in picking out the main points, reducing the story within narrower compass without weakening the effect, and giving to each part of the story its fair amount of space.

1. No stir in the air, no stir in the sea,
The ship was still as she could be,
Her sails from heaven received no motion,
Her keel was steady in the ocean.

2. Without either sign or sound of their shock
The waves flowed over the Inchcape Rock;
So little they rose, so little they fell,
That they did not move the Inchcape Bell.

3. The good old Abbot of Aberbrothok
Had placed that bell on the Inchcape Rock;
On a buoy in the storm it floated and swung,
And over the waves its warning rung.

4. When the rock was hid by the surge's swell,
The mariners heard the warning bell;
And then they knew the perilous rock,
And blessed the Abbot of Aberbrothok.

5. The sun in heaven was shining gay,
All things were joyful on that day;
The sea-birds screamed as they wheeled round,
And there was joyance in their sound.

6. The buoy of the Inchcape Bell was seen,
A darker speck on the ocean green;

Sir Ralph the Rover walked his deck,
And he fixed his eye on the darker speck.

7. He felt the cheering power of spring,
It made him whistle, it made him sing;
His heart was mirthful to excess,
But the Rover's mirth was wickedness.

8. His eye was on the Inchcape float:
Quoth he, "My men, put out the boat,
And row me to the Inchcape Rock:
I'll plague the Abbot of Aberbrothok."

9. The boat is lowered, the boatmen row,
And to the Inchcape Rock they go;
Sir Ralph bent over from the boat,
And he cut the bell from the Inchcape float.

10. Down sank the bell with a gurgling sound,
The bubbles rose and burst around;
Quoth Sir Ralph, "The next who comes to the rock
Won't bless the Abbot of Aberbrothok."

11. Sir Ralph the Rover sailed away,
And scoured the seas for many a day;
And now grown rich with plundered store
He steers his course for Scotland's shore.

12. So thick a haze o'erspreads the sky
They cannot see the sun on high;
The wind hath blown a gale all day,
At evening it hath died away.

13. On the deck the Rover takes his stand,
So dark it is they see no land.
Quoth Sir Ralph, "It will be lighter soon,
For there is the dawn of the rising moon."

14. "Canst hear," said one, "the breakers roar?
For methinks we should be near the shore."
"Now where we are I cannot tell,
But I wish I could hear the Inchcape Bell."

15. They hear no sound, the swell is strong;
Though the wind hath fallen they drift along,
Till the vessel strikes with a shivering shock—
"Oh Christ! it is the Inchcape Rock!"

16. Sir Ralph the Rover tore his hair,
And beat his breast in his despair;
The waves rush in on every side,
And the ship sinks down beneath the tide.

SOUTHEY.

The main points, which may be called the skeleton or outline of the story, are four in number:—

(*a*) The dangerous character of the reef called the Inchcape Rock;

(*b*) The bell-buoy placed there by a monk to warn mariners not to come near;

(*c*) The removal of the bell by a pirate, who was jealous of the monk's good name;

(*d*) The destruction of the pirate's ship on the very rock from which he had removed the bell some time before.

In the prose reproduction shown below we have given a separate paragraph to each of these points.

Off the coast of Scotland there is a dangerous reef called the Inchcape Rock, on which many ships used to be wrecked: for the rocks even in clear weather can scarcely be seen above the surface of the water, and at one time there was nothing to warn mariners that they were in the neighbourhood of danger.

To give mariners the necessary warning, a kind monk, known as the Abbot of Aberbrothok, had placed a bell-buoy in the water and fastened it to one of the rocks with a chain, so that it could not be carried away from that rock by wind or tide. The floating buoy moved with every motion of the waves, and the motion of the buoy caused the bell with which it was mounted to ring. Mariners understood from this ringing that they were approaching the dangerous reef, and steered clear away from it.

A notorious pirate, named Sir Ralph the Rover, who was cursed for his evil deeds as much as the Abbot was blessed for his good ones, envied the Abbot his good name and was bent on finding some means of gratifying his spleen. On a bright and cloudless day, while his ship was becalmed and received no motion from wind or wave, he was walking up and down the deck enjoying the pleasant sunshine, when he descried the bell-buoy, which in the distance looked like a dark speck on the green ocean. With a wicked smile he ordered his men to lower the boat and row him to the rock. On reaching it he cut off the bell, exclaiming, "The next visitor to this rock will not bless the Abbot!"

After this the pirate scoured the seas for many a long day, and having taken much plunder was steering his way back to Scotland. One evening, before the moon had risen, a thick haze overspread the sky, and neither he nor his men could tell where they were. One said that he thought he heard breakers, and that land could not be far off. Another said it might be so, but he wished he could hear the Inchcape bell. While they were still talking, the ship, borne along by the swell, (for the wind had gone down), was driven against the very rock from which the bell had been removed by the wicked Rover. The waves rushed in on every side and overwhelmed the shattered vessel. He, who had removed the bell and silenced the voice of kindly warning, perished with all his crew, in an agony of despair.

We append a few specimens of poems that appear suitable for reproduction in prose; but the teacher will select any other poems that he may consider more suitable for his class. We recommend, however, that poems which have been committed to memory should *not* be used for this purpose, as the student in such a case could hardly avoid repeating the words of the original, which would defeat the object of this kind of exercise. Let the poem be studied well beforehand in class, and let the teacher draw the attention of the students to the salient points of the story, and give any comments that will help the students to reproduce the substance in prose.

1. The Parrot's Recollection of Country.

1. The deep affections of the breast,
    That Heaven to living things imparts,
Are not exclusively possessed
    By human hearts.

2. A parrot, from the Spanish main,
    Full young and early caged, came o'er
With bright wings to the bleak domain
    Of Mulla's shore.

3. To spicy groves where he had won
   His plumage of resplendent hue,
His native fruits, and skies, and sun,
   He bade adieu.

4. For these he changed the smoke of turf,
   A heathery land, and misty sky,
And turned on rocks and raging surf
   His golden eye.

5. But petted in our climate cold,
   He lived and chattered many a day,
Until with age from green and gold
   His wings grew grey.

6. At last when blind, and seeming dumb,
   He scolded, laughed, and spake no more,
A Spanish stranger chanced to come
   To Mulla's shore.

7. He hailed the bird in Spanish speech;
   The bird in Spanish speech replied,
Flapped round the cage with joyous screech,
   Dropped down, and died.

T. CAMPBELL.

2. OSCAR, THE DOG OF SANDA.

1. The sun was sinking in the west,
   Lurid and red sank he,
While a little band stood on the land,
   And gazed out on the sea.

2. The farewell gleam of dying day
   Shone on a sailor's form,
As he clung to the deck of a battered wreck
   That drove before the storm.

3. "Alas! alas!" the gazers cried,
   As darker grew the sky,
"Must he find a grave 'neath the rushing wave?
   What a dreadful death to die!"

4. A giant billow sweeps the deck;
   He has loosed his hold at last,
And his drowning cry came shrilly by
   Upon the stormy blast.

5. See! see! a dog with leap and bound
   Speeds down the rugged steep:
Ere the eye can wink, from the rocky brink
   He plunges in the deep.

6. High on the waves, and low between,
   He breasts the angry sea;
Away from the shore, through the stormy roar,
   Right onward swimmeth he.

7. Speed, Oscar! speed, thou noble dog!
   Upon thy fearful path;
Speed, Oscar! speed, nor hear nor heed
   The raving tempest's wrath.

8. He hath seized the sailor, ere he sinks,
   He holds him firm and tight;
And back to the shore, through the stormy roar,
   He strains with all his might.

9. No word is said, no breath is drawn,
   Among the little band,
As through surf and spray he breasts his way,
   And gains the rocky land.

10. Long, long in Sanda's lonely isle,
   This story shall be told;
And coming days shall hear the praise
   Of Oscar true and bold.

3. Sir Philip Sidney on the Field of Zutphen.
A.D. 1586.

1. O come with me to Zutphen's plain
   Across the Northern Sea;
There Sidney falls, the fairest flower
   Of England's chivalry.

2. He quits the fatal battle-field,
   Struck by a mortal wound:
See how his friends and followers come,
   In pity gathering round.

3. His fevered lips are parched with thirst,
   His sight grows faint and dim,
One drop of water were a boon
   Beyond all price to him.

4. No flower exposed to noonday heat,
   Upon some thirsty plain,
E'er longed so much for dewy night
   Or grateful summer rain.

5. No traveller on Arabian sands,
   Amid the wilderness,
E'er yearned to reach some desert spring
   With greater eagerness.

6. See! see it comes! his languid head
   Upon your shoulders prop,
And let him drink the precious draught,
   Refreshed by every drop.

7. Why stays he thus? he will not taste,
   And with averted eye
Points to a fellow-soldier stretched
   Upon the ground hard by:—
"Take this and drink, O wounded man,
   Thou need'st it more than I."

8. Then from th' untasted flask his lips
   The suffering hero moves,
And on the soldier at his side
   Bestows the draught he loves,

9. Rejoicing, in the midst of pain,
   And weakness, that he can
To other's sorrows bring relief,
   And cheer his fellow-man.

10. O victor in a nobler strife
   Than those of shield and spear,
Sidney, thy hardest struggle and
   Thy highest praise is here!

11. A conquest o'er the love of self
   More worthy of renown,
Than his who takes by force or guile
   A long beleaguered town.

12. True manly valour shines most clear
   In love's celestial light,
And charity with courage leagued
   Makes up the perfect knight.

E. Wordsworth.

4. Child Lost in Snow.

1. It was a clear, cold, winter night,
   The heavens were brightly starred,
When on St. Bernard's snowy height
   The good monks kept their guard.

2. Around their hearth that night they told
   To one, who shelter craved,
How the brave dog he thought so old
   Full forty lives had saved;

3. When suddenly with kindling eye
   Up sprang the old dog there,
As from afar a child's shrill cry
   Rang through the frosty air.

4. In haste the monks unbarred the door,
   Rugs round the mastiffs threw;
And as they bounded forth once more,
   Called, "Blessings be with you!"

5. They hurried headlong down the hill,
   Past many a snow-drift wild,
Until the older dog stood still
   Beside a sleeping child.

6. He licked the little icy hand
   With his rough, kindly tongue;
With his warm breath he gently fanned
   The tresses fair and long.

7. The child looked up, with eyes of blue,
   As if the whole he guessed;
His arms around the dog he threw,
   And sank again to rest.

8. Once more he woke and wrapped him fast
   In the warm covering sent:
The dogs then with their charge at last
   Up the steep mountain went.

9. The fire glowed bright with heaped-up logs;
   Each monk brought forth a light;
"Good dogs!" the stranger cried, "good dogs!
   Whom bring you here to-night?"

10. In with a joyous bound they come;
    The boy awoke and smiled:
"Ah me!" the stranger cried, "some home
    Mourneth for thee, fair child."

11. With morning light the monk and boy
    Sought where the village lay:
I dare not try to paint the joy
    Their coming gave that day.

5. The Dog and the Water-lily: No Fable.

1. The noon was shady, and soft airs
    Swept Ouse's silent tide,
When 'scaped from literary cares
    I wandered on his side.

2. My spaniel, prettiest of his race,
    And high in pedigree,
(Two nymphs adorned with every grace
    That spaniel found for me),

3. Now wantoned lost in flags and reeds,
    Now starting into sight
Pursued the swallow o'er the meads,
    With scarce a slower flight.

4. It was the time when Ouse displayed
    His lilies newly-blown;
Their beauties I intent surveyed,
    And one I wished my own.

5. With cane extended far I sought
    To steer it close to land;
But still the prize, though nearly caught,
    Escaped my eager hand.

6. Beau marked my unsuccessful pains
    With fixed considerate face,
And puzzling set his puppy brains
    To comprehend the case.

7. But with a cherup clear and strong,
    Dispersing all his dream,
I thence withdrew, and followed long
    The windings of the stream.

8. My ramble ended, I returned;
   Beau trotting far before,
The floating wreath again discerned
   And plunging left the shore.

9. I saw him with that lily cropped
   Impatient swim to meet
My quick approach, and soon he dropped
   The treasure at my feet.

10. Charmed with the sight, "This world," I cried,
   "Shall hear of this thy deed:
My dog shall mortify the pride
   Of man's superior breed.

11. "But chief myself I will enjoin,
   Awake at duty's call,
To show a love as prompt as thine
   To Him who gives me all."

COWPER.

6. JOHN MAYNARD: SELF-SACRIFICE.

1. In North America once lived
   A man unknown to fame;
Methinks that very few have heard
   Of brave John Maynard's name.

2. A skilful pilot he was bred;
   In God was his delight;
His head was clear, his thoughts were pure,
   His hopes were ever bright.

3. On Erie's broad and placid lake
   A steamer ploughed her way;
And honest John stood at the helm
   That lovely summer-day.

4. Well filled with merry passengers,
   She cut the water wide,
Leaving a silver line of light
   Along the foaming tide.

5. But suddenly her captain starts,
   His cheek as white as snow;
O sight of dread!—Light wreaths of smoke
   Come curling from below.

6. Then rose the dreadful shout of "fire!"
   Appalling, wild, and drear:
No boat was on the steamer's side,
   Nor human aid was near.

7. All hands to instant work were called:
   Alas! all toil was vain.
The fury of the raging flames
   No effort could restrain.

8. "When, Pilot, can our port be reached?"
   Arose an eager cry.
"Three-quarters of an hour from hence,"
   John Maynard made reply.

9. Then forward rush the passengers,
   Dismayed with terror sore.
John Maynard at the helm still stands,
   As steadfast as before.

10. Now dreadful clouds of smoke arise,
   And sheets of flame divide.
"John Maynard, are you at the helm?"
   The captain loudly cried.

11. "Aye, aye, sir!" was the quick reply.
   "Then say, how does she head?"
"South-east by east"—the answer came
   Above the uproar dread.

12. "Head her south-east!" the captain shouts,
   "And run her quick ashore;"
"Aye, aye, sir!" but the quick response
   Was feebler than before.

13. "John Maynard! can you still hold on,—
   Five minutes longer still?"
The captain's ear scarce caught the words—
   "By God's help, sir, I will!"

14. Scorched were the old man's face and hair,
   One hand disabled hung;
Yet with the other to the wheel,
   As to a rock, he clung.

15. He beached the ship; to all on board
   A landing safe was given;
But, as the last man leaped on shore,
   John Maynard rose to heaven.

7. An Elephant saves the Flag.

1. Long, long ago, on India's plains,
   There raged a battle fierce and strong;
The din of musketry was heard,
   And cannon's roar was loud and long.
Old Hero marched with stately tread
   His part to act in the affray;
And on his back above all heads
   The royal ensign waved that day.

2. Fondly the soldiers viewed their flag,
   Which shook its colours to the air,
Proudly the driver rode, and sent
   His watchful gaze now here, now there,
Till "Halt!" he cried; and Hero heard,
   And instantly the word obeyed,
When, lo! a flash, a shriek, and then
   His driver with the slain was laid.

3. Oh, fierce and hot the conflict grew:
   Yet patiently old Hero stood
Amidst it all, the while his feet
   Were stained, alas! with human blood.
His ears were strained to catch the voice
   Which only could his steps command,
Nor would he turn when men grew weak,
   And panic spread on either hand.

4. But yet the standard waved aloft;
   The fleeing soldiers saw it. "Lo!
We are not conquered yet," they cried,
   And rallying, closed upon the foe.
Then turned the tide of conquest, and
   The royal ensign waved at last
Victorious o'er the blood-stained field,
   Just as the weary day was past.

5. Yet waited Hero for the word
   Of him whose sole command he knew—
Waited, nor moved one ponderous foot,
   To his own captain's orders true.
Three lonely nights, three lonely days,
   Poor Hero "halted." Bribe nor threat

Could stir him from the spot. And on
His back he bore the standard yet.

6. Then thought the soldiers of a child
Who lived one hundred miles away.
"The driver's son! fetch him!" they cried:
"His voice the creature will obey."
He came, the little orphaned lad,
Scarce nine years old. But Hero knew
That many a time the master's son
Had been the "little driver" too.

7. Obediently the brave old head
Was bowed before the child, and then,
With one long wistful glance around,
Old Hero's march began again.
Onward he went, the trappings hung
All stained and tattered at his side,
And no one saw the cruel wound
On which the blood was scarcely dried.

8. But when at last the tents were reached,
The suffering Hero raised his head,
And trumpeting his mortal pain,
Looked for the master who was dead;
And then about his master's son
His trunk old Hero feebly wound,
And ere another day had passed,
A soldier's honoured grave had found.

MARY D. BRINE.

CHAPTER II.—GENERAL HINTS ON WRITTEN COMPOSITION.

SECTION 1.—HOW TO WRITE CLEARLY AND EFFECTIVELY.

5. **How to give Force to Particular Words.**—In conversation, *i.e.* in oral composition, the method by which we usually give more force to one word than to another is by pronouncing it more loudly and more distinctly. In written composition this effect has to be produced by certain devices of language, of which we will now mention a few.

(*a*) *Placing a word out of its usual order.*—As a general rule, the order that has become established by custom should be adhered to. Sometimes, however, it is expedient to invert the order, provided this can be done without destroying the rhythm of the sentence. When a word is thus placed out of its ordinary position, it excites more attention and thereby acquires greater force :—

Silver and *gold* have I none ; but *such as I have* give I thee : in the name of Jesus Christ of Nazareth rise up and walk. —*Acts* iii. 6. (*Direct object before its verb.*)

They held their peace, and glorified God, saying, "Then hath God *to the Gentiles* also granted repentance unto life."—*Acts* xi. 18. (*Indirect object before its verb.*)

Great is Diana of the Ephesians.—*Acts* xix. 28. (Complement before its verb.)

I appeal from Philip *drunk* to Philip *sober*. (Adjective after its noun.)

(*b*) *Emphatic positions.*—The middle of a sentence is the least emphatic of all positions. The most emphatic is either the beginning or the end.

Romulus founded Rome.

In this sentence the words all follow their natural order, and thus there is no particular force attaching to any one of them. First comes the subject "Romulus," then the Trans. verb "founded," and lastly its Object "Rome."

If we wish to give more prominence to the word *Romulus*, we can do so by placing it last and altering the construction of the sentence :—

The man who founded Rome was *Romulus*.

Or, if we wish to give more prominence to *Rome*, we can do so by placing it first and making the requisite alteration in the construction of the sentence :—

Rome was the city that Romulus founded.

(*c*) "*It is*," "*it was*."—These words placed before a noun or adjective give increased force to it. Suppose the original sentence to be the following :—

Nelson destroyed Napoleon's fleet.

Here, as in the example given under (*b*), the words all stand in their natural order,—"Nelson" Subject, "destroyed" Transitive verb, "Napoleon's fleet" Object,—and hence there is no particular force attaching to any one of them. We can, however, give a good deal more prominence to each of them in turn by the use of the phrase "it was":—

1. It was *Nelson* who destroyed Napoleon's fleet.
2. It was *Napoleon's fleet* that Nelson destroyed.
3. It was the *destruction*, not merely the defeat, of Napoleon's fleet, that was accomplished by Nelson.

(*d*) *Setting one word against another.*—The process of setting one word against another by way of opposition or contrast adds much to the force of language, since we can always understand a thing better by seeing its opposite. This device is called *antithesis*, which means "setting against," *i.e.* setting one word against another.

The use of language is to conceal the thoughts.

In such a saying as the above, the most important word is "conceal," since it asserts a fact which most persons would deny; for it is generally held that we use language to make our thoughts known, not to hide or disguise them. In oral composition the speaker, in order to draw attention to the word "conceal," would throw a good deal of stress upon it by the tone of his voice. A writer might, with the same object in view, draw a line under it. To underline a word, however, is but a clumsy device, far less effective than the use of an antithesis, as shown below:—

The use of language is not to express, but to conceal, the thoughts.

(*e*) *Repetition.*—Force is sometimes added to a word or statement by repeating it, as a blacksmith repeats his blows on the anvil:—

1. Christ being raised from the dead dieth no more; *death hath no more dominion over him.*—*New Test.*

The second sentence (italicised) is a mere reassertion of the first in other words; but it adds greatly to its force.

2. How *weary, stale, flat* and *unprofitable,*
Seem to me all the uses of this world !—SHAKSPEARE.

There is not much difference in sense between the adjectives italicised. Their combined effect, however, is much greater than the single effect of any one of them could have been.

6. The use of Simple Words.—Big words, uncommon words, and roundabout phrases should be avoided, whenever a short and easy word will do equally well. Simple facts should be told in simple terms. A narrative loses much of its effect, if it is not told in words that express the genuine feelings of the writer. Dr. Johnson, in the course of his tour to the Hebrides, expressed himself as follows in a letter to a friend :—

When we were taken upstairs, a dirty fellow bounced out of the bed on which one of us was to lie.—*Letter on the Journey to the Hebrides.*

But in the *Journey to the Hebrides* that he prepared for the press, the same incident is dished up for the public in the pompous terms quoted below :—

Out of one of the couches on which we were to repose there started up at our entrance a man as black as a Cyclops from the forge.

The same writer, when asked for his opinion on the comedy called the *Rehearsal,* said without any restraint :—

It has not wit enough to keep it sweet.

Then, correcting himself, he added in more formal, but less effective, terms :—

It has not vitality enough to preserve it from putrefaction.

The use of high-sounding or uncommon words, far from adding to the beauty or dignity of composition, exposes the beginner to the risk of being ridiculed for using words which he does not understand.

7. Avoidance of Slang Words.—Simplicity, which has just been commended as a virtue in composition, must not be allowed to degenerate into the vice of slang. Language may be simple and direct without being colloquial or vulgar, just as it may be simple and dignified without being pompous or affected. Such colloquialisms as the following should be avoided in written composition, and there is nothing gained by using them in conversation :—

> *Peckish* for "hungry." To be *sat upon* for "blamed," "censured." To *do the handsome thing* for "act a liberal or generous part." *Boss* for "head man." *Fluke* for "lucky stroke." *Out of sheer cussedness* for "without any reasonable purpose." *Jiffy* for "instant." *Tanner* for "sixpence." *Quid* for "pound." *End in smoke* for "have no tangible result." *You bet* for "you may bet anything you like," "you may be quite certain." *Awfully* for "very." *Jolly* for "very." *Quite plenty* for "amply sufficient." *For all he was worth* for "to the best of his power." *Dance attendance* for "go backwards and forwards to meet some one, who takes his own time for seeing you." *Too utterly utter* for "intolerable." *Beastly* for "disagreeable." *Hang out* for "lodge" or "live." *Funk* for "fear," etc.

Trivial and childish words should be avoided no less than slang. The word *nice*, for example, we hear spoken on all sides to describe anything that is not considered objectionable :—

> A nice hat, a nice sleep, a nice song, a nice fire, a nice dog, a nice parrot, a nice flower, a nice girl, a nice cat, a nice book, a nice walk, a nice field, a nice house, a nice bed, a nice pie, a nice fruit, a nice breeze, a nice sunshine, a nice shower, a nice phrase, a nice poem, a nice story, a nice park, a nice theatre, a nice actor, a nice curtain, a nice pudding, a nice game, a nice ride, a nice coat, a nice horse, etc.

The teacher would do well to prohibit the use of this word altogether. The student will then be forced to seek for another, which he will very easily find, if he tries.

8. Avoidance of Unnecessary Words.—It has been shown in § 5 (*e*) that repetition is sometimes useful for adding force to a word or statement. As a general rule, however, brevity, or the avoidance of unnecessary words, gives as much force to a sentence as diffuseness takes from it. A word that does no good does harm. If a fact can be expressed in five words, there is a want of strength in employing ten.

There are four offences against brevity to be guarded against:—

(*a*) *Tautology;* the employment of a superfluous word or words in the same grammatical relation with some other word. The superfluous words are italicised in the following sentence:—

> In the Attic commonwealth it was the privilege *and birthright* of every citizen *and poet* to rail *aloud and* in public. —SWIFT.

(*b*) *Redundancy;* the employment of superfluous words not in the same grammatical relation. (The superfluous words are as before italicised.)

> He had the *entire* monopoly of the whole trade.
> I must decline *to accept* your offer.
> Charles V. of Spain and Francis I. of France *mutually* helped each other to extirpate the heretics of their time.

(*c*) *Verbosity;* the employment of a multiplicity of words, by the weight of which the drift of the sentence, far from being strengthened, is like David in Saul's armour encumbered and oppressed:—

> For seeing those things which are equal must needs have all one measure, if I cannot but wish to receive all good, even as much at every man's hand as any man can wish unto his own soul, how should I look to have any part of my desire herein satisfied, unless myself be careful to satisfy the like desire which is in other men?—HOOKER.

The above is a languid and clumsy way of saying—

> How can I expect to have my own desires satisfied, if I pay no heed to those of other men?

(*d*) *Prolixity.*—In prolixity it is not redundancy of words that harasses the reader, but the enumeration of twaddling and irrelevant details, amongst which it is not easy to catch the main point at a glance:—

On hearing the news he got off his chair, went out of the room, took down his hat, brushed it, put on his great-coat, went round to the stable, saddled his horse, mounted, and after giving a few directions to the cook, rode off to the town.

A prolix and pointless way of saying—

On hearing the news, he rode off at once to the town.

9. **Smoothness of Language.**—The writer himself must have a good ear, if he wishes to know what will please the ear of his readers. A few hints, however, are herewith offered.

(*a*) Avoid (if possible) the use of two different constructions in the same sentence:—

They suspected that he *had been bribed* and *given* an unjust sentence.

Here there is an abrupt change from the Passive voice "had been bribed" to the Active voice "given." It would sound much better to say—

They suspected that he had received a bribe and given an unjust sentence.

(*b*) Avoid using the same word twice in the same sense, but in a different connection:—

To enable us to make the *necessary* arrangements it is *necessary* for us to hear not later than noon on Friday, 21st current.—*Daily Telegraph*, Jan. 20, 1898.

Write "the *requisite* arrangements" for "the *necessary* arrangements."

(*c*) Avoid using words of the same or nearly the same sound within a very short distance of each other:—

(1) If all local authorities *affected acted* in the same manner, ratepayers might receive some benefit from unity.—*Daily Tel.*, Feb. 8, 1898.

Write *concerned* for *affected.*

(2) The darling of his old age killed *before* him *before* her time.

Write "killed *in front of him*" for "killed *before him.*"

(*d*) Avoid mixing Present participles with Verbal nouns:—

The Epistle to the Hebrews, *bearing* in its title a special form of address, is yet universal in its drift, as *designing* to convince all mankind of the necessity of *seeking* for happiness in a future life, and *avoiding* all things *leading* men to sin.

It will add to the clearness as well as to the smoothness of the sentence, if the sentence is rewritten as follows:—

The Epistle to the Hebrews, though it bears in its title a special form of address, is yet universal in its drift, as its design is to convince all mankind of the necessity of seeking for happiness in a future life and avoiding everything that may lead to sin.

(*e*) Avoid awkward constructions to which the ear is not accustomed:—

Flying visits to settlements of Finns, Poles, Bohemians, and Russians, located along the Northern Pacific, *disclosed them to have attained* a degree of Americanisation, etc.—*Harper's Magazine*, Feb. 1898.

Write "disclosed *the fact that these foreign settlers had attained*," etc.

(*f*) Avoid using the same word in different senses within the same sentence:—

He *means* (intends) to take advice as to the best *means* (method) of testing the fact.

(*g*) Avoid using verbs in different tenses within the same sentence without necessity:—

The lion *roared* to a false note, and then *rates* the jackals for yelping in unison.—*Daily Tel.*, Feb. 5, 1898.

Write *rated* for *rates;* or change *roared* into *roars.*

10. **Clearness of Language.**—We have placed this quality of composition last, because it is the most important. All other qualities of composition lead up to it. If a writer does not make himself understood, he writes to no purpose. We offer a few hints which may assist the beginner to avoid obscurity and cultivate clearness or perspicuity.

(*a*) Repeat the Subject, if there is any fear of a wrong Subject being construed with the next verb:—

He is endeavouring to help some friends, who are very grateful for his assistance, and will not allow any one else to help them.

What is the Subject to *will not allow?* If *who* is meant to be the Subject, there should be no comma after *assistance.* If *he* is meant to be the subject, then to avoid all ambiguity it should be repeated,—"and he will not allow any one else," etc.

(*b*) Repeat a Preposition, if the nouns governed by it are at some distance apart:—

As soon as he had the power, he took vengeance on all those persons, who had injured his friends and relatives, and especially ^ his cousin John.

To what word is *cousin John* the Object? If it is meant to be an Object to the verb *injured*, there should be no comma after *relatives.* If it is meant to be an object to the preposition *on*, then *on* should be repeated—"and especially on his cousin John."

(*c*) Repeat an Auxiliary verb, when the Principal verbs are far enough apart to cause any uncertainty as to the meaning:—

My powers had been cultivated at Oxford from the age of nineteen, when I was still young enough to be moulded into the shape that my advisers considered best for me, and ^ trained to the study of science in preference to that of ancient philosophy.

It is not clear what Auxiliary verb is to be supplied before *trained.* It might be either "*had been*" (carried forward from "My powers *had been* cultivated)," or "*to be*" (carried forward from "young enough *to be* moulded)."

(*d*) Repeat the verb or use some form of the pro-verb *do* after the conjunctions "than" and "as," if the omission of the verb causes any doubt as to the meaning:—

The Presbyterians of Scotland disliked the Independents led by Cromwell as heartily as, or even more heartily than, ^ the Royalists ^.

What are we here to understand by *Royalists?* Is this word an Object to the verb *disliked?* If so, the sentence should be "as heartily as or more heartily than *they did* the Royalists." Or is *Royalists* intended to be the Subject of *disliked?* If so, the sentence should be rewritten "as heartily as or more heartily than the Royalists *did.*" (If the writer prefers it, he can repeat the verb *disliked* instead of using the substitute-verb *did.*)

(*e*) Antecedent clauses must not be mixed up with consequent ones :—

The prosperity of England will decline, if she loses her command of the sea, and other countries step into her place.

This sentence may be rewritten in two different ways.

(1) If England loses her command of the sea, her prosperity will decline and other countries will step into her place.

(2) If England loses her command of the sea and other countries step into her place, her prosperity will decline.

(*f*) Repeat a noun in preference to using a pronoun, if there is any doubt as to the noun to which the pronoun refers. No good writer is afraid to use the same word twice, if by doing so he can escape from the greatest of all faults, ambiguity :—

(1) The lad cannot leave his father: for if he should leave his father, *his father* would die.—*Gen.* xliv. 22.

Here there is no uncertainty: but if for *his father* we write *he*, then *he* might refer either to "lad" or to "father."

(2) They were persons of moderate intellects, even before *they* were impaired by *their* passions.

The first *they* refers to persons, the second to "intellects," while *their* refers back again to persons. The sentence would be much clearer, besides sounding better, if it were rewritten—

They were persons of moderate intellects, even before their intellects were impaired by their passions.

(3) The captain swam ashore, and succeeded in also saving the life of his wife. She was insured in the Northern Marine Insurance for £5000, and carried a full cargo of cement.—Quoted in *Cornhill*, March 1899.

For *she* write *the ship.* Otherwise *she* will denote "wife."

(*g*) Be very careful to place a word as close as possible to the word with which it is connected in sense :—

I did not see what you had in the wheelbarrow, coming suddenly into the garden.

If *coming* is intended to be taken with *I*, place it first, and say, "Coming suddenly into the garden, I did not see," etc. If *coming* is intended to be taken with *you*, change *coming* into *as you were coming.*

Exercises on Section 1.[1]

(*a*) *Rearrange, or if necessary rewrite, the following sentences so as to give more force to certain words as directed*:—

1. No man hath greater love than this. (Emphasise *greater love.*)

2. The battle of Hastings was fought in 1066. (Emphasise (1) *the battle of Hastings*, (2) *in* 1066.)

3. A greater mistake was never made. (Emphasise *never.*)

4. Thou didst not anoint mine head with oil. (Emphasise *mine head.*)

5. The wind blows keen, and night is coming on. (Emphasise *keen.*)

6. If I have told you earthly things, and ye believe not, how shall ye believe, if I tell you of heavenly things?—*New Test.* (Emphasise *earthly* and *heavenly.*)

7. When all were seated, a noise was suddenly heard outside. (Emphasise *suddenly.*)

8. Moses led the children of Israel out of Egypt. (Emphasise (1) *Moses*, (2) *the children of Israel*, (3) *Egypt.*)

9. The reign of Constantine marks the epoch when Christianity was made the religion of the Roman Empire. (Emphasise *the reign of Constantine.*)

10. All classes of the Roman people did not with equal rapidity adopt the Christian creed. (Emphasise (1) *not with equal rapidity*, (2) *all classes of the Roman people.*)

11. Nature adapts the mind of man to his condition. (Emphasise (1) *nature*, (2) *mind.*)

12. Which of you by taking thought can add one cubit to his stature?—*New Test.* (Emphasise *one cubit.*)

(*b*) *Revise the following sentences, using easier words, or shortening the language, or cutting out redundancies*:—

1. He breathed his last in indigent circumstances.

2. At ten o'clock the fatal noose was adjusted to the criminal's neck, and he was launched into eternity.

[1] The teacher, if he thinks fit, can cause the students to go through these sentences with him orally in class, before they begin to write.

3. A vast concourse of people collected to witness the event.

4. Votes were taken by members exhibiting their hands above the heads of dissentients.

5. The rider was precipitated from his horse, but he met with no serious injury.

6. Your meaning does not come within my comprehension.

7. They called into immediate requisition the services of the physician who was accustomed to attend the family.

8. The contest of boats terminated in a victory to our crew.

9. I enjoy a short post-prandial slumber in a chair made for ease of posture.

10. An unwise man, if he is possessed of money, soon parts company with it.

11. Clouds of passion which might obfuscate the intellects of meaner females.—SCOTT.

12. She was tripping it on the light fantastic toe the greater part of last night.

13. Sarah Bernhardt is recuperating from the operation she underwent a week ago.—*Daily Telegraph*, Feb. 25, 1898.

14. Nature seemed to tremble under the fierce rays of the incandescent luminary.—*Mariam*, p. 2.

15. During the month the hebdomadal figures of the fatalities directly due to this undoubted scourge have been 43, then 40, followed by 73, and now 88.—*Daily Telegraph*, Feb. 2, 1898.

16. It is no way germane to such proceedings that I should strike off that County Council, which was the object of legislation ten years ago.—*Lord Salisbury's Speech*, Feb. 3, 1898.

17. Mr. Wheeler introduced an old friend, and brought up the apologue of the body and its members.—*Ibid.*

18. This happy consummation was adumbrated last night at a social gathering of the London Spiritualist Alliance.—*Daily Telegraph*, Feb. 8, 1898.

19. He has vanished with the order of things in which he existed; his lamp cannot be relumed.—*Fortnightly Review*, p. 259, Feb. 1898.

20. We learn without immoderate surprise that there is reason to apprehend the breakdown of the negotiations for a Chinese loan.—*Times Weekly*, Feb. 11, 1898.

21. Experienced members of the feathered tribe are not entrapped with husks of corn.

22. In Queensland the Labour party has antagonised even

the most advanced portions of the community.—*Review of Reviews*, p. 86, Jan. 1898.

23. He instituted a strict investigation and inquiry into the circumstances attending the bankruptcy of that insolvent firm.

24. The meeting gave one unanimous vote in favour of re-electing him as their chairman.

25. It was the universal opinion of all who saw him that he looked none the worse for his prolonged and obstinate attack of fever.

26. We should study the literature of England in chronological order, beginning with the most ancient books and coming down gradually to the most recent.

27. Never did Atticus succeed better in gaining the universal love and esteem of all men.—*Spectator*, No. 467.

28. There cannot be a greater gratification to our barbarous and inhuman wit than to expose whole families to derision, while the traducer remains unseen and undiscovered.—*Ibid.*, No. 23.

29. This week is in a manner set apart and dedicated to serious thoughts.—*Ibid.*, No. 23.

30. Lampoons and satires, that are written with wit and spirit, are like poisoned darts, which not only inflict a wound, but make it incurable.—*Ibid.*, No. 23.

31. A quite unique compliment was paid to the navy.—*Daily Telegraph*, Feb. 14, 1898.

32. Payment of a dividend for the past half-year, at the rate of 20 per cent per annum, making 20 per cent for the year, is recommended by the Directors of the Machinery Trust.—*Ibid.*, Jan. 29, 1898.

(*c*) *Revise the following sentences so as to improve the sound or rhythm*:—

1. So it is that I must be forced to get home partly by stealth and partly by force.—SWIFT.

2. Buildings should not be put up unless in conformity with the by-laws, unless we wish to encourage the jerry-builder.—*Mid. Co. Times*, July 23, 1898.

3. Two great sins, one of omission and the other of commission, were committed by him.

4. Far and wide the plain of the Vardu softened by a delicate blue haze, and in the extreme distance a thread of silver light—the Gulf of Salonica—stretches.

5. Of the western provinces which obeyed the Cæsars, Britain was the last that was conquered, while they (the Cæsars) gave it away before any other province.

6. Knowledge in one of its senses is synonymous with sensation.

7. If the profession of anything is good for anything, practice is better.

8. It is a remarkable fact that some of the most remarkable men in ancient times combined warlike pursuits with political ambition.

9. The blessings of fortune are the lowest; the next are the bodily advantages of health and strength; but the superlative blessings, in fine, are those of the mind.

10. A. came here daily; every other man came every other day.

11. Innumerable failures occur every day in the numerous careers of life.

12. As one peruses the accounts, as they are issued, the outlook seems to be very serious.

13. We should cease persisting in trying to put a quart into a pint pot.

14. Your not having hitherto paid the tithe, should such be the case, and the fact that the sum you are now called upon to pay does not rateably correspond with any previous payment made by you, cannot be raised as an objection.—*Tithe-Collector's Notice.*

15. The friendless state that he was in, and that he wished to die, made every one pity him.

16. Accident having opened a new and most congenial career to him, and having become a great favourite of, and of much use to, Mr. Nash, he ultimately accompanied his patron to London.—C. J. MATHEWS.

17. I have a book printed at Antwerp, and which was once possessed by Adam Smith.

18. He discourses more or less discursively upon the various changes, etc.—*Rev. of Reviews*, p. 165, Aug. 1898.

19. The Carlists possessed an army of their own, now disbanded, but many of whose officers would now expect to be reinstated in their former positions.—*Fort. Rev.*, Aug. 1, 1898.

20. The rest of the evening was devoted to voting away the nation's money.—*Standard*, Aug. 9, 1898.

21. This army is incapable because of sickness of marching anywhere except to the transports.—*Daily Tel.*, Aug. 8, 1898.

22. With a ministry without any authority any sudden course of action may be looked for.—*Ibid.*, p. 9, June 1898.

23. The Americans are perhaps sincere in saying that the United States are not contemplating seizing Cuba in order to annex it.—*Times Weekly*, p. 276, May 6, 1878.

24. Our ministers cannot understand that England is sick of the parish pump and sickest of all of the Manchester school.—*Rev. of Reviews*, p. 354, April 1898.

25. It is the men who have bridged the ocean with the steamship, who have tunnelled the mountains and severed the isthmus, who have made the empire.—*Daily Tel.*, p. 130, Feb. 1898.

26. Mr. J. H. C. said that there had been innumerable instances of bribery in the Guardians' Boards, leading to their supersession by the Government by paid Guardians.—*Ibid.*, April 28, 1898.

27. B. is a handy man with his fists, and maintains after long experience that he would prefer to rely on the clenched hand to defend himself to any weapon yet invented.—*Ibid.*, p. 129, Feb. 1898.

28. When a person has attracted to himself by an elevated moral bond several other persons, when he dies, it always happens that the survivors, often divided up to that time by rivalries, beget a strong friendship the one for the other.—*Translation of* RENAN'S *Apostles*.

(*d*) *Revise the following sentences so as to make the language clearer or otherwise more correct, or point out where the ambiguity lies*:—

1. I will spend a hundred or two pounds rather than be enslaved.—SWIFT.

2. My Christian and surname begin and end with the same letters.—*Spectator*, No. 505.

3. Lysias promised his father never to abandon his friends.

4. A box tree was planted between each plane tree.

5. A river adds much beauty to natural scenery; but a mountain is the thing that carries grandeur in its idea.

6. Mr. Dryden makes a very handsome observation on Ovid's writing a letter from Dido to Æneas in the following words.—*Spectator*, No. 52.

7. This prevents their attending enough to what is in the Bible, and makes battle for what is not in the Bible, but they have put it there.—ARNOLD.

8. Allahabad, one of the principal cities of Northern India, is situated between the junction of the Ganges and the Jumna.

9. All orders not issued by the Managing Director must not be attended to.

10. The history of Natal during the past year has been, except for agricultural depression caused by rinderpest and locusts, the happy history of a colony which has none.—*Times Weekly*, Jan. 7, 1898.

11. The German Mercantile Marine has since 1871 more than trebled its capabilities; and since 1880 has more than doubled them.—*Daily Tel.*, p. 9, Jan. 27, 1898.

12. The trial resulted in the binding over of the two boys who were charged with the stealing and the acquittal of the man who was charged with receiving.—*Ibid.*, Aug. 8, 1898.

13. By a narrow majority the Australian Federal Convention has reversed its decision making it compulsory for the Federation to take over the debts of the individual states.—*Ibid.*, March 3, 1898.

14. The amount which we annually devote to increasing our navy is, roughly speaking, identical with that expended by France, Russia, and Germany.—*Ibid.*, April 22, 1898.

15. Antony was not less desirous of destroying the conspirators than his officers.

16. Sir Morton Peto spoke of the notion that the National Debt might be repudiated with absolute contempt.—*Spectator*, Nov. 15, 1855.

17. They forget to consult, and, as far as they are not vicious, conform to the tastes, feelings, and habits of those whose happiness they would promote, and think only of their own.—W. J. Fox.

18. There is probably no one of this generation who bestows any thought upon the problems of history and politics, who will not acknowledge his indebtedness to Mr. Carlyle.—*Times*, Nov. 18, 1870.

19. We have just heard that the two boys leave school at the end of next week, and hope that they will not return to the same school again.

20. He is a great admirer of the artist who painted that picture and lives at Brompton.

21. The hopes of parents are blighted, if their children are indolent, and the money spent on them is wasted.

22. It is out of the question that Germany and Austria

will join in using force against Turkey.—*Daily Tel.*, Feb. 2, 1898.

23. In view of recent changes, and especially since the war between China and Japan, it seemed desirable that Germany should have a seaport there for safeguarding her interests.—Speech from Berlin quoted in *Daily Tel.*, Feb. 9, 1898.

24. The more faulty we consider this protective system to which Germany, in common with all the other Great Powers of Europe except Great Britain and the United States of America, adheres, the more surprising is the progress recorded.—*Daily Tel.*, Jan. 28, 1898.

25. As it is necessary to have the head clear as well as the complexion, to be perfect in this part of learning, I rarely mingle with the men, but frequent the tea-tables of the ladies. —*Guardian*, No. 10.

Section 2.—Common Errors in the Use of Common Words.

11. **Common Errors.**—Under this heading we have placed a miscellaneous collection of words and usages, about which mistakes are rather commonly made.

Nouns.

(1) **Concrete, Abstract.**—If a noun admits of being used in either a concrete or an abstract sense, take care to use it in one sense only within the same sentence:—

> He is a man of clear *judgment*, but as regards this case I think that the *judgment* he gave was too severe for the offence.

Here the first *judgment* means "the faculty of judging" (Abstract), while the second means "sentence," "verdict" (Concrete). Say "I think that the sentence he gave," etc.

(2) **Collective** nouns must not be connected with adjectives that imply individual qualities, nor with verbs that imply individual action:—

> (1) The average *population* of England is *tall.*
> (2) *Mankind seeks* for happiness in both worlds.

In (1) the Collective noun *population* does not suit the adjective *tall*, which is used only of individual men or women. Say "The average Englishman is tall," or "Most Englishmen are tall."

In (2) the Collective noun *mankind* does not suit the verb *seeks.* Say "Men in general seek," etc., or "Most men seek," etc.

(3) **Abstract** nouns must not be pluralised without authority :—

Leave off such *stupidities.* (Say *acts of stupidity.*)

(4) **Possessive case.**—Be careful how you use this case with nouns denoting anything inanimate or not personified :—

(1) Beware of *life's* shortness.
(2) Look at this *letter's* signature.

In (1) say "the shortness of life." In (2) say "the signature of this letter."

(5) **Apostrophe "s."**—If the apostrophe "*s*" is given to the ear, it should also be given to the eye. In other words, it should be written, if it is pronounced :—

Epps' cocoa. (Write *Epps's* cocoa.)
For *conscience's* sake. (Write *conscience'* sake.)

Pronouns.

(6) **We, I.**—If *we* is substituted for *I*, avoid coupling it with a Singular noun :—

We did things better, when we were *manager.*

Either change *we* to *I*, or change *were manager* to *held the office of manager.*

(7) **I.**—Take care to place this pronoun last, if it occurs in company with other pronouns or with nouns :—

I and James were equal. (Say *James and I.*)

(8) **Them.**—Avoid using this Demonstrative pronoun as if it were a Demonstrative adjective :—

Leave *them* books alone. (Say *those* or *these.*)

Note.—Worse still is the phrase "*them there* books" for "*those* books."

(9) **Myself,** etc.—A Reflexive (or Emphatic) pronoun cannot be the Subject of a verb :—

Myself saw him come. (Say *I myself.*)

(10) **They.**—This is less suitable than *those* as an antecedent of "who":—

They who are rich need no help. (Say *those.*)

(11) **One.**—When this is used, as it often is, as an Indefinite Demonstrative pronoun, it should not be followed by *he*, *his*, *him*, or any other form of Definite Demonstrative; for a Definite Demonstrative cannot have an Indefinite for its antecedent:—

One must not boast of *his* own success. (Say *one's own.*)

(12) **My, our, your, his, her, their.**—Avoid using these Possessives as antecedents to a Relative:—

It astonished *our* eyes *who* saw it. (Say *the eyes of us who.*)

Note.—The construction here discredited is found occasionally among good writers, but too rarely to warrant imitation.

(13) **Who, which, that** (as Subjects of a verb).—These must not be left out in prose, though they sometimes are in poetry:—

I had several men in my ship died of calentures.—SWIFT. (After *ship* say "*who* died.")

(14) **Whom, which, that** (as Objects of a verb).—When one of these Relatives is the connective of two rather long clauses, it is better not to leave it out:—

The action of libel recently brought in the City Magistrate's Court by Miss ——, a nurse, against Mr. ——, in respect of a letter the latter had written to a relative who was being nursed by the plaintiff, terminated in favour of the defendant.—*Daily Telegraph.*

Insert *which* between *a letter* and *the latter.*

(15) **Which, that.**—These Relatives, if they represent different cases, must be mentioned twice, once for each case:—

This is a point, which is of great importance and I cannot impress upon you too strongly.

Here *which* is Subject of the verb *is* in the second clause, and Object of the verb *impress* in the third. As this is bad grammar, we must say "*and which* I cannot impress," etc.

(16) **Same.**—After "same" use *as* or *that* for the following Relative, not *who* or *which* :—

This is the same man *who* came yesterday. (Say *that.*)

(17) **As.**—This must not be used as a Relative, unless it is preceded by *such* or *same* :—

This is not the book *as* I bought. (Say *that.*)

(18) **And who, and which.**—These words must not be used to introduce a Relative clause, unless another Relative clause similarly introduced by *which* has been expressed already :—

It is a doctrine not very easily adapted to his habitual creed, *and which* soon drops out of his mind.

Say "which is not very easily adapted to his habitual creed, and soon drops out of his mind." The Relative need not be repeated after *and*, unless it is in a different case.

Adjectives.

(19) **A, an.**—The *n* of *an* must be written if it is pronounced, but not otherwise :—

A clock is an useful thing.
He is an one-eyed man. } For *an* write *a*.

That is not a hotel.
A historical record. } For *a* write *an*.

In the last two examples the *h* of the first syllable is silent, because the second syllable is accented.

(20) **A, the.**—Take care to repeat the article after *and* when a separate person or thing is introduced by *and* :—

The styles of a poet and orator are not the same. (Say "and *an* orator.")

I like to see a black and white kitten playing together. (Say "and *a* white kitten.")

(21) **Other.**—Take care to use this word with a Positive or a Comparative, and to abstain from using it with a Superlative :—

He is as learned as any person now living. (Say "as any *other* person now living.")

He is more learned than any person now living. (Say "than any *other* person now living.")

Of all other scholars he is the most accurate. (Say "of all scholars.")

(22) **Other . . . but.**—Avoid using the preposition *but* after *other*. If *other* is used, it must be followed by *than*. If *but* is used, *other* must be struck out :—

He had no *other* object *but* to get money. (Say "no other object than," or "no object but.")

(23) **Few, little.**—Observe that these adjectives, unless they are preceded by *a*, are implied negatives :—

(1) *Few* men escaped, and these were rewarded.

(2) *Little* hope remained, and that was soon disappointed.

In (1) say "A few men." *Few men* means "not many men." There is no sense in saying, "Not many men escaped, and these were rewarded." In (2) say "A little hope." *Little hope* means "not much hope." There is no sense in saying, "Not much hope remained, and that was soon disappointed."

(24) **Any, either.**—Observe that *either* is used for two persons or things, and *any* for more than two :—

He was first groom, then coachman, then stable-boy; and he did not do well in *either* capacity. (Say "any capacity," or "any of these capacities.")

(25) **Comparatives.**—Use the Comparative in preference to the Superlative, when two things are mentioned or referred to :—

This picture is the *best* of the two. (Say *better*.)

(26) **Comparatives in "or."**—Avoid using *than* after Latin Comparatives in *or* :—

His work is superior and deserves to be better paid *than* yours. (Say "superior *to* yours, and deserves to be better paid.")

(27) **Like.**—This is an adjective, and therefore must not be used as if it were a conjunction :—

A timid child *like* he is. (Say "*as* he is.")

Verbs.

(28) **Shall, will.**—To express future time in its simplest sense, *shall* is used in the first person, and *will* in the second and third :—

I will be drowned : nobody shall save me.

I will be drowned means "I intend or wish to be drowned." *Nobody shall save me* means "nobody is permitted to save me." Both express a great deal more than merely future time. So unless the person intended to drown himself, he should have said, "I *shall* be drowned, nobody *will* save me."

(29) **Infinitive, Gerund.**—The Noun-Infinitive and the Gerund express the same sense, both being equivalent to Abstract nouns. But if the verb or other word going before requires a preposition, the Infinitive must not be used, since a preposition cannot be placed before it :—

> He persisted *to say* this. (Say *in saying.*)
> I insisted *to have* my fee paid. (Say *on having.*)
> I am confident *to win.* (Say *of winning.*)
> I assisted *to do* this. (Say *in doing.*)
> Disqualified *to compete.* (Say *for competing.*)

(30) **The Qualifying Infinitive.**—When this is used to qualify an adjective, the Active voice is more common than the Passive :—

> The road on account of robbers was difficult *to be passed.* (Say *to pass.*)

(31) **Two Direct objects to the same verb.**—If the same verb does not suit the sense of one of the two Objects mentioned, add a second verb which suits the sense of this object :—

> Few of the Sultans of Turkey have enjoyed a life of peace or a natural death. (Say "*or died* a natural death.")

(32) **One Auxiliary with two Principal verbs.**—Repeat the Auxiliary, if the voice of the two Principal verbs is not the same :—

> The growth of tobacco has been established in India for the last 300 years and overspread the country. (Repeat *has* after *and.*)

(33) **Two Auxiliaries with one Principal verb.**—When two Auxiliaries are used with the same Principal verb, take care to use the Principal verb in two forms, if one form is not sufficient :—

> I never *have* and I never *will* accuse a man falsely.

Here the first Auxiliary (*have*) cannot be followed by a

Principal verb in the form of *accuse.* We must therefore say, "I never *have accused* and I never *will accuse* a man falsely."

(34) **Mixed use of verbs.**—Repeat the full form of the tense in each clause, if the use of the verb is not the same in two successive clauses:—

> Happily we have not and could not have seen a repetition of the scandalous scenes which took place at the Assize Court.—*Times Weekly*, p. 213, April 8, 1898.

The sentence should begin, "Happily we have not *seen* and could not have seen." In the first clause "have seen" is a Present Perfect tense, *Indicative* mood. In the second clause "have seen" is the Perfect *Infinitive*, object to the verb *could.*

Adverbs.

(35) **Quite.** —Avoid the impropriety of using this adverb as if it were an adjective and competent to qualify nouns. *Quite* means "perfectly," "entirely," and should not be used in any sense or for any purpose except an adverbial one:—

> *Quite* an item. (A considerable item.)
> *Quite* a place. (An important place.)
> *Quite* a sensation. (A startling sensation.)

(36) **Since, ago.**—These adverbs mean "from the present time dating backwards." They must be preceded by a verb in the Past Indefinite tense, and be used after some word or words denoting a *period*, not a point, of time:—

> My house *has fallen* two weeks since (or ago.) (Say *fell.*)

(37) **That.**—Avoid the vulgarism of using *that* as if it were an adverb signifying "so":—

> I am *that* tired that I must sit down. (Say *so.*)

(38) **Scarcely, hardly.**—Avoid the vulgarism of using a negative with these adverbs:—

> I *don't hardly* know. (Say *I hardly know.*)

Prepositions.

(39) **Sequence of Prepositions.**[1]—Take care that nouns, adjectives, verbs, and adverbs, if they have to be followed

[1] A great deal of practice in the use of prepositions has been given in Chapter vii. of *Oral Exercises in English Composition*, by the same author.

by prepositions, are followed by the right prepositions, *i.e.* such prepositions as are required by idiom and express the sense :—

> China's resistance *of* Japan was vain. (Say *to.*)
> I have no sympathy *for* his opinions. (Say *with.*)
> A testimonial *of* my industry. (Say *to.*)
> I do not concur *with* that. (Say *with you in that.*)
> I prevailed *with* him to let me go. (Say *on.*)
> I never interfere *with* these matters. (Say *in.*)
> I never interfere *in* other people. (Say *with.*)
> He was killed *with* unkindness. (Say *by.*)

(40) **One Preposition for two.**—If one preposition is not fit to do the work of two, fill up the gap with a second preposition :—

> This fact did not add but detract from his merits. (Say "did not add *to*, but detract from, his merits.")

(41) **Than.**—This must not be used after "different," nor after "prefer," nor after "scarcely" :—

> His ideas are different *than* those of the majority. (Say *from.*)
> He had scarcely gone *than* a letter was brought in. (Say "No sooner gone *than*," or change *than* to *when.*)
> I prefer to do this *than* that. (Say "I prefer doing this *to* doing that.")

(42) **Except, without, against.**—These words are now used only as prepositions. They are not now used as conjunctions :—

> *Except* ye repent. (Say *unless.*)
> *Without* you apologise. (Say *unless.*)
> Have it ready *against* I come. (Say "*by the time that* I come," or "*against my coming.*")

Conjunctions.

(43) **Since.**—This word, when used as a conjunction, must be preceded by some kind of Present tense and followed by a Past Indefinite :—

> Two years *passed* since my father *has died.* (Say *have passed* for *passed*, and *died* for *has died.*)
> It *is* two years since my father *died.* (Correct.)

Note.—In Indirect speech, however, a Present Perfect tense is changed to a Past Perfect:—

Direct. { He exclaimed: "Two years *have* passed since my father died."

Indirect. { He exclaimed that two years *had* passed since his father died.

This is the only exception to the rule given above.

(44) **Not only . . . but also, both . . . and.**—Take care that the first of these is followed by the same part of speech as the second:—

He not only built a house, but also a stable. (Say "built *not only a house*.")

Overwork is bad both for mind and body. (Say "*both for* mind *and for* body," or say "for *both mind and body*.")

(45) **Than . . . as.**—*As* must not be placed after a Comparative:—

My prospects are no better, and not even as good as, they were before. (Say "are no better *than*," or rewrite the sentence thus: "My prospects are no better than they were before, and not even as good.")

(46) **That.**—This must not be used to save the repetition of *when*, *though*, *if*, *whether*, *unless*, etc.:—

If I do not refer to them, it is because they do not come within my subject, not *that* I consider them beneath notice. (Say *because*.)

Far distant be the day when lolling on an easy-chair takes the place of games, or *that* lectures multiply while sports decrease. (Say *when*.)

If it were attempted, and *that* any trouble came of it, you would not be answerable. (Say *if*.)

I had a sensation as though I had been walking through a long dark alley, and *that* I now saw daylight in front of me. (Strike out *that*. The conjunction need not be repeated.)

It must remain fixed for the latter end of April, unless very bad weather should set in, or *that* you can find agreeable travelling company. (Say *unless*.)

(47) **As.**—Avoid the vulgarism of using *as* for *that* to introduce a noun-clause:—

I do not know *as* I need say anything more. (Say *that*.)

(48) **And that.**—If this is used for introducing a noun-clause, take care that it is preceded by another noun-clause which also begins with *that*. When *that* has been mentioned in the first clause, it need not be repeated in the second, unless the subject of the verb is changed :—

(1) I fancied I should get on well by degrees, and *that* I had a good chance of ultimate success.

Insert *that* after "fancied," and strike out *that I* in the subsequent clause. Cancel the comma.

(2) There seemed to be some hope of his recovery, and *that* he would live to make a fresh effort.

For *of his recovery* say *that he would recover*, and omit *that he would* in the subsequent clause. Cancel the comma.

(3) Physicians declare lung-disease to be difficult to cure in England, and *that* the patient must go to a more equable climate.

Say "that lung-*disease is difficult*," etc. In the subsequent clause we must not strike out *that*. The conjunction must be repeated, because the subject is changed. Retain the comma.

(49) **Though, but.**—Remember that *though* is a Subordinative conjunction, while *but* is a Co-ordinative one and therefore more emphatic than *though* :—

He is an honest man, *but* poor; and honesty is always rewarded.

The last clause shows that the emphasis is on the word *honest*, not on *poor*. "But" must therefore be reduced to the weaker "though"; and the sentence should be rewritten: "Though poor, he is an honest man; and honesty is always rewarded."

(50) **Whether . . . whether.**—When contradictory or very different alternatives are offered, repeat the conjunction *whether* after *or*; otherwise simply say *or* :—

(1) I beg to ask whether our minister at Pekin has protested against or in any way recognised the claims made by the German minister and consul.—*House of Commons*, 10th August 1898.

Since the alternatives are very different, the wording should be: "I beg to ask whether our minister at Pekin has protested against or whether he has in any way recognised," etc.

(2) I beg to ask whether our minister at Pekin has protested against or in any way opposed the claims, etc.

Here *or* is sufficient, because protesting against and opposing are kindred actions, and not opposite alternatives.

(51) **Or.**—When the noun following *or* is contrasted with the noun preceding it, put an article or a preposition, if possible, before the second noun.

Has he gained a prize or scholarship? (Say *or a scholarship.*)

Did he influence you with promises or threats? (Say *or with threats.*)

Exercise on Section 2.

Correct, improve, or justify the following[1]:—

1. The ancient creed of Persia assumes the coexistence of a good and evil power, which divide the sovereignty of the world between them.

2. The failure of the spring and autumn harvest, one succeeding the other in the same year, led to a serious famine in India in 1897.

3. He mistook James' hat for his own.

4. A coxcomb, flushed with many of these infamous victories (over young women), shall say he is sorry for the poor fools, protest and vow he never thought of matrimony.—*Spectator*, No. 288.

5. The jury summoned to attend the court was a clever body of men.

6. Mazzini did more for the emancipation of Italy than any living man of his own time.

7. The squadron consisted of about 200 men, and divided the booty among themselves after the victory.

8. A masterly genius does not care what men say of him.

9. I heard the multitude's shout.

10. Bring them books down from the shelf.

11. No one as yet had exhibited the structure of the human kidneys, Vesalius having examined them only in dogs.—HALLAM.

[1] *To the Teacher.*—We are of opinion that to save time, and to encourage quickness and competition, many of the examples in this exercise should be done orally in class, and not in writing. The teacher, however, will of course be the best judge of this.

12. The claim, which is made for these persons, and they would not perhaps claim for themselves, cannot be proved.

13. In the time of Christ the three chief sects among the Jews were the Pharisees, Sadducees, and the Essenes; and they thoroughly disliked each other.

14. My readers, too, have the satisfaction to find that there is no rank or degree among them who have not their representative in this club.—*Spectator*, No. 43.

15. You shall seldom find a dull fellow of good education, but, if he happens to have any leisure upon his hands, will turn his head to one of those two amusements for all fools of eminence,—politics or poetry.—*Spectator*, No. 43.

16. Your Englishman is just as serious in his amusements as in any act of his life.

17. I prefer a profitable occupation, and which I can look back upon afterwards without regret.

18. There is no popular *Life of Oliver Cromwell* in print, those by Guizot and Carlyle being too bulky for general use.

19. I have read of a man who was very rich, but he considered himself poor all the same.

20. On a subject in which the feelings of others are entitled to respect, one must keep his thoughts to himself.

21. How do you distinguish between a poet and orator?

22. I have few things more to talk about, but there is no time now; you shall hear them to-morrow.

23. "A little knowledge," says Pope, "is a dangerous thing"; but, with all due deference to Pope, little knowledge is better than none.

24. My friend sent me a pair of turkeys to choose from; but I returned them with thanks, and told him I did not want any of them.

25. Several neighbouring gentlemen contributed works, for which they had either given commissions direct to our most distinguished artists, or had purchased them from the Royal Academy.

26. You will perceive that this is the same horse which yourself possessed four years ago.

27. I do not think that the squire and myself ever had better sport together than we had that day.

28. On comparing his gun with mine, they pronounced his to be the best.

29. In selecting this house, I had no other object but to get the one nearest the railway station.

30. In commerce it often happens that they who have abilities want capital, and they who have capital want abilities.

31. I never have and never will attack a man for speculative opinions.—BUCKLE.

32. Quite an innovation in the mode of dressing the hair has come into fashion this year.

33. My almost drunkenness of heart.—BYRON.

34. My success or otherwise will be communicated to me by post this evening.

35. I really believe that except to doctors and clergymen, and the very few intimate friends who have seen me frequently, even my state of extremity has been doubted.—MISS MITFORD.

36. In his translation of the *Iliad*, Pope has sometimes given us a picture of a very different kind than what Homer intended.

37. Breaking a constitution by the very same errors, that so many have been broken before.—SWIFT.

38. The trees have cast their leaves a month ago.

39. I will not let thee go, except thou bless me.—*Gen.* xxxii. 26.

40. He not only gave them his advice, but a good deal of pecuniary help besides.

41. It is contrary both to justice and common-sense to do such a thing as that.

42. This building is both superior in size and more suitable in design than any other town-hall that I have seen.

43. No one ever worked more regularly or so carefully as he.

44. We decidedly prefer reading the *Swiss Family Robinson* at this moment than the rather characterless *Masterman Ready*. —MISS YONGE.

45. The modern Germans are fond of metaphysics like the ancient Athenians were.

46. But scarce were they hidden away, I declare,
Than the giant came in with a curious air.—TOM HOOD.

47. I am not that fond of my books that I like to stay in the house reading them all the afternoon.

48. I consider him to be very clever, and that he will do great credit to his teachers.

49. If any such rash project were attempted and that any serious trouble came of it, the fault would be yours, not mine.

50. I pass over this subject in silence, because it does not

come within my present purpose, and not that I feel at all incompetent to deal with it.

51. He is an industrious boy, but naturally rather dull, and industry is almost always rewarded in the long run.

52. Whether this conflagration was the work of an incendiary, or that some one employed by the firm was guilty of carelessness, will never be ascertained.

53. The man as came here yesterday went away to-day.

54. That operation was first performed on rabbits; it is now performed with success on the human family.

55. It is interesting to observe the various substitutes for paper before its invention.

56. The virtuous and the vile, the learned and ignorant, the temperate and debauched, all give and return the jest.—BROWN'S *Characteristics*.

57. How should I look to have any part of my desire herein satisfied, unless myself be careful to satisfy the like desire which is in other men?—HOOKER.

58. Air, when carefully tested, is found to contain something else than nitrogen and oxygen.—GEIKIE.

59. The misreading of a person's character is an error rather difficult to be avoided.

60. He is as likely to make a good living for himself as his brothers have done.

61. Driving down the street, his horse ran off, and he was thrown out.

62. There have been three famous talkers in Great Britain, either of whom would illustrate what I say about dogmatists well enough for my purpose.—HOLMES.

63. We already possess four times as great a trade with China as every other nation put together.—*Report of G. Balfour's Speech*, Feb. 4, 1898.

64. No one would accuse the representative of an English newspaper as an Irishman desirous of exaggerating the distress and grievances of his country.—*Dillon's Speech*, Feb. 10, 1898.

65. Quite a record gallop fell to the Whaddon Chase from Wing, where Lord Orkney kept open house.—*Daily Tel.*, Feb. 10, 1898.

66. We were no sooner sat down, but after having looked upon me a little while, she said, etc.—*Spectator*, No. 7.

67. It is difficult to imagine a rougher experience than that involved by his attempt to carry out the adventurous project of

reaching Paris from New York by land.—*Times Weekly*, p. 92, Feb. 11, 1898.

68. It (the work of Abbé Dubois) records the impressions of an acute and a patient observer of the actual life of the Hindus. —*Times Weekly*, p. 92, Feb. 11, 1898.

69. The predicate of a sentence always is or contains a verb.

70. Few of his friends except myself knew of his being in the kingdom.

71. The public and private good are so far from being inconsistent that they promote one another.

72. Men and women who have no object or aim than amusement.—*Daily Telegraph*, p. 8, Feb. 16, 1898.

73. Though these nine warships were built in different dockyards, the design of the whole nine is the same, with slight differences in points of detail.—*Daily Telegraph*, p. 9, Feb. 16, 1898.

74. Bounteous harvests in the Punjaub and in the wheat lands of the River Plate are expected to furnish supplies from the Southern Hemisphere to the extent of about 5,000,000 quarters, etc.—*Daily Telegraph*, April 29, 1898.

75. Mr. Gladstone was able to sit for a short while in an easy chair on the small lawn by the side of the house, which is charmingly sheltered by quite a small pine-forest.—*Daily Tel.*, March 22, 1898.

76. I shall leave this house at once without you put it in proper repair.

77. You will have to get that lesson by heart like I did.

78. He preferred to take a sweep-crossing than beg his bread from door to door.

79. I am anxious for the time when he will talk as much nonsense to me as I have to him.—W. S. LANDOR.

80. From this coalition, and not from the spirit of its own laws and institutions, he attributed the harsh and ungenerous treatment of our fallen enemy, Napoleon Buonaparte. — MRS. FLETCHER.

81. The position of the Cabinet is exceedingly difficult between the danger of foreign and civil war, either of which may be precipitated by a simple error. — *Telegram from Madrid*, April 14, 1898.

82. The image and name of Goethe occurs to us at once when we try to evoke the man of most perfect brain who ever existed.—*Fortnightly Review*, p. 766, May 1898.

83. The condition of Mr. Gladstone, who is without pain, is not quite so favourable.—*Daily Telegraph*, April 21, 1898.

84. By that time he will have come in contact with some of the most gifted genius of the earth.—*Cassell's Family Magazine*, p. 158.

85. Here is a specimen from *Hamlet* which illustrates the unmethodical character conversation will assume when a principal interlocutor is pursuing a private train of thought with intense eagerness.—ABBOTT AND SEELEY, *English Lessons for English Readers*, p. 231.

86. The whole question is accordingly remitted to a committee, the composition of which has already been announced in our columns, who will consider and report upon with all convenient speed the proposals of the Government of India.—*Times*, May 3, 1898.

SECTION 3.—SENTENCE AND PARAGRAPH.

12. Unity of Sentence.—A sentence should express one main fact at a time, and not more than one. This is called the **Unity** of a sentence. The sentence as a whole may, it is true, consist of several clauses or smaller sentences; but if it does, the clauses must be so closely connected in sense, as to leave the impression that *one main fact* has been stated, and not more than one. Such a sentence as the following is devoid of unity, because here two perfectly distinct statements are muddled together as if they were one:—

> He invaded France, but Philip wisely declined a pitched battle, and having exhausted his money and loaded himself with debt, Edward returned the next year to England.—RANSOME, *Short Hist. Eng.*, p. 48, ed. 1897.

This sentence should be broken up into two, a separate sentence being given for each separate statement:—

> Edward invaded France, but Philip wisely declined a pitched battle. Having exhausted his money and loaded himself with debt, Edward returned the next year to England.

To take one more example:—

> The battles are adequately illustrated, and we have seen no better boy's book of late than *Helmet and Spear*.—*Spectator*, p. 505, April 6, 1901.

There is little or no connection between the two statements made in the above sentence, which should be divided into two sentences by striking out the conjunction "*and*" and placing a full stop between them.

Note.—Since a sentence is commenced with a capital letter to show that it stands apart from any preceding sentence, it ought not as a rule to be commenced with the conjunction *And*. The practice of commencing a sentence with *And* is, however, very common among beginners. Its use in such a position should be not merely condemned, but prohibited. This is the best way of putting an end to a practice which is liable to so much abuse.

13. **Unity of Paragraph.**—A paragraph is a group of sentences.[1] An essay is a group of paragraphs concerning a given subject. On what principle, then, is the division into paragraphs to be made? On the principle of Unity. A paragraph should be a separate whole; *i.e.* it must deal with one main division of the essay at a time, just as a sentence must make one main statement at a time. The subject or main point of a paragraph, on which its unity depends, is called the **theme.** This is generally expressed in a sentence of its own at the commencement of the paragraph. All other sentences included in the same paragraph should have some direct bearing on the theme, and this by way of comment, explanation, enlargement, illustration, or contrast. We give one example:—

> Of Pau I shall say nothing. It would be real impertinence in one, who spent only three days in it, to describe a city which is known to all Europe; which is a permanent English colony, and boasts of one, sometimes two packs of English foxhounds. But this I may be allowed to say. Of all delectable spots that I have yet seen, Pau is the most delectable. Of all the landscapes which I have yet beheld, that from the Place Royale is for variety, richness, and grandeur the most glorious; at least as I saw it for the first time.—KINGSLEY, *Prose Idylls*, v. p. 182.

[1] A paragraph is usually a *group* of sentences; but sometimes, for purposes of exposition, one very important or leading statement is placed in a paragraph by itself.

Observe that every sentence in the above paragraph has some bearing upon the first sentence, and that the first sentence expresses the theme. In describing his tour, the author disclaims any intention of dwelling upon the beauties of Pau: "Of Pau I shall say nothing." In the remaining sentences he gives his reasons for this decision, and makes one or two passing comments before bringing the paragraph to a close.

We now give an example of a paragraph which contains a flagrant breach of the rule of Unity:—

The Royal Tour in Australia.

The great event of the month in the Colonies has been the opening of the Australasian Parliament by the Duke and Duchess of Cornwall. The Royal progress in Australia has been one long triumphal procession. Colony has vied with colony as to which could make the most overwhelming manifestation of their loyalty and enthusiasm. So far everything has gone without a hitch, and when the Royal party returns, it will have to report that the stately ceremonial of the christening of the Commonwealth passed off in a fashion which bodes well for the future relations between the Commonwealth and the Empire. The King had a narrow escape from drowning last month. He was on board the *Shamrock II.* when Sir T. Lipton's yacht suddenly capsized in a squall. Fortunately no one was hurt.—*Rev. of Reviews*, p. 529, June 1901.

Here the theme of the paragraph, as distinctly given by the writer himself, is the "Royal Tour in Australia." Yet before concluding the paragraph he darts off, without giving a word of warning, into an entirely new subject,—an accident off the English coast. "Empire" should have been the last word of the paragraph. A new paragraph should begin with the words "The King."

A letter or an essay always gains in clearness as well as in force, if a new paragraph is commenced with every new turn of the argument or description. In the report by the Cambridge Syndicate on the Local Examinations of December 1900, the examiner gives a note of warning:— "The essays were well written and well expressed. Punctuation and *the proper division* of the essays *into paragraphs* were, however, still much neglected at many centres."

14. Sentences Periodic and Loose.—A complex sentence can be either Periodic or Loose. It is *periodic*, if the sense is completed by the time the sentence comes to an end; *loose*, if after the principal clause has been stated, a qualifying clause or clauses are tacked on to it:—

> Though I speak with the tongues of men and of angels, and have not charity, I am become as sounding brass, or a tinkling cymbal.—1 *Cor.* xiii. 1.

This is Periodic, because the qualifying clauses are stated first. The following sentence is Loose, because the qualifying clause is placed last instead of first:—

> A crowd is not company, and faces are but a gallery of pictures, where there is no love.—BACON.

As a general rule, a Periodic sentence is to be preferred to a Loose one, on account of its superior force and lucidity. But sometimes it improves a sentence to place the principal clause between two qualifying clauses, as in the following example:—

> As the sun at this time of the year sets as early as four o'clock, we had better start at once, if we are to get to our journey's end in daylight.

The sentence would have an awkward sound, had the order of the clauses been as follows:—

> As the sun at this time of the year sets as early as four o'clock, if we are to get to our journey's end in daylight, we had better start at once.

15. Use of a Parenthesis.—If the writer wishes to say something, which is useful by way of comment or explanation, but has no direct bearing on the main point, he may do so by inserting a parenthesis into the body of the sentence: *provided the parenthesis is short*, this is not felt to be a breach of unity (§ 12):—

> This gentleman (for I found he was treated as such by his audience) was entertaining a whole table of listeners with the project of an opera.—ADDISON, *Spectator*, No. 31, para. 4.

The unity of the sentence is not marred by the brief remark here made in brackets. In the following sentence, however, the length of the parenthesis creates an awkward break in the sense, and we feel that the unity of the sentence has been violated :—

> Failing as he does to recognise the obligation to speak the truth imposed by any of our solemn affirmations (you cannot make him put his hand on his son's head, and declare that the youth may die, if the witness speaks not the truth,—which is about the only way to save him from lying), and conscious that whatever course he may adopt, he will not lose the respect of his fellows, the mind of the (Hindoo) witness is almost in an equilibrium, till the weight of his interest thrown into the scale decides the matter.—CURRIE, *Behind the Surface*, pp. 165, 166.

This sentence might be broken up into two, in the following way :—

> Failing as he does to recognise the obligation to speak the truth imposed by any of our solemn affirmations, and conscious that whatever course he may adopt, he will not lose the respect of his fellows, the mind of the witness is almost in an equilibrium, till the weight of his interest thrown into the scale decides the matter. The only way to save him from lying would be to make him put his hand on his son's head, and declare that the youth may die, if the witness speaks not the truth ; but this you are not allowed to do.

16. **Length of Sentence.**—No absolute rule can be laid down as to the length of a sentence. We may, however, safely advise the beginner to abstain from making very long sentences. When sentences are spun out to a great length, there is always a risk of the construction becoming confused or the sense obscured. Nothing in the way of clearness or force is gained, but much is lost in such a prolonged sentence as the following :—

> There are girls, however, on whom the education and independence of to-day are having a deeper effect, and whose intellectual qualities and sympathies, being largely

> developed, welcome the freedom they enjoy, not from the standpoint of amusement or pleasure, but from the prospect it opens up to them of a wider and deeper life in which their mental powers may find an outlet, and who may probably be more impatient of old-fashioned opinions and restraints than were girls of a former generation.—*Fort. Review*, p. 635, Oct. 1900.

It cannot be said that this sentence is deficient in unity, since the parts are all well connected with one another in sense. The fault of the sentence is that it is long and straggling, that the construction is rather involved, and that the attention of the reader is somewhat wearied before it is finished. Most readers, we think, would prefer to see it broken up into three sentences as follows:—

> There are girls, however, on whom the education and independence of to-day are having a deeper effect. The intellectual qualities and sympathies *of such girls*, being largely developed, welcome the freedom they enjoy, *and this* not from the standpoint of amusement or pleasure, but from the prospect it opens up to them of a wider and deeper life, in which their mental powers may find an outlet. *Girls so influenced* may probably be more impatient of old-fashioned opinions and restraints than were those of a former generation.

Observe that we have detached the second sentence from the previous one by substituting *of such girls* for *and whose;* and to give it more point we have inserted the words *and this.* In the last sentence we have written *girls so influenced* for *and who;* in the original sentence this Relative is separated from its antecedent "girls" by no fewer than fifty-nine words.

Though a long sentence is to be avoided, when the sense can be more lucidly expressed in two or three shorter ones, yet a succession of little periods, which are obviously connected in sense and could easily be put together in a single sentence, is a fault in the opposite direction. One extreme should be avoided as much as the other:—

(1) Northumberland's triumph seemed to be complete. The heir to the throne was a Protestant, and his own son's wife.

(2) Hyde's party opposed the Remonstrance. It was carried by a small majority of eleven. It was then printed and published.

The periods in (1) and (2) can be easily put together, so as in each case to make a single sentence of very moderate length :—

(1) Northumberland's triumph seemed to be complete, since the heir to the throne was a Protestant and his own son's wife.

(2) The Remonstrance was opposed by Hyde's party, but carried by a small majority of eleven, and then printed and published.

On the other hand, the little periods quoted below cannot be combined into a complex or compound sentence, and no attempt should be made to do so :—

With the dead there is no rivalry. In the dead there is no change. Plato is never sullen. Cervantes is never petulant. Demosthenes never comes unseasonably. Dante never stays too long. No difference of political opinion can alienate Cicero. No heresy can excite the horror of Bossuet.—MACAULAY.

17. Length of Paragraph.—The length of a paragraph depends upon the scope of the "theme" (§ 13), and the selection of the theme and the mode of stating it are at the option of the writer himself. We advise the beginner, however, to make his paragraphs short rather than long. A lengthy paragraph in a long book or a long essay may be quite appropriate, but in a short essay or in a letter a lengthy paragraph amounts almost to a fault; for in such compositions several different points have to be touched upon within a narrow space, and a separate paragraph should be given to each of them.

In the essay (3) quoted below in § 41, the reader will find that all the paragraphs, ten in number, are short; and that out of these ten there are three that consist of a single sentence. We consider that the separation of that essay into ten paragraphs is correct, because each paragraph deals with a distinct sub-division of the subject, "The Uses of Books."

Exercise on Section 3.

Rewrite the following extracts in such a way as to remove the violation of unity (if it exists) or reduce the length of the sentence :—

1. Welbeck Abbey, the seat of the Duke of Portland, was seriously damaged on Thursday night by a fire which broke out in the Oxford wing, from which the Marquis of Titchfield, the heir, and his sister and brother were rescued.—*Daily Telegraph*, p. 8, Oct. 6, 1900.

2. Women are seeking for means to escape the mission that nature has cast on them, and they will probably continue so to struggle, while they will not realise how ineffably feeble they are in the fight, and until they are vanquished, we may possibly see even more wonderful developments than any we have yet witnessed.—*Fort. Review*, p. 636, Oct. 1900.

3. What is still worse, there is throughout the whole of this biography a dark uncharitable cast, by which the most unfavourable construction is put upon almost every circumstance in the character and conduct of my illustrious friend, who I trust will by a true and firm delineation be vindicated both from the injurious misrepresentations of this author, and from the aspersions of a lady who once lived in great intimacy with him.—BOSWELL'S *Life of Johnson*.

4. When his father's unsuccessful speculations reduced the family to straits, he obtained through the good offices of Lord Houghton a post in the British Museum, which he held for twenty years, until his second marriage made him a rich man, when he bought an estate in Sussex, and settled down as a country gentleman, afterwards migrating to Hastings, and finally to Lymington.—*Spectator*, p. 845, Dec. 8, 1900.

5. A very widespread expression of sympathy has been obtained for the broad general principle, that the names of all our dead should be permanently preserved in an appropriate building in London, whether they were British born or whether they came from the colonies, whose assistance in this campaign has marked the birth of a coherent and united empire, in which every part is ready to share in the common responsibility and to bear the common burden.—*Daily Telegraph*, p. 5, Aug. 2, 1900.

6. As regards the education of the Irish Catholics of the better class, where Catholic Ireland is plainly and greatly

wronged—Mr. Balfour has candidly acknowledged the fact—his eloquent and earnest speeches do him infinite credit—the Government has been silent and has done nothing.—*Fort. Review*, p. 265, Feb. 1901.

7. Without dwelling upon a most unlucky appointment, believed to be the result of a crooked intrigue, for which he must be held in part responsible—an avowed abetter of the "Plan of Campaign"—a swindling conspiracy of the basest sort—is not exactly a personage to place in high office—he has deeply offended thousands of the best men in Ireland.—*Ibid.*, p. 264, Feb. 1901.

8. The Queen will with her own gracious hands lay the foundation-stone of the new buildings, which, under the name of the "Victoria and Albert Museum," and together with the "Science College," to be simultaneously constructed, are destined to complete the magnificent idea which the Prince Consort cherished in establishing at South Kensington the centre of the artistic life of the kingdom.—*Daily Telegraph*, p. 8, May 17, 1899.

9. Mr. Treves follows all the movements and activities of the hospital in his little book, which Messrs. Cassell and Co. have produced in admirable taste as to paper, binding, and type.—*Ibid.*, p. 11, Nov. 1, 1900.

10. General Buller was brought into telegraphic communication with Lord Roberts, who has returned to Pretoria, on Saturday afternoon, at which time he was advancing against the enemy's position at Spitz Kop.—*Ibid.*, p. 8, Sept. 12, 1900.

11. Archbishop Tillotson died in this year. He was exceedingly beloved both by King William and Queen Mary, who nominated Dr. Tennison, Bishop of Lincoln, to succeed him.—BURNET.

12. In this uneasy state both of his public and private life, Cicero was oppressed by a new and cruel affliction, the death of his beloved daughter, Tullia; which happened after her divorce from Dolabella, whose manners and humours were entirely disagreeable to her.—MIDDLETON, *Life of Cicero.*

13. Their march was through an uncultivated country, whose savage inhabitants fared hardly, having no other riches than a breed of lean sheep, whose flesh was rank and unsavoury by reason of their continual feeding upon sea-fish.—PLUTARCH, *Eng. Trans.*

14. At length the sun approaching melts the snow, sets

longing men at liberty, and affords them means and time to make provision against the next return of cold. It breaks the icy fetters of the main, where vast sea-monsters pierce through floating islands, with arms which can withstand the crystal rock; whilst others, who of themselves seem great as islands, are by their bulk alone armed against all but man, whose superiority over creatures of such stupendous size and force should make him mindful of his privilege of reason, and force him humbly to adore the great composer of these wondrous frames, and the author of his own superior wisdom.—SHAFTESBURY.

CHAPTER III.—PUNCTUATION, CAPITALS, SYLLABIC DIVISION, UNDERLINING.[1]

SECTION 1.—PUNCTUATION: HOW TO USE THE VARIOUS MARKS OR STOPS.

18. Necessity of Stops in Written Composition.—Punctuation or the use of stops divides one sentence from another sentence, or one part of a sentence from another part. Its object is to make what is written or printed more readily intelligible to the reader; and it does this partly by showing the reader when and where he is to make a **pause** (an actual pause, if he is reading aloud,—a mental one, if he is reading to himself), and partly by helping him to see how the different parts of a sentence are related to one another by **grammatical construction**. In fact, punctuation is an attempt to indicate in writing the stops or pauses that we should make in talking. Punctuation therefore is an important element in written as distinct from oral composition. In the Syndicate's report on the Cambridge Locals for 1900, the

[1] *To the Teacher.*—Punctuation is a difficult subject to a beginner. Unfortunately it is very important in written composition. As this chapter is long and rather difficult, we recommend that it be taken up by instalments; first §§ 20, 21 on the Comma; then §§ 22-24 on the Full Stop, the Colon, and the Semicolon; then §§ 25-33 on the remaining marks. Sections 2, 3, and 4 can be taken up after the three instalments of punctuation have been finished.

examiner makes the following comment respecting the "Junior" paper on Composition: "The lack of punctuation caused loss of marks in many instances" (p. xxii.).

Much confusion may be caused by using wrong stops, or by putting stops in wrong places, or by leaving them out where they are wanted. To take the following example:—

> Mr. A. was standing near the house where we lived was not a desirable place of residence.

This will bear two meanings according to the punctuation that we give to it:—

(1) Mr. A. was standing near the house. Where we lived was not a desirable place of residence.

(2) Mr. A. was standing near. The house where we lived was not a desirable place of residence.

In talking, *i.e.* in oral composition, the speaker, to express the first sentence, would drop his voice at the word *house*, and make a pause before uttering the word *where*. To express the second sentence, he would drop his voice at the word *near*, and make a pause before uttering the words *The house*. Punctuation, then, is a system of marks, by which a writer endeavours to show to the eye of the reader what, if he were speaking instead of writing, he would express by his voice.

19. System of Marks or Stops.—The following are the principal marks or stops used in the English system of punctuation:—

Comma	,	Apostrophe	'
Full Stop or Period	.	Dash	—
Colon	:	Brackets	( ) [ ]
Semicolon	;	Hyphen	-
Note of Interrogation	?	Diæresis	..
Quotation marks	" "	Asterisk	*
Note of Exclamation	!	Omission mark	^

Comma.

20. Comma.—This is the shortest and most frequently used of all the marks or stops employed in English composition. As a general rule, a comma should be inserted, whenever a *slight* pause is to be made in reading. But in the use of commas there is much diversity of practice, and it is difficult to lay down precise rules. What is called "close punctuation" consists in the frequent use of commas, which some writers and printers carry to a fault. The sparing use of commas is called "open punctuation." It is better to err on the side of this extreme than on that of the other. As an example of the excessive use of commas we quote the following:—

> There are girls, however, on whom the education, and independence, of to-day, is having a deeper effect, and whose intellectual qualities, and sympathies, being largely developed, welcome the freedom they enjoy, not from the standpoint of amusement, or pleasure, but from the prospect it opens up to them of a wider, and deeper life, in which their mental powers may find an outlet.—*Fortnightly Review*, p. 635, Oct. 1900.

The superabundance of commas here used is a hindrance rather than an aid to the reading and understanding of the text; it thus defeats one of the main objects for which stops are used at all. The punctuation of the above passage might well be reduced by one-half,—seven commas being used instead of fourteen.

> There are girls however, on whom the education and independence of to-day is (are ?) having a deeper effect, and whose intellectual qualities and sympathies, being largely developed, welcome the freedom they enjoy, not from the standpoint of amusement or pleasure, but from the prospect it opens up to them of a wider and deeper life, in which their mental powers may find an outlet.

As an example of the too sparing use of commas we quote the following sentence, in which, though it consists of no fewer than six clauses, not a single comma occurs:—

> The man who allows public affairs to be carried on in a way he dislikes because he is too indifferent or too indolent to vote for a Deputy who will see that they are carried on differently is not the man to make a revolution.—*Spectator*, p. 43, Jan. 12, 1901.

There is obviously a pause in the sense after the word *dislikes* and after the word *differently:* any one who read out the sentence without making these two pauses would be considered a bad reader. We might therefore rewrite the sentence as follows, inserting two commas where at present there are none :—

> The man who allows public affairs to be carried on in a way he dislikes, because he is too indifferent or too indolent to vote for a Deputy who will see that they are carried on differently, is not the man to make a revolution.

21. Uses of Commas.—We will now attempt to show how commas (according to what we believe to be the generally received practice) should be used in the composition of (1) Simple, (2) Compound, (3) Complex sentences.

(1) *Simple sentences:* the chief positions of commas are—

(*a*) Between nouns or pronouns in apposition :—

> Alexander, the king of Macedon, conquered Persia.
> My cousin, William, has gone out to sea.

(*b*) Between two or more words of the same part of speech, not connected by the conjunction *and.* If the last two words in a series are connected by *and,* a comma must still be used before *and* :—

A dull, heavy sound was heard outside. (*Adjectives.*)
Greece, Italy, and Spain are peninsulas of Europe. (*Nouns.*)
He lived soberly, prudently, and industriously. (*Adverbs.*)
Steam propels, elevates, saws, prints, threshes, etc. (*Verbs.*)

Similarly a comma is placed between repeated words and phrases :—

> Hark, hark, the lark at heaven's gate sings.
> Never again, never again, shall such a thing happen.

(*c*) After the Nominative of Address :—

> Friends, Romans, countrymen, lend me your ears.

If the Nom. of Address comes in the middle of the sentence, a comma must be also placed before it :—

> I saw it, my friends, I saw it with my own eyes.

(*d*) Absolute constructions are marked off from the rest of the sentence by commas :—

Nominative absolute.—The sun having set, we all went home.
Impersonal absolute.—Supposing this to be true, you are guilty.
Imperative absolute.—We have gone, say, ten miles.
Infinitive absolute.—I am, to tell you the truth, thoroughly dissatisfied.

(*e*) Before and after words interpolated in the middle of a quotation :—

"Leave the room," said he, "and do not come back."
"Great is truth," says a Latin proverb, "and it will prevail."

(*f*) After an adverbial phrase at the beginning of a sentence :—

In fact, his poetry is no better than prose.

Note.—Here, however, the use of a comma is optional. The pause produced by the comma that is placed after "fact," arrests the reader's attention and thereby throws a little more emphasis on the sentence that follows.

(*g*) To separate words or phrases that go together in pairs from other words or phrases similarly related :—

By night or by day, at home or abroad, asleep or awake, he is pursued with remorse.
We shall be wise to assume that ship for ship, gun for gun, and man for man, we are no more than equal to our neighbours for fighting power.—*Empire Review*, p. 52, Feb. 1901.

(*h*) Before and after a participial or adjectival phrase, provided that the said phrase has a force equivalent to that of a subordinate clause, and is not used in a merely qualifying sense :—

Caesar, having defeated the Gauls, led his forces into Britain.

Some persons would not use commas in such a sentence as the above. It seems more appropriate, however, to put them in, since they would certainly be needed if we substituted a subordinate clause for the participial phrase :—

Caesar, after he had defeated the Gauls, led his forces into Britain.

Note.—When a participle is used in a merely qualifying sense, it should *not* be separated from its noun by a comma any more than an adjective should be :—

A man convinced against his will is of the same opinion still.

(*i*) Explanatory phrases are separated by commas :—

The field was oblong, 60 yards in length, 40 in breadth.

(*j*) Parenthetical clauses can be marked off by commas :—

He was not aware, it would seem, how wrong his accounts were.

Note.—There are other ways, as will be shown below, by which parentheses can be marked off. But for short parentheses such as the above, a comma at either end is sufficient.

(*k*) To introduce words used by a speaker. The sentence so quoted must begin with a capital :—

What I say unto you I say unto all, Watch.—*New Test.*

People are asking the question, What is to be done with the army?—*Spectator*, p. 17, Jan. 5, 1901.

Note.—The comma is frequently thus used when the quotation is short. For longer quotations the colon followed by a dash and quotation-marks is more frequently used. See § 23 (2).

(*l*) To mark the omission or save the repetition of a verb; here, however, the use of a comma is optional :—

My regiment is bound for India; yours, for Gibraltar.

(*m*) When two prepositions are used with a single noun, a comma should be placed after both of them :—

He is in the same grade with, but junior to, me in service.

(2) *Compound sentences.*—The chief rules are the following :—

(*a*) If the co-ordinate clauses are connected by *and*, and if the verb of each clause has a separate Subject of its own, the separation of clauses is marked by a comma :—

His vanity is greater than his ignorance, and what he lacks in knowledge is supplied by impudence.

Note.—No comma should be used, if the verbs of the connected clauses have only one subject between them :—

I made haste and caught him.

He took up a stone and threw it at the mad dog.

(*b*) If the co-ordinate clauses are connected by some conjunction other than *and*, and if the separation of the clauses is not intended to be strongly marked, or if the verbs in both clauses have the same subject, a comma is sufficient (see § 24 (3), *Note*) :—

High wages do not necessarily increase the cost of production, but often lower it by increasing the labourer's power.

(*c*) If there is no conjunction whatever for connecting the co-ordinate clauses, each clause must be separated by a comma at least, and (if the writer desires to emphasise each clause in succession) by a semicolon : see § 24 (1).

Steam propels, elevates, lowers, pumps, drains, pulls, etc. (Here a comma is evidently sufficient, since there is the same Subject to all the verbs.)

(3) *Complex sentences.*—The chief rules are the following :—

(*a*) A **Noun-clause** should *not* be separated by a comma from the word to which it stands in grammatical relation as equivalent to a noun :—

(1) *That the art of teaching is difficult* is allowed by all.
It is allowed by all that the art of teaching is difficult.

Here the use of a comma would evidently be wrong, since the noun-clause indicated by italics is the subject of the verb "is."

(2) No one knows *when he will come.*

Here too it would evidently be wrong to use a comma, since the noun-clause indicated by italics is the Object of the verb "knows."

(3) His pardon depends upon *whether he will confess his fault or not.*

Here too a comma would be wrong, since the noun-clause is the object of the preposition "upon."

(4) He made a promise *that he would work hard next term.*

Here the noun-clause is in apposition with *promise.* No comma is used in such cases.

But when two or more noun-clauses stand in the same relation to the same word, they should be separated by commas :—

No one knows *when he will come*, or *whether he will come at all*, or *whether he is even alive.*

(*b*) An **Adjective-clause**, unless it is rather long, is not separated from its noun by a comma :—

The man *we saw yesterday* has come again to-day.

The man, *who reflects carefully before acting*, is more likely to be successful than one, *who thoughtlessly takes a leap in the dark.*

Note.—Relative clauses that are not restrictive, but are merely continuative, must always be marked off by commas :—

By nine o'clock in the evening we reached York, *which* (=and this) is a fine old historical town.

(*c*) An **Adverb-clause** is separated by a comma from the clause, to which it is subordinate :—

He will succeed, *because he works hard.*
I will gladly do this, *if I am allowed.*

The comma, however, can be omitted, if the adverb-clause is either very short or is expressed elliptically :—

He likes you better *than me.*
Send me word *before you start.*

Exercise on § 20. (To be done orally and at sight.[1])

(*a*) *Insert commas, where they are needed, in the following; but avoid putting in any comma unnecessarily :—*

1. The triple alliance consists of Germany Austria and Italy.
2. A dog barking at nothing is a nuisance.
3. The roof of the house having caught fire the inmates fled and remained outside until the fire was put out.
4. My son so far from being blamed for his conduct was commended and even rewarded.
5. Towns villages and hamlets were all alike attacked with the epidemic of cholera.
6. I shall be happy to make the attempt that you advise if I am permitted.

---

[1] *To the Teacher.*—We advise the teacher not to waste the time of the class in having these examples written out. The class can show more readily by word of mouth than by the slow process of writing where the comma or commas ought to be in each sentence.

7. From morning till noon, from noon to evening, from evening to midnight, the same grief never leaves him.

8. Athens the eye of Greece mother of arts and sciences.

9. Early this morning when we had just left the house we met the man that we had been looking for.

10. He found as I expected he would that the house he had lately purchased was badly built.

11. What was the cause of so much grief to him or why the grief lasted so long was never known to any of us.

12. I hope my friend that you will come and spend at least a week with us.

13. He has now grown so old and infirm that he spends most of his time in sleeping taking his food or sitting in an easy-chair.

14. I shall not leave home for business unless you set the example.

15. Example as the proverb says is the sincerest form of precept.

16. To tell you the plain truth I should be glad to retire from business altogether considering that I am now past sixty years of age and have a son to succeed me.

17. And Reuben said unto them do the lad no harm.

18. A snake sleeping in the grass will bite if any one treads upon it.

19. The prisoner having been convicted of the crime of which he was accused must make up his mind to suffer the penalty.

20. The building is a noble structure of red brick and comprises a reading-room a library a writing-room and a room for refreshments.

21. It is quite true that this fine building was erected by private subscriptions but it took a good deal of trouble to collect the money and the building continued to be in debt for several years.

22. This might have been all very well had George III. been a man of genius capable of guiding and ruling a great country.

23. Had he been able to direct affairs himself all might have been well but before the year was out he was prostrated with sickness and forced to retire from public life.

24. A similar increase having been proposed in the previous year the mind of the public was not taken by surprise.

25. Maid of Athens ere we part
Give O give me back my heart.—BYRON.

26. My son is in preparation for the army; yours for the navy.

27. Three poets in three different ages born
Greece Italy and England did adorn.—DRYDEN.

28. Hope springs eternal in the human breast;
Man never is but always to be blest.

29. The last years of George III. were years of peace but not of rejoicing.

30. To have isolated if only for a day or two the head of the army in South Africa would have delighted the hearts of the enemy.

(*b*) *Remove redundancies or supply deficiencies of commas in the following sentences, if you see reason*:—

1. After a brief rest Nelson was called upon to meet the threatened invasion of England, by the flotillas of Buonaparte. —*Nelson*, by S. L. Brome, p. 267, 1891.

2. Until some definite plan has been decided on all official pressure should cease.—*Pioneer Mail*, p. 9, May 11, 1900.

3. We needed a man whom the public trusted, who was experienced in war, and above all, fear of popular clamour.—*Review of Reviews*, p. 352, April 1900.

4. His father, being denounced by the populace, the family fled to Lyons.—*Literature*, p. 47, July 21, 1900.

5. The lake was at least two miles broad six miles long well wooded all round.

6. Sir L. R., who was in command at Dover previously to his proceeding to South Africa is to take up an appointment at the War Office on his return.—*Daily Telegraph*, p. 9, Sept. 12, 1900.

7. When the riff-raff foreigners, who have been looting in the Transvaal, stream over the border into Portuguese territory the Portuguese will have plenty of work for their police to do. —*Ibid.*, p. 7, Sept. 19, 1900.

8. So far as wounds are concerned the results of this war have not borne out the forecast made of the long range of these guns.—*Fortnightly Review*, p. 493, Sept. 1900.

9. Several officers ranking with, but junior in service to Sir R. Buller may be passed over in silence.—*Ibid.*, p. 624, Oct. 1900.

10. The supposition that this village was a Saxon settlement is strengthened if not established by certain facts.—MRS. JACKSON, *Annals of Ealing*, p. 12.

11. In these days some persons will generally be found ready to explain away actions, and passions, of a questionable character.—*Fortnightly Review*, p. 632, Oct. 1900.

12. The interest which he threw over the fate of the Italian city, and the heroic efforts of the last of its tribunes marked him out to be a great writer.—GRAHAM, *Vict. Lit.*, p. 64.

13. The different sections of the party desire to obtain office in order to advance their several ideas, interests and hopes.—*Fortnightly Review*, p. 803, Nov. 1900.

14. The sky was covered with inky clouds, and the ground being damp, deadened the sound of our footsteps as we crossed the yard.—*Blackwood's Magazine*, p. 177, Aug. 1900.

15. The lives and interests bound up in hers, are anchors from which she can only swing a certain distance.—*Fortnightly Review*, p. 632, Oct. 1900.

16. As long as they existed, united, and powerful, while we shook our heads over the innovations we deplored, we could have no fear for the safety of English social life.—*Ibid.*, p. 633.

17. We do not find many of them, among the women, and girls, with whom this paper deals.—*Ibid.*, p. 635.

18. The new king married Matilda, daughter of Malcolm, king of Scots and Margaret, the sister of Edgar Atheling.—RANSOME'S *Short Hist. Eng.*, p. 53.

19. While this enthusiasm lasted the service done to civilisation by the monks was immense.—*Ibid.*, p. 58.

20. His claim was allowed in 1231, and in 1238, Henry gave him his sister Eleanor in marriage.—HUNTER'S *Short Hist. Eng.*, p. 100.

21. With the sanction of the Pope, and of the Spanish king, conspiracies were set on foot to assassinate Elizabeth, to bring foreign troops into England and to make Mary queen.—*Ibid.*, p. 225.

22. He ordered the seven bishops to be tried for publishing a false, malicious and seditious libel.—*Ibid.*, p. 303.

23. It was resolved that James II., having broken the original contract between king and people, having ruled tyrannically, and having abdicated, the throne was vacant.—*Ibid.*, p. 305.

24. The possession of Calais served to keep up yearnings for

conquest, and to misdirect the policy of the island-monarchy.—GOLDWIN SMITH, *United Kingdom*, vol. i. p. 262.

Full Stop, Colon, Semicolon.

22. **Full Stop** (sometimes called a Period).—The full stop has three main uses:—

(1) It indicates the close of a complete sentence, Simple, Compound, or Complex: the sentence that follows is always commenced with a capital.

(2) It indicates an abbreviation, as A.D. for *Anno Domini;* i.e. for *id est*, "that is"; MS. for *Manuscript* and MSS. for *Manuscripts;* cf. for *confer*, "compare"; ibid. for *ibidem*, "in the same place" or "with the same author"; Bart. for *Baronet;* The Hon. for *The Honourable;* Rev. J. Thompson for "Reverend John Thompson."

(3) It is placed at the close of Roman numerals (upright and expressed by letters). Thus we say, Charles I., Charles II. A full stop is also placed after Arabic figures (the figures that we use in writing on slate or paper), when these are not enclosed in brackets, and are made to number sections, paragraphs, etc. Observe, for example, how all the paragraphs in this book have been numbered.

Note.—If the last letter of a word is given, the stop is not always used; as Dr Jones, Mr Clarke, Messrs Scott and Sons.

23. **Colon.**—Next to the full stop this is the strongest of all the dividing marks. It is intermediate in strength between the full stop and the semicolon; and may often be interchanged with either. It has, however, certain uses peculiar to itself.

(1) It introduces a statement which is intended to repeat, confirm, or slightly extend the drift of a previous statement, without taking the reader into entirely new ground:—

> Strive above all things, in whatever station of life you may be, to keep good health: without good health there can be no happiness in life.

(2) It introduces a quotation: the colon in this case is usually followed by a dash.

He rather exaggerates Napoleon's greatness, when he says:—"If greatness stands for natural power, for something human beyond humanity, then Napoleon was assuredly great."—*Fortnightly Review*, p. 132, Jan. 1901.

(3) To introduce or sum up a series of co-ordinate clauses, all bearing upon the same cardinal fact. Here too the colon is usually followed by a dash:—

You must now hear what I have to say about the uses of iron:—We sleep on iron; we traverse the earth on iron; we navigate the sea on iron; we plough the fields with iron; we shoot with iron; we chop down trees with iron; we pump water with iron; we bore into mines with iron; we print with iron:—in fact, there is scarcely anything that we can do without the help of this marvellous metal.

(4) To introduce an enumeration of particular objects, all dependent on the same word:—

Send me the following objects:—a penholder, a brush, a pencil, a portfolio, an envelope, three sheets of foolscap, and a dozen nibs.

24. **Semicolon.**—This word literally means "half a colon." It therefore separates sentences by a division not so strong as that indicated by a colon, though stronger than that indicated by a comma.

(1) A semicolon is used for separating co-ordinate clauses, when these are not joined together by conjunctions, and when the writer desires that full attention shall be given to each statement in succession:—

To err is human; to forgive divine.—POPE.

The things which are seen are temporal; the things which are not seen are eternal.—*Epistle to Corinthians.*

Reading makes a full man; speaking a ready man; writing an exact man.—BACON.

We sleep on iron; we traverse the earth on iron; we navigate the sea on iron; we plough the fields with iron; we shoot with iron; we chop down trees with iron; we pump water with iron; we bore into mines with iron; we print with iron.

Honesty of purpose in worldly affairs has many advantages over deceit. It is a safer way of dealing with men; it is an easier mode of dispatching business; it inspires men with greater confidence; it acquires in the course of its progress more and more confidence in itself, while deceit becomes more and more diffident of the success of its own operations.

(2) A semicolon is used for separating co-ordinate clauses, when the parts of the co-ordinate clauses are themselves divided by commas. A semicolon is necessary in such a case, even though the subordinate clauses are combined by the conjunction *and*. Here a semicolon is required, because the comma has been already used to indicate smaller divisions.

Look down upon the willow and aspen copses, where over the heads of busy washerwomen the nightingale and the hippolais shake the copses with their song; and then toil upward to the grey fortress-tower on the grey limestone-knoll, and pass out of nature and her pure sunshine into the bleak shadow of the unnatural Middle Age, into the region of dirt and darkness, cruelty and fear.—KINGSLEY'S *Prose Idylls*, v. p. 200.

(3) A semicolon is commonly used for separating coordinate clauses, when these are distinguished from one another by a conjunction expressing contrast or alternative, as *but*, *and yet*, *but yet*, *yet*, *still*, *nevertheless*, *otherwise*, or by a conjunction expressing inference, as *for*. Here, if a semicolon is used in preference to a comma, it indicates that the reader should take full note of the contrast, the alternative, or the inference:—

I met him as he was leaving the house; *otherwise* I should not have known where he lived.

I refused to do what he asked me to do; *for* I was convinced that he had been misinformed of the facts.

Note.—It often happens, however, that a comma is sufficient at the end of a clause, which is followed by *but*. Sometimes we may even go to the other extreme and place a full stop at the end of such a sentence. It all depends upon the length of pause which the writer wishes to produce in the reader's mind.

(1) High wages do not necessarily increase the cost of production, but often lower it by increasing the labourer's powers.—*Spectator*, p. 17, Jan. 5, 1901.

Here a comma is obviously sufficient, since the same Subject, "high wages," does for both verbs, "increase" and "lower."

(2) Many proposals have been put forward for improving the army, but I have not noticed any proposal for doing away with the army altogether.—*Ibid.*

Here too a comma is sufficient. The union of clauses makes a very good Compound sentence.

(3) Heaven and earth shall pass away, but my words shall not pass away. But of that day and that hour knoweth no man, no, not even the angels of heaven.—*Matt.* xxiv. 35, 36.

Observe the difference of punctuation. In verse 35 *but* is the connecting link between two clauses of a Compound sentence, and therefore a comma is sufficient. On the other hand, in verse 36, *But* is the first word of an entirely new sentence, and is preceded by a full stop, because with verse 36 there is a complete change in the subject-matter.

Exercise on §§ 22-24.

Insert the proper stops (including commas) in the following:—

1. We bent our course towards the northern part of the island the heat was suffocating the moon had risen and was surrounded by three black circles a frightful darkness shrouded the sky but the frequent flashes of lightning disclosed to us long rows of thick and gloomy clouds hanging very low and heaped together over the centre of the island being driven in with great rapidity from the ocean although not a breath of air was perceptible on the land

2. As we walked along we thought we heard peals of thunder but on listening more attentively we perceived that it was the sound of cannon at a distance repeated by the echoes these ominous sounds joined to the tempestuous aspect of the heavens made me shudder I had little doubt of their being signals of distress from a ship in danger in about half an hour the firing ceased and I found the silence still more appalling than the dismal sounds which had preceded it

3. We hastened on without uttering a word or daring to communicate to each other our mutual apprehensions at midnight by great exertion we arrived at the sea-shore in that part of the harbour called Golden Dust the billows were breaking against the beach with a horrible noise covering the rocks and the strand with foam of a dazzling whiteness blended with sparks of fire by these phosphoric gleams we distinguished notwithstanding the darkness a number of fishing canoes drawn up high on the beach

4. At the entrance of a wood a short distance from us we saw a fire round which a party of the inhabitants was assembled we repaired thither in order to rest ourselves till the morning while we were seated near this fire one of the bystanders related that late in the afternoon he had seen a vessel in the open sea driven towards the island by the current that the night had hidden it from his view that two hours after sunset he had heard the firing of signal-guns of distress but that the surf was too high to enable them to launch a boat to go off to her that a short time after he perceived the glimmering of the watch lights on board the vessel which he feared by its having approached so near the coast had steered between the mainland and the little island of Amber and that if this were the case of which however he would not take upon himself to be certain the ship he thought was in very great danger

5. Other inhabitants gave different opinions on the subject they continued to discuss it in the usual desultory manner of creoles Paul and I observed a profound silence we remained in this spot till break of day but the weather was too hazy to admit of our distinguishing any object at sea for everything was covered with a fog all we could descry to seaward was a dark cloud which they told us was the Isle of Amber at the distance of a quarter of a league from the coast on this gloomy day we could only discern the point of land on which we were standing and the peaks of some inland mountains which started out occasionally from the midst of the clouds that hung around them.—Extracts from *Paul and Virginia.*

25. Note of Interrogation.—This is used after sentences which ask questions. It might therefore be called the question-mark. The sentence following must be commenced with a capital. (Observe, however, that the question-mark must *not* be used when the question is expressed in the Indirect form.)

Where was he born? When did he die?
I beg to inquire where he was born, and when he died.

26. **Quotation marks.**—A pair of *inverted* commas marks the beginning of a quotation or of an interrupted quotation. Another pair of commas, *not inverted*, marks the close.[1] If a quotation is introduced within a quotation, a single comma is used at either end, an inverted one at the beginning, a non-inverted one at the close:—

"What did they say to you?" inquired the man.
"They gave me," he answered, "strict orders, 'That gate is not to be opened under any circumstances whatever.'"

Great confusion and uncertainty may arise, if the quotation marks are omitted or not put in their right places:—

The plaintiff said the witness was guilty of perjury.

This sentence as it stands makes very good sense. But if quotation-marks have been unintentionally omitted, and if these are now supplied, the sense is entirely changed:—

"The plaintiff," said the witness, "was guilty of perjury."

27. A **Note of Exclamation** is used after words or sentences which are intended by the writer to express an emotion or a wish:—

How are the mighty fallen, and the weapons of war perished!
—2 *Samuel* i. 27.
May every blessing attend him!
O, what a fall was there, my countrymen!—SHAKSPEARE.
I to say such a thing! Never!
Bacon far behind his age! Bacon far behind Sir Edward Coke! Bacon clinging to exploded abuses! Bacon withstanding the progress of improvement! Bacon struggling to push back the human mind! The words seem strange.—MACAULAY.

28. An **Apostrophe** (consisting of a comma placed *above*

[1] Some writers and printers, instead of using a pair of commas to mark a quotation at each end, use only one comma. If there is a second quotation enclosed within the first, it is put within double quotation marks. There is no harm in this method, provided it is consistently carried out.

the body of a letter instead of below it, as ordinary commas are) is inserted to show that some letter or letters have been left out :—

The Hon'ble (for *Honourable*); 'tis (for *it is*); ta'en (for *taken*); don't (for *do not*); shan't (for *shall not*); tho' (for *though*); an ox's head (for *oxes* head; and all other instances of the Possessive case).

29. **Dash.**—This is indicated by a single horizontal line, as the hyphen is, but the line is about twice as long. The dash as a mark in punctuation has at least ten different uses. The common property that runs through all these uses is that the dash signifies a rather lengthy pause, which the reader must make with his voice, if he is reading aloud, or with his mind, if he is reading to himself.

(*a*) It marks a sudden stop or abrupt transition in the progress of a sentence :—

Here lies the great—false marble where?
Nothing but sordid dust lies here.—*Epitaph.*

(*b*) It marks the omission of a word or name which the writer does not wish to mention :—

The historian, when quoting personal testimony, must make up his own mind whether he is listening to Herodotus or Mr. ——. Every reader can fill up the blank.—*Spectator*, p. 615, April 27, 1901.

(*c*) It marks words in apposition or in explanation :—

They plucked the seated hills with all their loads—
Rocks, waters, woods—and by their shaggy tops
Uplifting bore them in their hands.—*Paradise Lost.*

Nothing comes amiss to her nimble fingers — spoons and forks as well as purses.—*Daily Tel.*, p. 9, May 7, 1901.

(*d*) It resumes a scattered subject :—

Health, friends, position—all are gone.

Intellect, imagination, power of expression, humour, taste, truth to life, and truth to human nature,—these are not the qualities which to-day make a writer popular.—*Fort. Review*, p. 280, Feb. 1898.

(*e*) It indicates a long and significant pause (such as a

person would make if he were speaking), with a view to increasing the effect of the word or words that follow :—

> Captain Dreyfus was brought back, retried, again condemned in the face of evidence, and—pardoned.—*Spectator*, p. 523, April 13, 1901.
>
> She has charms of person and of mind, and is rich, but—she is a kleptomaniac.—*Daily Tel.*, p. 9, May 7, 1901.
>
> They would have made an ill-matched pair, but happiness may still be theirs — in other company. — *Ibid.*, p. 9, May 7, 1901.

(*f*) It indicates a hesitating or faltering speech :—

> Few words will—er—suffice to refute—er—the arguments by which this gentleman—er—endeavours to prove his case.

(*g*) It is used to insert a parenthesis. Here as in (*c*) and (*f*) two dashes are required, one at the beginning, and one at the end. A parenthesis may be in the form of a phrase or of an entire sentence. When it takes the form of a sentence, the sentence does not begin with a capital :—

> *Phrase.*—The Republic in France is despised by the aristocrats, detested—with too much reason—by the clerics, and only just tolerated by the Imperialists.—*Spectator*, p. 524, April 13, 1901.
>
> *Sentence.*—A treatise of his on Bills of Exchange—of course, as it has passed through many editions, it has been largely altered and added to — is still the recognised text-book on the subject. — *Fortnightly Review*, p. 93, Jan. 1901.

(*h*) It marks the repetition of a noun or other word at the end of a clause :—

> He retained his virtues amidst all his misfortunes,—misfortunes which no one could have foreseen or prevented.

(*i*) It marks the omission of intervening figures. Thus "houses 6—12" means "houses 6, 7, 8, 9, 10, 11, 12." "The years 1899—1901" means "the years 1899, 1900, 1901."

(*k*) It is placed before the name of an author or book,

when this name is given at the end of an extract or quotation ending with a full stop:—

An honest man's the noblest work of God.—POPE.

30. Brackets are used like a couple of dashes, as explained in § 29 (*g*), for inserting a parenthesis:—

At the age of ten (such is the power of genius) he could read and translate Greek with facility.

At the age of ten—such is the power of genius—he could read and translate Greek with facility.

Note.—As explained above in § 20 (*j*), commas are sometimes used to indicate a parenthesis. Hence we could write the above sentence as follows:—

At the age of ten, such is the power of genius, he could read and translate Greek with facility.

But commas have enough to do already; and therefore it would be better to use either dashes or brackets to indicate the insertion of a parenthesis.

Brackets are also used for introducing some word or words in apposition or in explanation. (The same work is done by dashes: see § 29, *c.*)

I gave all I had (two pounds) to that cause.

31. Hyphen.—A hyphen is used for joining the parts of a compound word. It is of the same shape as the dash, but is usually rather shorter. See specimens of both in § 19.

Geography is a mind-expanding subject.

A war-indemnity is usually claimed by the side that conquers.

Note.—If the compounds are well established, as *bathroom*, *nobleman*, *priestcraft*, *fiddlestick*, etc., the hyphen is not used.

A hyphen is also used to indicate the separation of one syllable from another:—

For-mer-ly. Hand-some. Hos-pit-a-ble.

32. Diæresis (separation) consists of two dots placed over the second of two vowels, to show that the two vowels are to be sounded separately. (The separation can also be indicated by a hyphen.)

Coördinative = co-ordinative.

33. **Asterisks** denote that some words or clauses have been intentionally left out:—

The Jews * * * * had to pay heavy taxes to the Norman kings.

SECTION 2.—WHEN TO USE CAPITAL LETTERS.

34. **When to use Capitals.** — Capitals are used as follows:—

(1) With the first letter of a sentence following a full stop:—

She adopted the boy and gave him an Egyptian name. He was educated as a priest and became a member of the University of Heliopolis.—READE, *Martyrdom of Man*, p. 185.

(2) With the first letter of a sentence following a note of interrogation:—

Who could disprove the evidence of a tradition? He made no secret of his design; it was to drive the Phœnician strangers out of Africa.—READE.

(3) With the first letter of proper names, and for that of all adjectives derived from proper names:—

England, English. Japan, Japanese. Milton, Miltonic.

Note.—When an adjective formed from a proper name has come into such general use that no thought of its origin is suggested to the mind on our hearing or seeing it, it is written without a capital:—as, *jovial*, *stoical*, *martial*, *quixotic*, *mercurial*, *gladstone* bag, etc.

(4) With the first letter of a common noun, when the thing denoted by the common noun is personified:—

Fair Science frowned not on his humble birth,
But Melancholy marked him for her own.—GRAY.

(5) With the first letter of the names of months, the days of a week, or the names of holidays, seasons, or festivals:—

He arrived on August 16th and left on the following Saturday. Good Friday. Christmas. Lent. A Bank Holiday.

(6) With the first letter of titles of honour or office, and in addressing any one as Mr. or Mrs. :—

The First Lord of the Treasury. The Commander-in-chief. The Prime Minister. The Colonial Secretary.

Similarly, when letters are used instead of whole words to represent titles, the letters are written with capitals :—

M.A. (for Master of Arts). M.D. (for Doctor of Medicine).

(7) With the first letter of a descriptive noun or adjective used as a kind of surname or additional name :—

Aristides the Just. Herod the Great. Charles the Fat. William the Conqueror. Edward the Confessor. Henry the Fifth. Edward the Seventh.

(8) With the first letter of the name of the Deity or any person of the Trinity, or a pronoun that stands for any such name :—

Trust in Providence. In all thy ways acknowledge Him, and He will direct thy paths.

(9) With the pronoun "I" and with the interjections "O" or "Oh" and "Ah!"

(10) With the first letter of every line of poetry :—

Only the pure and virtuous soul
Like seasoned timber never gives;
And though the whole world turn to coal,
Then chiefly lives.—HERBERT.

(11) With the first letter of a speech or sentence quoted in the Direct form :—

Another of the disciples said unto him, "Lord, let me first go and bury my father." But Jesus said unto him, "Follow me, and leave the dead to bury their dead."

(12) With the first letter of a technical term. When a technical term is first introduced and defined in a treatise, it is usual to print the first letter of every such term in a capital. As the work proceeds, the use of the capital may be continued or not at the option of the writer.

(13) With the first letters of titles of books, poems, chapters, and magazines, and of words expressing some great historical event :—

The Daily Telegraph. The Daily Express. The Ancient Mariner. The Norman Conquest. The Revival of Learning.

(14) In the "salutation" of a letter the words *sir* or *madam*, *lord* or *lady*, are capitalised, as in—

My dear Sir. Dear Madam. My Lord. My Lady.

SECTION 3.—HOW TO DIVIDE WORDS INTO SYLLABLES.

35. First Rule.—Take care that the group of letters which you separate from another group of letters does really make a syllable. Thus we cannot divide *first* into "fir-st," because *st* cannot be sounded as a syllable.

This rule applies to the terminations *-cial*, *-cious*, *-cean*, *-sion*, *-gion*, *-tion*, *-tial*, *-tious*. Since all these are sounded as one syllable (and it is the sound that makes the syllable or word, not the spelling), they cannot be divided into two :—

So′-cial, o′-cean, le′-sion, le′-gion, con′-scious, mo′-tion, par′-tial, cap′-tious, fi-nan′-cial.

In such words as the following the termination *-ion* or *-ious* has to be detached from the preceding consonant, in order to throw the accent on the consonant :—

Re-lig′-ion, con-trit′-ion, prec′-ious, con-dit′-ion, o-pin′-ion, on′-ion, ver-mil′-ion, de-cis′-ion.

36. Second Rule.—Be guided by the pronunciation, not by the etymology. The etymology, even when it is known, is not a safe guide. For instance, *banquet* must be divided as "ban-quet," not as "banqu-et": yet etymologically the latter division would be correct; for the *-et* is merely a suffix, and the stem of the word is *banqu*.

The pronunciation of a word depends very largely upon the accent. Thus we divide *ocean* into "o′-cean," but *oceanic* into "o′-ce-an′-ic"; we divide *partial* into "par′-tial," but *partiality* into "par′-ti-al′-i-ty."

La-ment′, lam′-en-ta-ble. At′-om, a-tom′-ic. At′-tri-bute (noun), at-trib′-ute (verb). Pro-vide′, prov′-i-dence. Tel′-e-graph, te-leg′-ra-phy. Ex-pect′, ex′-pec-ta′-tion. Me-chan′-ic, mech′-an-ic′-ian. Dom′-i-neer, do-min′-ion. Fi′-nite, fin′-ish. Ta′-ble, tab′-let. Nu′-me-ral, nu-mer′-i-cal.

SECTION 4.—WHEN TO UNDERLINE A WORD.

37. **Uses of Underlining or Italics.**—When we draw a single line under a word or words in writing, this is intended to have the same effect on the eye of the reader as that which a printer indicates by italics.

There are three uses of underlining or italics :—

(1) To give particular emphasis to some word or words. If we were reading such words aloud, we should lay stress on them with the voice, *i.e.* we should utter them more loudly and distinctly. In reading a book out to an audience, or in conversation, it adds much to the effect to throw more stress of voice upon the more important words. But in written composition we should avoid the practice of frequent underlining, and rely more on the position of the words and the clearness of the language: see above, § 5.

(2) To indicate the name of a book or newspaper :—

> Have you seen the *Telegraph* office?
> I am well acquainted with *The Ancient Mariner.*

If the words italicised above were not underlined in writing, the sense of both sentences would be entirely different from what it is.

(3) To indicate that the word or words used are foreign :—

> I have studied this subject *ad nauseam.*
> We shall meet him *en route.*

We must point out, however, that though it is a very common practice to use foreign words (especially French and Latin ones) in English, it is very much better to shun the use of such words altogether. It would be quite as easy to say: "I have studied this subject, till I am sick of it"; "We shall meet him on the way."

Exercises on §§ 20-37. (To be done in writing.)

Put in all the stops or other marks required in the following, and supply the necessary capitals :—

(*a*) *Preceptors' Third Class Examination.*

1. useful indeed said the man come you had pinched and ground me down for some years before that but i had served you faithfully up to that time in spite of all your dogs usage had i ralph made no reply had i said the man again you had had your wages rejoined ralph and had done your work—June 1889.

2. at last calling serjeant thompson aside i asked him am i too old to be accepted in johns place why i dont know said he you are rather old to be sure but yet money may do much i put the money into thompsons hand and said jack you are free i will go in your stead—Xmas 1889.

3. impatient of the silent horn now in the gale her voice was borne father she cried the rocks around loved to prolong the gentle sound awhile she paused no answer came malcolm was thine the blast the name less resolutely uttered fell the echoes could not catch the swell a stranger i the huntsman said advancing from the hazel shade—June 1890. (Write out in proper metre.)

4. huntsman rest thy chase is done while our slumbrous spells assail ye dream not with the rising sun bugles here shall sound reveille sleep the deer is in his den sleep thy hounds are by thee lying sleep nor dream in yonder glen how thy gallant steed lay dying huntsman rest thy chase is done think not of the rising sun far at dawning to assail ye here no bugles sound reveille—Xmas 1890. (Write out in proper metre.)

5. then while his plaid he round him cast it is the last time tis the last he muttered thrice the last time eer that angel voice shall Roderick hear it was a goading thought his stride hied hastier down the mountain side sullen he flung him in the boat and straight across the lake it shot—June 1891.

6. the man was a rough bearded old sea dog who had just burst in from the tavern through the low thatch upsetting a drawer with all his glasses and now came panting and blowing straight up to the high admiral my lord my lord theyre coming i saw em off the lizard last night who my good sir you seem to have left your good manners behind you the armada your

worship the spaniard but as for my manners tis no fault of mine for i never had none to leave behind me—Xmas 1891.

7. curse on him quoth false sextus will not the villain drown but for this stay ere close of day we should have sacked the town heaven help him quoth lars porsena and bring him safe to shore for such a gallant feat of arms was never seen before—June 1892. (Write out in proper metre.)

8. but north looked the dictator north looked he long and hard and spake to caius cossus the captain of the guard caius of all the romans thou hast the keenest sight say what through yonder storm of dust comes from the latian right—Xmas 1892. (Write out in proper metre.)

9. we all withdrew mr rochester stayed a moment behind us to give some further orders poole the solicitor addressed me as he descended the stair you madam said he are clear from all blame your uncle will be glad to hear it if indeed he should still be living when mr mason returns from madeira my uncle what of him do you know him—June 1893.

10. soldier rest thy warfare oer sleep the sleep that knows not breaking dream of battlefields no more days of danger nights of waking in our isles enchanted hall hands unseen thy couch are strewing fairy strains of music fall every sense in slumber dewing.—June 1894. (Write out in proper metre.)

11. miss matty could hardly drink for looking at her brother peter and as for eating that was out of the question i suppose hot climates age people quickly she said almost to herself when you left cranford you had not a grey hair in your head but how many years ago was that said mr peter smiling ah true yes i suppose you and i are getting old—Xmas 1894.

12. O tiber father tiber to whom the romans pray a romans life a romans arms take thou in charge this day so he spake and speaking sheathed the good sword by his side and with his harness on his back plunged headlong in the tide—June 1895. (Write out in proper metre.)

13. it is not unlikely that your highness will one day command your governor to show you some of our productions to which he will answer for I am informed of his designs by asking your highness where are they and what is become of them and pretend it is a proof that there never were any because they are not then to be found not to be found who has mislaid them your highness will exclaim—Xmas 1895.

14. The pass of thermopylæ was favourable to the greeks for

the persians could not avail themselves of their superior numbers xerxes sent messengers to leonidas king of sparta bidding him give up his arms he replied come and take them lands were then offered to the defenders of the pass on condition that they should become allies of the great king but the lacedæmonians answered it was their custom to win lands by valour not by treachery—June 1897.

15. You are mad said the curate starting up astonished is thy master such a wonderful hero as to fight a giant at two thousand leagues distance then they heard don quixote bawling out stay villain since i have thee here thy scimiter shall but little avail thee—Xmas 1897.

16. i opened the boxes and to andersons surprise i counted out gold coin to the amount of four hundred pounds not a bad legacy said mr wilson then you knew of this of course i answered i have known it some time ever since the attempt to rob her but what are these papers said the lawyer—June 1898.

17. the traveller made three quick steps towards the jail then turning short tell me said he has that unnatural captain sent you nothing to relieve your distress call him not unnatural replied the other gods blessing be upon him he sent me a great deal of money but i made a bad use of it—Xmas 1898.

(b) *Calcutta Matriculation Papers.*

1. a valiant knight sir giles de argentine much renowned in the wars of palestine attended the king till he got him out of the press of the combat he would retreat no further it is not my custom he said to fly with that he took leave of the king set spurs to his horse and calling out his war cry of argentine argentine he rushed into the thickest of the scottish ranks and was killed—1891.

2. he invited heilburg to avail himself of the opportunity which would then be afforded to effect his escape what exclaimed the noble dutchman and leave my unfortunate countrymen to perish no I will never desert the brave fellows who have fought so well for their country the english officer affected by the generosity of heilburgs noble reply answered bravo my good fellow god bless you here is my hand i give you my word i will stay with you—1893.

3. indeed his whole character is most forcibly expressed in his own words which every young man might well stamp upon his soul the longer i live said he the more certain i am that the

great difference between men between the feeble and the powerful the great and the insignificant is energy invincible determination a purpose once fixed and then death or victory that quality will do anything that can be done in this world and no talents no circumstances no opportunities will make a two-legged creature a man without it—1894.

4. in the wise words of Shakspeare all places that the eye of heaven visit are to the wise man ports and happy havens happiness indeed depends i repeat it much more on what is within than without us o how careful we should therefore be that we be well furnished within written on friday the sixth of june in london england by john grant solicitor—1895.

5. after school in the evening as he was standing silently beside hardy who was ruling a sheet of paper for him tarlton in his brutal manner came up and seizing him by the arm said come along with me lovatt ive something to say to you i cant come now said lovatt drawing away his arm ah do come now said tarlton in a voice of persuasion well ill come presently nay but do pray theres a good fellow come now because ive something to say to you what is it youve got to say to me i wish youd let me alone said lovatt—1896.

6. having arrived at cardiff he called on blind walter ross the baker for lodgings what caused you to come here asked the blind man and what may be your business in cardiff robert jones the peat cutter advised me to come here he said you were honest and respectable my business is to build for mr john morris in high street theres a clear ring in your voice young man yes yes I shall be glad to have you come in sir—1897.

CHAPTER IV.—EXPANSION OF OUTLINES: ESSAY-WRITING.

38. **Expansion of Outlines.**—In Chapter I. we supplied the student with materials for composition by giving him an entire extract in prose or verse and telling him to reproduce its substance in his own words. In the present chapter we shall give him an outline and tell him to expand it in the form of a continuous narrative. This is a new step in advance towards original composition; but we trust that the student, after the experience gained in

working out such exercises as those given in Chapter I., will not prove unequal to the task. We give outlines on three sets of subjects, arranged in the order of increasing difficulty:—

(1) Outlines of Æsop's Fables;
(2) Outlines of Object Lessons;
(3) Outlines of Short Essays on General Subjects.

SECTION 1.—OUTLINES OF ÆSOP'S FABLES.

39. **The Plan followed.**—In the first two examples, underneath each outline, we have given a specimen of the kind of way in which the outline may be expanded. In all the other examples the student will fill up the outline himself. Each figure (not to be repeated in the expanded narrative) is intended to mark the commencement of a new paragraph.

1. *A Lion and a Bear fight over the Carcass of a Fawn. Fighters lose what they fight for.*

Outline.

1. A lion and a bear, once friends, fight over the carcass of a fawn till both are exhausted.
2. A fox comes up and carries off the carcass.
3. They are sorry that they had not agreed to divide the carcass instead of fighting over it.

Expansion of Outline.

A lion and a bear, who up to that time had been friends, came accidentally upon the carcass of a fawn. As each claimed to have seen it first, and neither would give way to the other or consent to a division, a fight ensued. The contest was so fierce, and the combatants were so equally matched, that at last they could fight no longer. Both of them lay on the ground, half-blinded with wounds, panting for breath, and too exhausted to move.

A fox, seeing what a helpless state they were in, walked in between them and carried off the prize.

"What fools we have been!" said the combatants; "we might have agreed to divide the booty in a fair and friendly spirit.

Instead of that we have wasted our strength and wounded each other only to give a dinner to a rogue, who had no right to it; and we have now nothing left to dine upon ourselves."

2. *The Lion and the Bulls. Union is strength.*

Outline.

1. Three bulls feed together in perfect safety in the same field.
2. A lion separates them by spreading evil reports.
3. The lion falls upon each of them singly.

Expansion of Outline.

Three bulls were accustomed to graze together in the same field. They were so friendly to one another, that they were never seen apart at any hour of the night or day.

A lion watched them, hoping to make a prize of one of them; but so long as they remained together, he saw he had no chance. They were indeed quite safe, so long as their friendship lasted. But a quarrel at last arose through the cunning of the lion, who set one against the other by spreading evil reports and sowing distrust amongst them. Then they parted company, and each grazed in solitude in a different part of the field.

The lion, seeing that they no longer fed together, fell upon each of them singly, until all were devoured.

3. *The Fighting Cocks and the Eagle.*
The penalty of bragging.

1. Two cocks fight for the first place in a fowl-yard.
2. The defeated one retires in silence: the conqueror stands on the top of a barn and crows with delight.
3. An eagle, hearing it crow, swoops down and carries it off.

4. *The Wolf and the Crane.*
Make sure of your fee before you begin to work.

1. A wolf employed a crane to pull a bone out of his throat.
2. The crane with her long neck extracts the bone and asks for the fee.
3. "Be thankful," says the wolf, "that you have got your neck out safe."

5. *The Crow and the Jug.*
Necessity is the mother of invention.

1. A thirsty crow tries in vain to reach some water at the bottom of a jug.
2. By dropping pebbles into the water he raises the water to the rim and drinks it.

6. *The Fox and the Stork. Returning like for like.*

1. A fox asks a stork to dinner, and places before her some thin food in a shallow saucer. The stork goes away hungry.
2. The stork invites the fox to dinner next day, and places before him a vessel with a long narrow neck. The fox goes away hungry.

7. *The Dog and the Shadow.*
Grasping at too much and losing all.

1. A dog, holding a piece of meat in his mouth, sees his shadow in the water, while crossing a brook on a plank.
2. Thinking that the shadow is another dog with another piece of meat, he drops his own piece to seize the other.

8. *The Fox and the Crow. Listening to flatterers.*

1. A fox sees a crow perched on a tree, and holding a piece of cheese in her mouth.
2. The fox flatters her for her good looks, but pities her inability to sing.
3. The crow opens her mouth to sing, and drops the cheese.

9. *The Frogs ask for a King.*
Going further and faring worse.

1. The frogs beg Jupiter for a king. He sends them a log.
2. Finding the log inactive and stupid, they beg for a king who has more energy.
3. He then sends them a stork, who gobbles them up.

10. *The Wolves and the Sheep.*
Sacrificing old friends to new ones.

1. The wolves offer friendship to the sheep, if they will send away the dogs.
2. The sheep assent, dismiss the dogs, and are devoured.

11. *The Wind and the Sun.*
Gentle means better than rough ones.

1. Between wind and sun there is a dispute who can take a cloak off a traveller's back first.

2. The violence of the wind makes him fasten it on all the tighter.

3. The gentle warmth of the sun makes him take it off.

12. *The Hare and the Tortoise.*
Slow and steady wins the race.

1. A tortoise challenges a hare to a race.
2. The hare, confident of victory, takes a nap on the way.
3. The tortoise goes steadily on and reaches the goal first.

13. *The Shepherd-boy and the Wolf.*
A liar is not believed even when he speaks the truth.

1. A shepherd-boy makes fun of his neighbours, crying "Wolf!" when there is no wolf.

2. One day a wolf comes; no one believes him; and the sheep are devoured.

14. *The Lion and the Mouse. One good turn deserves another.*

1. A lion spares the life of a mouse, who had run against his nose while he was asleep.

2. The same lion, being afterwards caught in a net, roars with distress.

3. The mouse, having heard the roaring, nibbles the cord and releases the lion.

15. *The Belly and the Members.*
Capital and labour mutually dependent.

1. The hands, arms, and legs refuse to work any longer for the idle belly.

2. In starving the belly they grow weaker and weaker themselves.

3. At last they find out that the belly was doing some work too, though not of the same kind as theirs, and that they depend on the belly as much as the belly on them.

16. *The Horse and the Stag. Help can be bought too dear.*

1. There is a contest between a horse and a stag for the right of pasture.

2. The horse, being worsted, gets the help of a rider, who expels the stag.

3. The horse, instead of being unharnessed, is taken away by the man, and becomes his servant for life.

17. *The Bundle of Sticks. Union is strength.*

1. A man who had quarrelsome sons told them each to bring some sticks.

2. Having tied them together in a bundle, he told them each to break the bundle. One after another tried and failed.

3. Having untied the bundle, he told them each to break separate sticks. This they did easily.

4. He then pointed the moral,—"Be united, and you will come to no harm."

18. *The Ass's Shadow.*
Losing the substance for the sake of the shadow.

1. A young man hires an ass, and rides, while the driver follows behind.

2. The sun is very hot, and the young man gets down to rest in the shadow of the ass.

3. The driver claims the shadow, as he had let out the ass, not the shadow.

4. While they fight about the shadow, the ass runs away.

19. *The Dog, the Cock, and the Fox.*
Cunning caught in its own trap.

1. A dog and a cock (who are friends) spend the night in a forest. The dog sleeps in a hole under the root of a tree. The cock roosts on a branch.

2. The cock crows as usual in the morning.

3. A fox, having heard the crowing, begs the cock to come down, and join him in a morning hymn.

4. The dog steals out of his hole, seizes the fox, and devours him.

20. *The Jackdaw in Peacock's Feathers.*
The danger of false pretensions.

1. A jackdaw, having stuck some peacock's plumes among his feathers, goes among the peacocks as if he were one of them.

2. They strip him of his false plumes, and drive him from their company.

3. On returning to his own kindred, he is jeered at and expelled from their company also.

21. *The Ass, the Cock, and the Lion.*
The danger of self-conceit.

1. A lion casts hungry eyes upon an ass.

2. A cock standing by sets up a vigorous crowing; the lion is startled and runs away.

3. The ass pursues the lion, and is devoured.

22. *Mercury and the Woodman. Honesty the best policy.*

1. A woodman let his axe slip into a river, of which Mercury was the god.

2. Mercury, pitying his grief, brought up first a gold axe, then a silver one, and lastly an iron one. Woodman declined the gold and silver axes, but accepted the iron one,—his own.

3. Mercury made him accept the gold and silver ones too.

4. Another woodman, having heard of this, intentionally threw his axe into the same river: he then wept and prayed to Mercury.

5. Mercury produced a gold axe as before. The woodman claimed it as his own. But Mercury refused to give it, and vanished.

23. *The Fox and the Goat. Look before you leap.*

1. A fox had fallen into a well, and could not get out.

2. The fox invites a passing goat to come in and taste the delicious water.

3. The goat leaps in. The fox mounts upon his head and jumps out.

24. *The Rustic and the Snake. The penalty of ingratitude.*

1. A rustic picked up a snake half dead with cold and took it home.

2. The snake, being revived with the warmth of the fire, attacked the children of the house.

3. The rustic then killed it with his hoe.

25. *The Wolf and the Lamb.*
One who is bent on mischief will always find a pretext.

1. A wolf was drinking in a stream; a lamb was paddling lower down.

2. The wolf complained that the lamb was making him drink muddy water: the lamb showed that this was impossible.

3. The wolf then complained that the lamb had spoken ill of him a year ago. "No," said the lamb, "I was not born."

4. "Then your father spoke ill of me." Saying that, the wolf devoured him.

26. *The Sick Lion.*

Avoid a place, where many go in, but none come out.

1. A lion, too old to hunt, retired to his cave, and announced that he was very ill.

2. Every beast that went in to see him was devoured.

3. A fox, invited by the lion to enter, declined, because he saw that all the footmarks pointed towards the cave, and none back again.

27. *The Eagle and the Fox.*

Where there's a will there's a way.

1. A fox kept her cub at the foot of a tree, whereon an eagle had built her nest and was rearing her young.

2. While the fox was away, the eagle swooped down and seized the cub.

3. The fox, having in vain asked the eagle to return the cub, seized a lighted brand from an altar, and threatened to set fire to the tree, if the cub were not returned.

SECTION 2.—OUTLINES OF OBJECT-LESSONS.

40. Description of Objects discussed in Object-lessons.[1] —We assume that object-lessons form part of the curriculum of the school, and that for every lesson either the

---

[1] The following extract from "Revised Instructions" issued to Inspectors of Schools (1900) by the Board of Education deserves attention:—"The attempt to teach children to be accurate in observation cannot be separated from the need of making them accurate in description. After they have been trained to observe a fact, they should be practised in making a correct statement of it in a sentence of their own. This oral answering in complete sentences will lead to correct use of the English language, both in talking and writing, and will store the mind with a useful vocabulary. In the higher standards they will be able to write brief weekly compositions, in which they may express in a written form the ideas which they have acquired through oral instruction."—*Revised Instructions*, 1900, p. 65.

object itself or some coloured picture of it, together with other necessary materials, is placed before the student for the sake of illustration. If the student's mind has been saturated with facts relating to some object or class of objects, it ought not to be very difficult for him to describe the object in the form of a continuous narrative, using his own words.

It is beyond the province of this book to show how object-lessons should be taught. But we give three specimens of the kind of description that a student might be expected to write, after he has received the lesson. We also give a few examples of outlines of object-lessons, such as a teacher might be supposed to ask a student to reproduce in narrative-form. The teacher will of course substitute any other sets of object-lessons that he may prefer.

We suggest that after an object-lesson has been completed orally by the teacher, each student be asked to show up an outline of it in writing, and that the expansion of the outline, *i.e.* its reproduction in the form of a continuous narrative or short essay, be not commenced until after the written outline has been returned to each student with corrections, additions, or other amendments. The outline as thus examined and revised can be used by the student as the basis of the essay. It is not at all necessary (as we need scarcely add) that all the outlines in the class should be of the same form or plan. So long as the outline prepared by a student gives a fairly complete version of the lesson as a whole, individuality of treatment and originality in preparation are to be encouraged.

1. *A Blackboard.*

Outline.

1. Of what material and in what shape it is made.
2. How its surface is made smooth and level, and for what purpose.
3. How a blackboard is supported: describe an easel. Shew why an easel is more convenient than any kind of immovable support.

4. Why the board is painted black, and why it is varnished.
5. The usefulness of a blackboard to a teacher.

Expansion of Outline.

A blackboard is to be seen in almost every school or classroom: in fact, a classroom is not properly furnished, if it is without one. Its name shows what it is made of and what its colour is. It is made of two or more broad boards, which are fastened together in such a way as to make one large level surface in the shape either of a square or (more usually) of an oblong, that is, a rectangular figure whose length is greater than its breadth.

Since a blackboard is used for writing on, its surface must be made perfectly smooth as well as level, and this is easily effected by a carpenter, who first levels it with his plane and then smooths it with sandpaper.

A blackboard is usually supported on an easel or movable wooden frame that tapers towards the top and stands on three legs, two in front and one behind. The board can be placed at any height that may be found most convenient for the teacher or for the class; for the two forelegs have a line of equidistant holes running up the middle, and the pegs on which the board rests can be fixed in any pair of holes that will give the height required. Sometimes a blackboard or series of blackboards is permanently fixed into one of the walls of the classroom; but this is hardly so convenient as the use of an easel, the position of which can be changed according to the variations of light or space.

The board is not only painted black, but varnished, so that it may have a clear and glossy surface, which will not retain much dust, and which, after it has been written on, can be easily wiped clean with a duster, or, if necessary, washed with a moist sponge. The board is painted black in preference to any other colour, so that the writing or drawing, which is put on it with a stick of white chalk, may be seen well against it: for there are no two colours so strongly contrasted as black and white, and a colour is always made more conspicuous when it is seen by the side of its opposite.

The eye will often teach more than the ear; but whether it does so or not, it is invariably an aid to the ear. The usefulness of a blackboard, then, lies in the fact that the class can not only hear, but see, what the teacher has to tell them.

2. *Chalk.*

Outline.

1. Chalk is a kind of mineral. Why is it called a mineral?
2. White chalk is the only real chalk. What is called black chalk and red chalk belong to different species of rock.
3. Chalk is extremely porous; a chalk-bed is sometimes the source of artesian wells.
4. Chalk useful as a dressing for cold and heavy soil.
5. Chalk, when it is burnt, useful for making mortar.
6. Chalk in its natural state useful for writing on a black-board.

Expansion of Outline.

Chalk is a kind of mineral. We give the name of "mineral" to every kind of solid substance, such as sand, gravel, stone, coal, gold, silver, copper, etc., that can be dug out of the earth. Such things are called "minerals" from the word "mine," which signifies a hole, pit, or other kind of excavation cut into the earth for the sake of obtaining some useful or valuable substance not found on the surface.

The chalk with which we are most familiar is white. In fact, this is the only kind of rock that can be called chalk in the proper sense of the word; for the black chalk used for drawing pictures on paper and the red chalk or reddle used for marking sheep, though we call them chalk for convenience, belong to different species of rock. What we call black chalk is a variety of slate reduced to clay; red chalk is a kind of ironstone reduced to clay; white chalk is not a clay at all, but a kind of limestone.

The white chalk mineral, with which alone we are now concerned, is extremely porous: when it is dry, it will take up nearly one-third of its bulk of water. As a storehouse of water a chalk-formation under ground is of great importance, the artesian wells of London and many other places being supplied from this kind of source.

This mineral, when it can be easily got, is much used as a dressing for land that is too cold and heavy. If, as sometimes happens, it is found immediately below the surface, the farmer digs it out with a pickaxe and scatters it in lumps over the heavy clods, where it crumbles into dust from the effects of frost, sun, and rain.

When it is burnt, it does not harden like clay, nor melt like metal, but crumbles into a fine dust as other limestones do, and is used as a lime-dust for making mortar, sand and water being mixed with it.

Lastly, chalk in its natural and unburnt state is the material used for writing on a blackboard. For this purpose it is convenient in two different ways:—the whiteness of its colour shows off well against the blackness of the board; and when the same board is needed for another lesson, what has been written on it can be very easily wiped off. Moreover, chalk costs very little and is procured without difficulty.

3. *Birds contrasted with Mammals.*

Outline.

1. Difference in the manner in which birds and mammals produce and rear their young. Birds lay eggs and hatch them. Mammals bring forth their young alive and suckle them. A whale and a bat are therefore mammals.

2. Bodies of birds lighter in proportion to size than those of mammals—(*a*) because feathers are the lightest kind of covering; (*b*) because the bones of most birds are hollow and filled with air.

3. Birds have wings instead of forelegs or arms. The wings are mounted with contour-feathers, strong, but light, which help it to fly; and are set in motion by muscles which meet at the breast-bone.

4. Birds have beaks for mouths. The habits of a bird depend upon the shape of the bill, in the same way as those of a mammal on the quality of the lips and teeth.

5. Birds have claws for feet. The habits of a bird vary with the shape of the claw, some claws being made for clinging to a branch, others for seizing prey, others for wading, others for swimming.

Expansion of Outline.

In comparing a bird with a mammal, the first point that we have to notice is the different way in which they produce and rear their young. The term "mammal" is limited to those animals which produce their young alive and feed them with milk. A bird does neither. It lays eggs, and produces the live bird from the egg by the slow process of hatching. When at last the young bird is strong enough to break the shell and come out, the mother-bird rears it not by giving it milk, but by dropping little fragments of dry food into its beak. A whale looks very like a fish, because it lives in water; a bat looks very like a bird, because it flies through the air. But both are really mammals, because both produce their young alive, and both rear them with milk.

The next point to be noticed is that the bodies of most birds are much lighter in proportion to their size than those of mammals. Considering that most birds are frequently on the wing, flying about from one place to another, sometimes even from one country to another, the lightness of body is to them a very valuable property. It will be asked, What is the cause of this lightness? Well, there are two causes;—firstly, feathers with which the body of a bird is covered make the lightest of all clothing,—much lighter than the fur coat or thick hide of most mammals; secondly, the bones of most birds, though not smaller in diameter than the bones of mammals of the same size of body, are hollow and filled with air, while the bones of mammals are solid and heavy. The larger bones of some mammals are hollow, it is true; but even then they are filled not with air, but with marrow, which makes them much heavier than if the space were filled with air. Whenever a bird breathes, air enters the bones; and the presence of this air adds much to their lightness, as we may gather from what we see of the lightness of an inflated football.

Birds have wings instead of forelegs or arms. Birds, quadrupeds, and men have each two pairs of limbs. The wings of a bird answer to the forelegs of quadrupeds and to the arms of men. The wings are mounted with strong, but light, feathers, which are called contour-feathers to distinguish them from down-feathers. The latter are for warmth, the former for flight. The bird moves through the air by flapping its wings. The wings are exactly of the same weight and length. If one of the wings is clipped shorter than the other, the bird loses its balance and is unable to fly. The great muscles by which the bird is enabled to move its wings with so much strength and rapidity are attached to the broad breastbone in front of its body.

Birds have beaks for mouths. While in mammals we find soft fleshy lips and hard rows of teeth, in birds we find nothing but a horny bill, which serves the purpose of both lips and teeth. The beaks or bills vary with the food. There is almost as much difference between the beaks of birds as between the mouths of the horse, the sheep, the cat, the dog, the rabbit, and many other kinds of mammals. The character of the bird depends upon the shape of the bill to the same extent that the character of the mammal depends upon the shape of its lips and teeth.

Birds have claws for feet. Among the claws of birds, too, there is as much variety as among the feet of mammals. Some claws are made for clinging to a branch or a roost; others for seizing prey and tearing it to pieces; others, viz. the long spreading claws, for wading in water; others, the webbed feet as they are called, for swimming in water. In short, the habits of birds vary with the form of the claw as much as those of mammals vary with the form of the foot.

4. *A River. Outline.*

N.B.—In this and the following outlines the figures represent paragraphs, and the italicised word or words immediately following each figure denote "the theme of the paragraph" (§ 13). The figures should not be repeated in the "expansion" of the outline, but the letters (*a*), (*b*) might for clearness of exposition be very properly retained.

1. *The source of a river.*—High mountains (the source of the Ganges), or an inconspicuous elevation (the source of the Thames). Fed by rain or by melted snow, both of which are more abundant on hills than on plains.

2. *The course of a river.*—Winding, not straight: straight lines not seen in nature. A river follows the line of least resistance. Makes its own bed, and by depositing mud and sand helps to make its own banks. Flows at last either into some sea or as a tributary into some larger river.

3. *The basin of a river.*—The whole area drained by a river and its affluents or tributaries is called the basin. The edge or rim of a river-basin is called its "watershed." Give an example from geography, such as the basin of the Ganges (India), or of the Ouse (England).

4. *The mouth of a river.*—The part where its waters enter the sea. Called an estuary, when the mouth is very wide and receives a high tide from the sea. Seaport towns are built at river-mouths: examples, Liverpool, Hull, Newcastle, and further inland, London, Calcutta, Rangoon, Bangkok.

5. *Rice. Outline.*

1. *What it is.*—One of the grain-bearing grasses. In appearance very like barley.

2. *Where it is grown.*—In countries where there is a great deal of water, and where there is great heat overhead. Examples: Egypt, parts of India, parts of China, Carolina, parts of Burma, Siam, and Tonquin.

3. *How it is cultivated.*—Two different ways: (*a*) sowing broadcast; (*b*) planting out in drills: both very common in India. When the plant is 3 or 4 inches high, the land is flooded either by irrigation or by natural overflow of river.

4. *The grain.*—Covered, like wheat and other grains, with a husk, and in that state called "paddy." The husk is removed by rubbing the ear between stones or by other methods. The removed husk is called "bran." The unhusked grain is called "rice."

5. *Uses.*—(*a*) For food, (*b*) for making starch.

6. *A Sponge. Outline.*

1. *Properties.*—(*a*) Porous, *i.e.* absorbs water. (*b*) Can be compressed, *i.e.* the water absorbed can be squeezed out again. (*c*) elastic; springs back again after compression. (*d*) Soft to the touch. (*e*) Tough, not brittle.

2. *Uses.*—The uses follow from the properties. Useful for mopping up water, for washing one's skin, for bathing a wound.

3. *What a sponge is.*—The skeleton of an animal that lives at the bottom of the sea, and is fastened by a kind of root to a rock. The flesh is soft and looks like that of a jelly-fish. When flesh is removed, we have a sponge.

4. *How procured.*—By divers. Diver has a heavy stone attached to his foot: why? If a diver's dress and pump are supplied, diver can remain about an hour under water; otherwise not more than two or three minutes at most.

7. *A Camel. Outline.*

1. *Two kinds of camels*, the Arabian with one hump, the Bactrian with two. The Arabian is spread through Arabia, Syria, Egypt, and India: lately introduced into Australia and Nevada (United States). The Bactrian is spread through Central Asia and Mongolia. More thickly covered with hair: why?

2. *Stomach.*—So constituted that it can store water—Arabian for five or six days, Bactrian for about half that time.

3. *Hump.*—A mass of fat, without any corresponding curve in backbone. This forms a reserve of nourishment, when fodder is scarce. The camel lives on its own fat.

4. *Foot.*—The sole is very broad and the toes spread out. Why is this useful for walking on sand?

5. *Usefulness* of camel for crossing deserts: hence called "ship of the desert." How it kneels to be loaded or unloaded. Refuses to rise, if overloaded.

6. *Character.*—Stupid, rather than docile. Patient and enduring, when fairly treated; but vindictive, when ill-used.

8. *India-rubber. Outline.*

1. *How procured.*—Made from the juice of a tree that grows in the East Indies, Brazil, and other hot countries. Holes are bored in surface-root, trunk, and branches. A little tube is put into the hole; and the milky juice that flows out is caught in a pot that is fastened under the hole.

2. *How manufactured.*—After standing some time the milky juice separates into two kinds of substance,—one sticky, and the other watery. The latter is evaporated either by exposure to the sun or by artificial heat. What remains is india-rubber.

3. *Properties and uses.*—(*a*) Sticky. Hence used for rubbing out pencil-marks. The black lead sticks to the india-rubber and is thus taken off the paper. (*b*) Waterproof. Hence cloth steeped in india-rubber, after the rubber has been dissolved in naphtha, becomes waterproof. (*c*) Elastic, *i.e.* springs back to its former place. If stretched and kept in cold water for some days, it becomes inelastic. While it is in the inelastic state, it is cut into narrow strips, and threads of silk, wool, or cotton are wound round them. These are woven into braces, bandages, spring-sides of boots, garters, etc. When they are passed over a hot roller, they immediately become elastic again.

Note.—A separate paragraph might be given to (*a*), (*b*), and (*c*) respectively; otherwise the paragraph will be inconveniently long.

9. *Cotton. Outline.*

1. *Tree and plant.*—There is a cotton-*tree* that lasts many years, and a cotton-*plant* that lasts for one season. Cotton falls from the former like a lump of wool, and is used for stuffing

beds and pillows. Cotton from the latter is made into calico. In both, cotton-fibre is the coating in which the seeds are encased.

2. *Cotton plant where grown.*—In India, Egypt, Brazil, and the warmer parts of United States. Requires a good deal of heat and some, but not excessive, moisture.

3. *How grown.*—Takes about seven months from date of sowing. Height from 2 to 4 feet. When the flower goes off, a pod is formed. After a time the pod bursts, and the white fibre peeps out. Gathered by the hand, and dried in sun.

4. *Ginning.*—Name given to the process of separating the cotton-fibre from the seed. Not done by hand, but by a machine called a gin or cotton-gin. Two kinds of gin: (*a*) the roller-gin; the cotton passes between two rollers, through which the seed cannot pass; (*b*) the saw gin; the cotton passes through the teeth of a saw, and the seeds are separated.

5. *Bales.*—A large bundle of cotton tightly pressed together for despatch to the mill is called a bale. In the mill the fibre is spun into yarn. Yarn is woven into calico.

6. *Seed.*—Used partly for the sowing of the next crop, and partly for the extraction of oil.

10. *Linen. Outline.*

1. *Calico and linen.*—The former made from cotton-plant, the latter from flax. The former warm, soft, and fluffy; the latter cold, hard, and glossy. Linen stronger and more durable than calico.

2. *The flax-plant.*—Is grown partly for its fibre, and partly for its seed, out of which linseed oil is made. Grown in temperate climates, as in Holland and Russia; also in India during the temperate season.

3. *Retting, or extraction of fibre.*—Fibre taken from stalk, not from pod, as in cotton. Two things in stalk—wood and fibre. Stalk is soaked till wood rots; the fibre is then set loose.

4. *Heckling.*—Fibres are straightened out by being made to pass through the teeth of a comb. Long fibres reserved for weaving into linen. Short fibres or tow used for making twine and cord.

5. *Linen.*—Fibre spun into yarn, bleached, and woven. Used for shirt-fronts, collars, household linen, tea-cloths, etc.

11. *Elephant. Outline.*

1. *Two kinds, African and Asiatic.*—African blacker, tusks in female as well as male, larger ears, and a saddle-shaped dip

near the shoulder. Asiatic (Ceylon, India, and Indo-China) has a muddier colour, tusks smaller and in male only, shorter ears, no dip anywhere in back.

2. *Properties common to both.*—A trunk, a very heavy and large head, small eyes, very short neck, long thin tail, very thick and hard hide, very massive body, and very thick legs. Contrast elephant's head and neck with camel's. Height from 8 to 10 feet. Both species live on herbs only.

3. *Tame and wild.*—All African, but not all Indian, elephants wild. African hunted for ivory. Some Asiatic elephants tamed to carry passengers on back and to haul logs in saw-mills.

4. *Character.*—When tamed, very intelligent and docile.

12. *Trunk of Elephant. Outline.*

1. *Length of trunk.*—Six or seven feet. Why so long? Elephant could get neither food nor drink without it. As useful as a neck is to other animals.

2. *Nostrils.*—The trunk is a prolongation of the nose and upper lip, which have coalesced. Two holes or nostrils can be seen at end of trunk.

3. *Serves as finger and hand.*—At end of trunk is a projection about five inches long, which serves as finger for handling little things or doing delicate work. Give examples of what it can do.

4. *Serves as arm and weapon.*—Enormous strength of trunk. Can be moved in any direction. How the elephant attacks its enemy with its trunk.

13. *Tea. Outline.*

1. *Tea-plant.*—Can grow to a tree 15 or 20 feet high. But it is kept to a height of about 6 feet. Why? That it may run to leaf rather than wood and that its leaves may be within reach. An evergreen.

2. *Where grown.*—In great varieties of climate, but must have a hot sun and much rain. China, Japan, hill tracts of India, Ceylon, and Indo-China.

3. *The gathering of the leaf.*—Three crops a year—spring, summer, autumn. Spring crop best, autumn crop worst. Only the new leaves plucked. Those who pluck the leaf often wear gloves to avoid bruising it.

4. *Green tea and black tea.*—The plucked leaves are left to

wither and dry. If they remain long enough in a heap, they change colour and become brown. From these the black tea is made. Green tea is made from the green leaf, which has not changed colour.

5. *Manufacture.*—The withered leaf, either green or brown, is first dried a little by fire and then rolled by hand or by machinery. After it is rolled, it is roasted in flat pans over a charcoal fire. It is the final roasting that gives the tea-flavour to the juice of the leaf. Care is taken that the leaf shall not be burnt.

14. *Coffee. Outline.*

1. *The coffee-plant.*—First found in Abyssinia; then reared in Arabia; now in Jamaica, Ceylon, and in most countries where the tea-plant grows. An evergreen. Kept down to a height of about 6 feet, but could grow to a height of 20. Kept short for the same reason that the tea-plant is.

2. *The coffee-bean.*—The coffee-plant bears a beautiful white flower, which is followed by a berry about as large as a cherry. Inside each berry are two hard oval-shaped beans face to face. It is from these beans that we get our coffee.

3. *The harvesting.*—The berries, when ripe, fall from the tree, and are picked up from the ground; not plucked from the tree. They are spread out to dry, till the outer pulp shrivels. This is rubbed off between stone-rollers.

4. *The preparation.*—The bean is prepared by roasting. The unroasted bean is greenish and has no taste or smell of coffee. It is the roasting which changes the colour, and gives the smell and flavour. Roasted in a cylinder that is kept constantly revolving: why?

15. *The Cuckoo. Outline.*

1. *Name.*—The bird named from its cry: a similar name in all countries where the bird is known. The cries are the love-notes uttered during the mating season.

2. *Summer visitant.*—Leaves its winter quarters in Africa at end of March, crosses the Mediterranean, visits the whole of Europe, going even into the Arctic Circle. Reaches England in the latter part of April, prepares to fly in July, goes for a certainty in August. Returns to Africa.

3. *Appearance.*—Length from beak to end of tail about 14 inches; black wings tipped with white; blue-grey feathers in

the back; between the wings and legs, feathers are white, streaked with slate-coloured stripes; tail spotted and tipped with white.

4. *Eggs.*—Has no time to build a nest. Lays an egg in a hedge-sparrow's or other bird's nests, one egg in one nest at a time. Cuckoo's egg is hatched with the other eggs. The young cuckoo throws the other young birds out. Early in September leaves England and follows its parents to the south.

16. *Slate. Outline.*

1. *What slate is.*—A kind of rock, chiefly of a dark blue colour. Can be split into even slabs by giving a chisel a sharp tap with hammer. Contrast effects on other kinds of rock.

2. *Uses.*—(*a*) For roofing houses. Very common in England. Tiles made of burnt clay answer the same purpose, where slate rock is not found. (*b*) For writing on. Slab is enclosed in a light wooden frame. Why?

3. *Preparation.*—For roofing houses cut into rectangular shape, but not polished. For making "a slate" to write on, it is rubbed smooth against a millstone or by some other method.

4. *Slate pencil.*—A short stick of slate. Leaves a white mark. Very convenient, since marks can be easily rubbed or washed off.

17. *Ostrich. Outline.*

1. *The largest bird* now extant: from 6 to 8 feet high. Chiefly found in South Africa; but not unknown in the deserts of Syria, Arabia, and North Africa.

2. *Legs.*—Of great length and strength. Runs more rapidly than the swiftest horse. Can break a man's leg with a kick. Has only two toes, one about half as long as the other.

3. *Wings.*—Small and weak in proportion. Cannot fly in air. Wings help it a little to run, as the wings help a fowl.

4. *Feathers.*—Those of wing and tail very large and valuable. The bird is hunted for these feathers, as a fox is for its tail. Horses run straight, but ostrich runs zigzag and so is caught.

5. *How reared.*—Wild ostriches scarce to what they once were. But ostrich farms are now kept in South Africa. In the wild state eggs chiefly hatched in the sun; in farms by artificial heat.

6. *Food.*—Vegetables, especially melons. Beak rather like a duck's, not at all like either a kite's or a hen's. Explain reason.

18. *Cork. Outline.*

1. *What it is.*—The outer bark of an oak that grows chiefly in Spain. Differs from English oak: (*a*) much smaller; (*b*) evergreen.

2. *How the bark is stripped off.*—Incision is made round trunk at top and bottom; but not deep enough to cut into the inner bark. Say why they avoid cutting the inner bark. Cuts are made in straight lines downward from upper to lower ring. Outer bark then gradually separates from tree and drops off.

3. *Times of stripping.*—Not commenced before the tree is over twenty years old. Can be repeated at intervals of ten years.

4. *How the bark is prepared.*—Pressed down flat in pits. Soaked in water, while it is pressed. Then dried and slightly charred to close the pores. When the pores are closed, we have cork: for water cannot pass through cork.

5. *Properties and uses.*—Elastic; so it can be pressed into necks of bottles. Impervious to water; so nothing escapes from bottle. Very light; so used as floats for fishing-nets and for life-belts.

SECTION 3.—OUTLINES OF SHORT ESSAYS ON GENERAL SUBJECTS.

41. Essay-writing.—In all essays, of whatever length and on whatever subject, there are two things to be considered,—the matter and the language.

As regards the *language*, we have, in Chapter II., given a few hints respecting force or energy of diction (§ 5), simplicity (§ 6), purity (§ 7), brevity or the avoidance of unnecessary words (§ 8), euphony or smoothness of diction (§ 9), and perspicuity or clearness of diction (§ 10). In the same chapter we have put the student on his guard against certain errors into which beginners are apt to fall in the use of common words and in the forming of common constructions. Finally, in the same chapter we have given some general hints about the structure of sentences and paragraphs.

As regards the *matter*, we have in this, as in the two preceding sections, furnished the student with an outline of the main headings, under which the subject that he is asked to write on can be treated, each heading to be expanded into a paragraph.

If the student prefers to substitute an outline of his own, he is of course quite at liberty to do so. But we think it advisable to put him on his guard on two points of no little importance. (1) Before he begins to prepare his headings, let him be quite sure that he understands the scope and purport of the subject on which he is required to write, and while he is preparing them let him be careful to confine himself to what is strictly relevant to the subject in hand. Matter that is not relevant to the subject of the essay or consistent with its main purpose must not be admitted. "An essay should be an artistic whole; it should have a central idea, to which all its parts are subordinated" (Fowler). (2) Let him take care to observe the principle of proportion, *i.e.* to give to each part of the essay as much prominence as is due to its relative importance. If an essay is an "artistic whole," proportion, which is one of the first principles of art, must not be neglected. Supposing, for instance, that the subject to be written on is the Magna Charta, it would be against all sense of proportion if the writer were to give three-quarters of his space to the acts of tyranny and oppression which provoked the barons to draw up the Charta, and leave only a quarter of the space for describing the contents of the Charta itself, the ceremony of the signing at Runnymede, and the king's attempts to evade the obligations that he had incurred by signing it.

One more precaution may be added. Whatever outline the student may decide upon, let him be quite sure before he begins to expand it that he knows his own mind, *i.e.* knows what he has to say on each point. There must be no such thing as vagueness of purpose or cloudiness of ideas. The matter must suggest the words, not the words the matter. If the writer is quite clear in his own mind about what he has to say, he is not likely to be at much loss to find words to express it. Whatever difficulty he may experience at first, this will become less and less by practice.

To show the standard of merit that may be aimed at in this early stage, we cannot do better than make use of the "Prize Competition" published by the *School World* in June 1900, when two prizes were offered by the editor for the two best English essays written by boys or girls of less than sixteen years of age. Candidates for these prizes were allowed to choose any one of the six subjects named below:—

The Uses of Books.	Prevention is better than Cure.
Holiday Tasks.	India.
Soldiers.	Comparative advantages of Town and Country Life.

Having received the permission of the editor to make free use of the essays that were sent to his office, we have selected three as typical specimens of various degrees of merit:—

(1) An essay on Prevention is better than Cure; (2) one on the Comparative advantages of Town and Country Life; (3) one on the Uses of Books.

The first is neither below nor above the average: several better ones on the same subject and several worse were sent in.

The second is somewhat above the average, but not as good as the essay to which the second prize was awarded.

The third is the essay to which the first prize was awarded.

All three essays have been printed in the form in which they were received in manuscript. The last needs no revision. The second needs some revision, and this we have shown in brackets by the side of the original. The first needs rewriting altogether; we have therefore given a revised version under it.

1. *Prevention is better than Cure.* Original essay as received (written by a girl of fourteen).

This old time-worn saying is so often repeated that more notice would be taken of it, if it were remodelled and put into other words. Then those who object to hackneyed expressions might perhaps stop to think what it means, and if they would but do so the millennium would begin very soon. Prevention in this phrase may mean either hindrance or caution, the one conveying the idea of stopping what has begun, the other of stopping before the beginning. Cure also may be taken either as care or healing; and care is the most wearying and depressing of things; so the world would be happier without it.

This proverb is generally used of physical matters such as health, but even in these it should be more used. That a good foundation of body and brain is necessary is beginning to be understood. If in the building up of the characters of the young this were insisted on, crimes and criminals would disappear. And, if in the building up of their bodies it were attended to, what fine-men and women we might be! Where it is, this proverb may be safely forgotten. In other matters also it should be remembered, as for instance art, music, politics, and such things.

The chief item in things not physical is also a firm foundation. In education the thorough mastery of the elementary subjects is the prevention of what cannot be cured afterwards. When prevention is taken into account, accidents will be averted, deaths delayed, sickness almost unknown. Animals and plants, especially when wild, show us how to prepare for the future; we see both laying up stores and preparing for hostile attacks. Thus in everything care is necessary, and those who begin any affair carelessly are almost always brought to a sudden standstill. With this proverb one other may be grouped, "Well begun is half done." The need of care shows that there has been thoughtlessness somewhere, and we are reminded of the quotation, "Evil is wrought by want of thought as well as by want of heart," and it is evils of this kind that are most numerous and need most trouble in curing.

There is one class of people who depend for their living on the proverb, "Cure is better than prevention." They are doctors. But it is pleasing to see that most of them urge prevention for health's sake.

The writer appears to have had four main points in her mind, while she was engaged in the above composition :—

1. The maxim has become so hackneyed that it is often overlooked in practice.

2. Prevention may mean either the stopping of an evil which has begun or the not allowing it to begin.

3. How the maxim holds good in physical matters, such as health.

4. How it holds good in things not physical, as education, the forming of habits, the building up of character.

For dealing with the subject named this is a very suitable outline to work upon; but there are several defects in the way in which it has been worked out. (*a*) "Physical matters" are mixed up in the second paragraph with "things not physical," whereas the two subjects should have been discussed in separate paragraphs, as the writer must have intended to do in placing the former phrase at the commencement of the second paragraph, and the latter at the commencement of the third. (*b*) The verbal reference to "care" and "cure" in the first paragraph is based on a false etymology; for there is no connection between the two words. (*c*) The allusion to animals and plants in the third paragraph is far-fetched and hardly serves the purpose of illustration. (*d*) The two senses ascribed by the writer to "prevention" are so much to the point that they deserve a fuller treatment than she has given to them in the first paragraph.

Taking the four headings given above as the basis, and giving a separate paragraph to each of them, we may rewrite the essay as follows, retaining the language of the original as nearly as we can, but omitting what is redundant or inappropriate, changing the position of one or two sentences that have been placed in a wrong connection, and adding one or two new sentences where more comment or point was required.

This time-worn maxim is so often repeated, that perhaps more notice would be taken of it in practice, if it were recast and put into other words. Then those, who make light of hackneyed sayings as if they were too common to be of much value, would stop to think what it means and how much truth there is in it. If they would but do this, the world would soon be better than it is; accidents would be averted, deaths delayed, and sickness almost unknown.

"Prevention" in this saying may mean either stopping what has already begun, or not allowing even a beginning to be made. The second kind of prevention, if it is practicable, is the more useful of the two. But we cannot always foresee the first beginnings of evil; and until these have shown themselves, no action can be taken. When such symptoms have appeared, there must be no delay in arresting their progress.

The proverb is generally applied to physical matters, such as health; but even in these it should be practised more than it is. Many an attack of small-pox, for example, which, even if it does not prove fatal, is not easily cured and is likely to leave its marks upon the face; could have been prevented by vaccination. If a good foundation of body and brain is laid in early years by healthy and industrious habits, there is less fear of weakness of body and brain in after life. It might seem that it would be more lucrative to a doctor, if the proverb were reversed, "Cure is better than prevention." But this is not true. A doctor who succeeds in stopping the progress of an illness before it has taken firm hold or in preventing it from breaking out, does good to himself as well as to his patient; for he raises his reputation and feels more pride and satisfaction in his work.

In things not physical the saying is equally true and, if not neglected, equally valuable. In education, for example, a thorough mastery of elementary facts will prevent a good deal of blundering and difficulty, which cannot be so easily removed afterwards. If in the building up of the characters of the young bad thoughts and bad habits were repressed at the outset, crimes would almost disappear. The need of a cure shows that there has been some neglect or thoughtlessness at an earlier stage; and we are reminded of the quotation, "Evil is wrought by want of thought as well as want of heart." In fact, those evils that spring from thoughtlessness, and not from intention, are the most numerous and sometimes the most difficult to cure.

2. *Comparative advantages of Town and Country Life* (written by a girl of fifteen). Outline of the essay as shown by the paragraphs.

1. The question stated,—Which is to be preferred?
2. Pleasures of country life in spring and summer: the beautiful scenery, the songs of birds, rural amusements and occupations.

3. Disadvantages of country life: dreariness in winter, absence of medical aid, of social gatherings, of schools.

4. Drawbacks of town life, especially in the summer months: danger of infectious diseases.

5. Advantages of town life: activity in all weathers, the best sights, the best medical attendance, and the best schools.

We print this essay in the form in which it was received. It has defects both in language and in matter. As regards the *language*, there are several well expressed sentences besides some faulty ones: the amendments most needed we have given in brackets side by side with the original. The hackneyed quotation from Goldsmith is pointless; such quotations should be avoided. As to the *matter* of the essay, the main defect is that it comes to no conclusion. It does not take up a definite position and sum up in favour of it. It see-saws, so to speak, now to this side, now to that, without giving a clear indication of the writer's own preference. "From a literary point of view decisiveness even in a wrong cause is preferable to shilly-shally." (See note appended to this chapter, where reference is made to "Argumentative Essays.")

A question we often hear asked is, Which is to be preferred, town or country life? [*say* "town-life or country-life"]. Well, the only answer to this question is, Both have their advantages; but, like everything else in this world, each is attended with disadvantages that must be placed to the opposite side of the account.

What can be more enjoyable than country life in spring and summer? In the country there are fields of various hues stretching all around one; the trees with their luxurious foliage, forming natural summer-houses for both man and beast; the thick hedges interwoven with sweet-smelling honeysuckle and all kinds of wild flowers; then there are the grass-grown or forest-clad hills that form the background, as it were, of this natural picture. But the picture is not a lifeless one [*insert* "like a picture on a wall"]. One may hear the sweet songs of the birds singing from every tree-top, the whistling of men whilst digging or ploughing in the fields, the bleating of the flocks, the merry laughter of some picnic party, and now and then the barking of some great farmyard dog. But the chief characteristics of the country are the freshness of the air and the peaceful, but not melancholy, calm. Then there are the outdoor amusements, —golf, tennis, driving, riding, cycling, gardening,—which afford so much pleasure to those who have the leisure and the means; while for the hard-working poor there is the harvest-time with all its festivities. In speaking of the country we may truly say in the words of Goldsmith—

> Where smiling Spring its earliest visit pays,
> And parting Summer's lingering bloom delays.

But it is not always spring and summer in the country. The dark days of winter visit it [*say* "set in"], and then we become aware of the disadvantages. In the long winter evenings there are no theatres, no concerts, no places of amusement; as the houses are far apart, there are few visitors, few gatherings, and on the whole life begins to seem rather monotonous. If [*insert* "at this or any other season of the year"] some one became [*say* "becomes"] suddenly ill, there is no doctor to be had, no telegraph office or telephone to send a message to him [*say* "no means of sending for one by telegraph or telephone"]. Then again, if a fire broke out [*say* "breaks out"], there is no fire-station near, and perhaps a very poor supply of water in the house. For those who have children to educate one great disadvantage of the country appears [*say* "is manifest"],—the absence of schools, which certainly cannot be done without [*say* "are certainly necessary"] in this age of enlightenment and competition.

Now, to turn to the town, we find there no nice [*say* "beautiful"] scenery, none of the freshness of the country. Everywhere [*say* "wherever"] we go, we see the same smoky, dusty, and gloomy-looking streets, where one feels inclined to think the sun never penetrates [*say* "which the sun never seems to penetrate"]; the busy road full of horses and carts; the crowded footpaths; the noise of machines in the great factories; the hubbub of many voices,—everything adding to the general din, until one almost feels it is again the Babel of centuries ago. If an illness commences [*say* "if an infectious disease breaks out"] in a town, there is danger of its rapidly spreading in the narrow space in which large numbers of persons are compelled to live.

In summer town is especially hot and dusty, and every one tries to get away to the seaside or the country; but as soon as winter sets in, they are all glad enough to return to town. Then we find the advantages of town life. If it is a rainy day, all does not look deserted as it does in the country. People go about as usual, and there is always something to see. In the evenings there are theatres, concerts, and parties [*say* "social gatherings"]. There are the delights of a day's shopping, or a visit to the picture galleries. There are plenty of visitors, and one does not seem to be alone in the world. In case of illness there is medical aid near; if a fire breaks out, one has only to telephone, and the fire brigade appears almost immediately. To the poor a town-residence seems, on the whole, more advantageous than living in the country; for there are schools without number, where the young can be taught not only to read and write, but to learn some trade by which they can earn their living.

3. *The Uses of Books* (written by a girl of fifteen). We give the essay as it stands: it needs no amendment or revision.

One of the most delightful things about a good book is, I think, its companionship. While we are able to enjoy good books, we need never lack friends. We are surrounded by an imaginary world which is peopled with good and noble characters, who let us share their inmost thoughts.

Books are, indeed, the only means we have of entering into the thoughts of the great men of all ages. While we commune with them, we are for the moment lifted up to something of the same height as that on which they stand, and we see the prospect beneath with their eyes. What is real and vital stands out sharp and clear; what is false and trivial is lost. Nor is the good we get from reading transitory. We read some noble thoughts, ponder on them, and find them true. They become also our own, a possession none can take away from us; for they mould our characters, and enter into our very being.

And if a book can form the character of an individual, can it not also form that of a nation? The Bible made Puritan England. The Puritans had many faults; they were narrow and uncultured; but they had moral dignity, moral fibre; they were God-fearing, God-serving men.

The ways in which books are of use to us are innumerable. Scientific books, for instance, help us to appreciate the manifold forces and beauties of nature that lie around us.

History has been called "Philosophy teaching by example." It makes us realise how people lived in past ages; how they built up our constitution and laws. Biographies of great men are very valuable, especially when they do not dwell too much on unimportant facts, but let us see something of the inner lives of the persons described.

Good novels, whatever may be said to the contrary, are of very real use in widening our sympathies. While we read a novel, we lose our own personality in that of the hero or heroine, and we feel emotions and go through experiences which we may never have in our own lives. Novels enable us to enter more sympathetically into the feelings of others.

Poetry leads us to the true and beautiful, makes us love beauty, and speaks to us as perhaps nothing else save music can.

The influence a book may have is incalculable. In Milton's noble words—a "good book is the precious life-blood of a master-spirit, embalmed and treasured up to a life beyond life."

But after all, the power of a book has some limitations. No two persons will read Shakespeare alike. One will understand more than the other; neither will understand more than what is already in some degree in himself. A book cannot create faculties in a man, nor can it give him any fresh qualities. No man ever became a genius by sheer force of reading. There must be some affinity between two minds, or they will never understand one another.

Finally, we may say that the chief end of a book is to awaken and develop those good qualities which might otherwise have lain dormant in a man for ever.

42. **Subjects with Outlines.**—We give a few subjects which may be useful for practice in the composition of short essays or descriptions. To each subject we append a brief outline, which the student may use or not according to his own choice or that of the teacher.

If he decides on accepting the outline that we have offered, he must shut the book before he begins to write. He might find it useful to redraft the outline in his own words. Under no circumstances should the book be referred to while he is engaged in the composition.

If, on the other hand, he prefers to prepare an outline

of his own, it might be expedient that he should show it to the teacher before he begins to expand it. On this point the teacher will be the best judge.

1. *Make Hay while the Sun shines.*

1. To show the point of the saying describe what hay is: long grass cut in the summer, dried in the sun, and ready to be stacked for winter use. It should have the juice dried in it. Rain washes out the juice, and makes the dead grass mouldy and unfit for fodder. Hence the importance of sunshine.

2. Uncertainty of dry and sunny weather in England: hence during hay-season the opportunity of such weather must not be lost.

3. The precept is sound for other purposes besides hay-making. Whenever a good opportunity occurs, it should be seized. No one can tell how long it may last, or, if it is lost, whether another one like it will come.

4. Parallel precepts or proverbs: "Strike while the iron is hot," "The mill cannot grind with the water that is past." Enlarge on these, and show importance of seizing an opportunity.

2. *Description of Hay-Field and Hay-Rick.*

1. Grass in England sprouts in spring; reaches full height in June or July; is then cut. Hay-harvest precedes wheat-harvest by one or two months. Convenience to farmer.

2. Grass cut either with a scythe or with a mowing machine. Scythe convenient on undulating ground; why? Machine preferable, wherever it can be used; why?

3. Grass, when cut, is left on the field to dry; is turned over with a prong or scattered by a machine; raked into "cocks"; then carted away for the hay-rick.

4. Hay-rick has four corners and sloping top, like a house. The top is thatched. Top why sloping and why thatched? Hay is cut in blocks as it is wanted; in what season? Much hay taken into cities and sold.

3. *Soldiers.*

1. What a soldier is: one trained to fight for his country, and bound to its service for a certain term of years. Not all soldiers of the same rank: a general commands an army, a colonel commands a regiment, etc.

2. Obedience the first duty of a soldier: example, the charge of the Light Brigade, which ran into the jaws of death without questioning the order. Without obedience, no discipline. Discipline as necessary in time of peace as on the battlefield. Necessity of good behaviour in barracks or among a conquered people.

3. Courage the next great duty of a soldier: bravery in attack; presence of mind; tenacity of purpose. Ambition of a soldier to win Victoria Cross.

4. All military service in British Empire voluntary: no compulsory service as in France, Germany, Russia, etc. Hence the high qualities of the English soldier; also of the Indian, Soudanese, and Egyptian troops serving under the British flag.

5. Conscription not needed in British Empire, as men are always found, when they are wanted. They join voluntarily, because they have confidence in their officers, and know that they will be regularly paid.

4. *The Volunteer Movement.*

1. Difference between a Volunteer and a Soldier. Volunteer gives only his spare time to soldiering, receives no salary as a soldier does, is rarely employed on foreign service, does not belong to the regular army.

2. Volunteer movement began in 1859, when invasion from France was feared. At first taken up only by those who could pay for their own arms, uniform, etc. Movement has since filtrated downwards to all classes; all expenses now paid by the Government.

3. Benefit to the country. A force of 250,000 young men armed and drilled, and ready for action. A home army for home defence. Some even went out on foreign service to South Africa. Have set a good example of patriotism, and made their country respected. Defence, not defiance, is their motto.

4. Benefit to themselves. Habits of obedience and discipline; sense of self-respect; pride in their country; physical training in the open-air, without having to give up ordinary occupations. Every large school in England has its cadet corps.

5. *Athletic Sports.*

1. Comment on the word "athletic" and on the word "sport." The former excludes such games as badminton, tennis,

golf, which require skill, but not such a high degree of muscular effort.

2. Athletic sports on land: chiefly cricket in summer and football in winter. On water: chiefly swimming and rowing.

3. Benefits to body. Exercise is necessary to health, and sport is the best way of taking it. No weariness, because the excitement destroys the sense of labour. A boy or man in training never eats or drinks more than is good for him.

4. Benefits to mind. A sound mind goes with a sound body. The best athletes often the cleverest at books. In all sport there is competition, and this arouses energy, ambition, and a sense of fair play. The captain of a football- or cricket-team, or the stroke in a boat-race, acquires a healthy sense of responsibility; those under him learn discipline and combination.

6. *Books for Recreation.*

1. Observe the scope of the subject. "Recreation" excludes books studied in school or for professional purposes. Applies to books read in intervals of leisure. We need recreation for the mind as much as exercise for the body. Prose generally preferred to poetry, because it is not such a tax on the attention.

2. Three main classes of books for recreation: biography, travel, fiction.

3. Biography. Teaches by example; valuable, because true; a good example stimulates to industry and emulation, as a bad one excites disgust.

4. Travel. Reading about foreign countries and foreign customs opens the mind; throws light on geography and sometimes on history.

5. Fiction. Called pre-eminently "light reading," enlarges our sympathies; extends our knowledge of mankind. But excessive reading of fiction not advisable; the mind, like the body, needs change of diet.

6. Men's characters are shown by the books they read as much as by the companions they keep. A bad boy will read bad books, whenever he can get them.

7. *A Rolling Stone gathers no Moss.*

1. Moss forms only on stones that remain fixed in the same place. Hence the proverb means:—Avoid unnecessary change. This admits of various applications.

2. Stick to one line of study, and persevere in it. Trying one study after another or one school after another, and giving up each in turn, is a waste of time. A rolling schoolboy gathers no knowledge.

3. Having chosen a calling, stick to it. Experience gained in one calling is of no use for another. Change of profession means beginning again at the bottom.

4. Having chosen a suitable place of residence, do not leave it without a good reason. Old residents are more likely to make friends and gain position than new-comers. Old friends are generally better than new ones.

5. Change of country, without any strong necessity, is not advisable. One who tries first England, then one colony, and then another, is almost certain to fail. Wherever a good start can be made, go on with it; it is rash to throw it up for some new craze in some other part of the world.

8. *April in England.*

1. April is the middle month of spring. "March winds and April showers bring forth May flowers." English climate uncertain: but April usually showery with intervals of sunshine. Describe rainbow in such intervals—how caused.

2. Vegetation everywhere sets in. Describe the meadows, the hedge-rows, the wheat-fields, the primroses, the trees breaking out into the first leaf.

3. The winter birds (the red-wing, the fieldfare, and the wood-lark) have gone farther north. The summer birds (the swallow, the house-martin, the nightingale, the cuckoo, each in succession) return to us from Africa; show why they come and why they go.

4. Our home-birds begin to build. Describe some of them.

5. Fishermen spread out their sails for the open sea.

9. *April in Northern India.*

1. The hot dry weather (to last for three months) has fully set in. Wind blows from west to east. The blue sky is often obscured with a dusty haze. No sign or expectation of rain. April the first month of the torrid season, July of the rainy, November of the temperate.

2. The wheat harvest was cut in March. The stumps and

roots remain in ground which cannot be ploughed till rain returns at end of June. Every blade of grass is burnt up by the sun. Cattle fed with chopped straw.

3. Snakes, which lay dormant in the ground during the winter, come out of their holes and warm themselves. Lie in shady nooks during the heat of the day, but move about in the open after sunset.

4. The rivers, which had shrunk in their beds in the previous months, begin to rise a little, swollen by melted snow from Himalaya mountains.

5. Marshes are all dried up, and the water-birds (ducks, snipe, etc.) are no more seen. They have returned to the cooler regions where they were bred.

10. *April in Canada.*

1. On account of vast extent of Dominion, the climate of Canada has considerable variations. East of the Rocky Mountains the more settled parts have two great seasons—a very cold winter lasting through November, December, January, February, March,—a very hot summer lasting through May, June, July, August, September. April is the transition-month between winter and summer.

2. April an unpleasant and uncertain month. The long reign of frost and snow gradually yields to returning warmth. Fresh snow sometimes falls, but soon melts. Early in April the alders and willows break out in bloom. As snow disappears, thin blades of wheat or rye, which was sown in the previous autumn and protected during the winter by the snow, are seen on the fields.

3. Fresh ploughing is commenced by middle of April, and must be rapidly done; for harvesting begins before the end of July, hay, grain, and root-crops following one another in rapid succession. Cattle, which were stalled at great cost during the winter, are turned out to graze in April: they nibble the tender shoots of trees and blades of reappearing grass.

4. Why the extraordinary difference between climate of England and that of Canada in similar latitudes? (1) The Gulf Stream makes England warmer in winter. (2) The surrounding ocean makes it cooler in summer. (3) Canada has no high mountain range from east to west to protect it during the winter from the excessive cold of the Arctic regions.

11. *Penny Saved, Penny Gained.*

1. Parallel proverb, "Take care of the pence and the pounds will take care of themselves." The proverb is meant to teach frugality or thrift. Beware of little expenses which can be saved. Little expenses added up make a large sum: "Many a little makes a mickle."

2. A savings bank is a great aid to the thrifty who desire to save. Describe one. Especially useful for those who can save only small sums, even a few pence, at a time.

3. Frugality is an aid to generosity. A man who saves nothing can give nothing. Charity begins at home; but when home-wants have been satisfied, a man who saves a little may be able to help others without stinting his own house.

4. Extravagance conduces to meanness. A man who runs into great expenses to indulge his own fancies or appetites, tries to recoup himself by being correspondingly mean to others. Such meanness often ends in dishonesty.

12. *A Contented Mind is a Continual Feast.*

1. What is the secret of happiness? So far as the body is concerned, health. So far as the mind is concerned, *contentment*. Contentment is the greatest good we can hope for in life. It does not bring wealth, but it banishes the desire of it, which is much more valuable. Contentment is natural wealth; luxury is artificial poverty. He who is perpetually striving to increase his wealth suffers as much anxiety as one who has to struggle against want.

2. Contentment is very much a matter of disposition: but the disposition may be cultivated by two or three considerations: (*a*) Have I already as much as I really require? (*b*) Have I already more than I really require? (*c*) How much worse off might I be than I really am?

(*a*) The fable of the dog and the shadow shows the force of this question. The dog had already as much as it needed,—a large piece of bone and flesh; and ought to have been contented with it. In seeking for more, it lost all.

(*b*) Many men have already much more than they need; but they go on grasping for more. They live in a state of perpetual want, while the contented man enjoys a continual feast. Such men have no peace.

(*c*) This consideration may be useful to those whose means

are small or who have suffered some loss. There is the story of the Dutchman, who broke his leg by a fall from the main-mast, but congratulated himself that he had not broken his neck.

13. *The Uses of Mountains.*

1. Mountains give motion to water. A river owes its current to some slope on the earth's surface. Without rivers there would be no inland navigation, no natural drainage, no fresh water. Rain would stagnate in pools and marshes, which would become more and more foul. The air would be polluted. The earth would not be fit to live on.

2. Mountains maintain a constant change in the currents and nature of air. Hills divide the earth not only into districts, but into climates. Mountain-ridges and table-lands much cooler than valleys and plains. Canada suffers much cold, because no mountain chain from east to west shuts off the cold from the Arctic circle.

3. Mountains cause perpetual change in the soils of the earth. Surface soil is carried from hills into plains by rivers. Egypt has been called "the gift of the Nile," having been formed from deposits of mud from mountains in equatorial Africa. The whole of Bengal is alluvial, formed by the Ganges and its tributaries.

4. Mountains help to divide nations and empires. Examples: the Pyrenees, the Alps, the Caucasus, the Hindu Kush, the Himalayas.

14. *Story of Crœsus: Call no Man Fortunate till you see his End.*

1. Crœsus, king of Lydia in Asia Minor, was the richest man of his age. His wealth has become proverbial. His capital, Sardis, was visited by the greatest men of ancient Greece, and among these was Solon, the wise man of Athens.

2. Crœsus asked Solon to tell him who was the most fortunate man that he had ever seen. Solon mentioned one private person after another, and gave their histories. Crœsus angrily dismissed him for not mentioning himself. Solon declined to call him fortunate, till he had seen his end.

3. A few years afterwards Crœsus, conquered by Cyrus the Great, was put on a pile of wood to be burnt alive, when he called out "Solon, Solon, Solon." Cyrus, learning his story, and thinking that he might some day be conquered himself, spared him.

4. The end of Cyrus himself was a similar example; for he was slain in battle not long afterwards. The end of Napoleon I. in St. Helena, and that of Napoleon III. in Chislehurst, are other examples. No one can tell what the future may have in store. Misfortune may befall the highest as well as the lowest.

15. *The Choice of a Calling.*

1. To any one who has a very decided bent in a certain direction, the choice is easy: follow that bent. If another career may appear more lucrative, do not be tempted. Live your own life, *i.e.* the life that nature intended for you. You will be more happy and more successful. Better to be a good mechanic than a bad doctor, a good farmer than a bad lawyer, a good blacksmith than a bad clergyman.

2. Those who have no decided bent must select work according to (*a*) their opportunities, (*b*) their faculties. Having once taken up a calling, stick to it, and be content. You will grow to like it, and excel in it in time. Perseverance will triumph.

3. If a boy can get the training and the opportunity, and has the ability, there is no harm in his aspiring to a position higher than that in which he was born. This is a laudable ambition. But without the ability and without the training it is sheer folly.

16. *Virtue its own Reward.*

1. A man must do his duty without fear of punishment or hope of reward. It very often happens that virtue brings respect, advancement, and prosperity. But to gain these must not be the motive; for sometimes virtue entails loss, and suffering, and even temporary ruin.

2. The real reward of virtue lies in the approval of one's own conscience. Aristides, the Athenian, was banished from Athens; yet he never swerved from his duty: he was recalled, and was surnamed the Just.

3. Never do evil that good may come. In such cases the good may not come at all, and only the evil, the guilt, the self-reproach remain.

17. *Strike while the Iron is Hot.*

1. Iron is one of the hardest of metals, but becomes soft by the action of fire. While soft, it can be beaten into almost any shape. That is the time to strike.

2. The saying is not less true in a metaphorical sense. If consent has been given to something, act upon it at once, before the consent is withdrawn. If there is a chance of buying or selling something on which much depends, seize the chance. A chance that has come once may never come again, and it very soon passes. If a good resolution has been formed, act on it at once before it has had time to cool.

3. "Too many irons in the fire." A caution against undertaking more than you can manage. There is only one time for striking the iron. It is therefore useless to have several irons in the fire at once, when there is only one man to strike.

18. *Beasts of Burden and Draught: England and India.*

1. Explain the words "burden" and "draught."

2. England. For burden no beasts are used; everything is put on carts or wheel-barrows. For draught the only animals used are the horse and the ass. The horse is used for dragging the plough, wagons, carts, and vans. The English cart-horse is a peculiar breed of enormous strength,—very broad and very tall. The ass is used for drawing light greengrocers' carts, bath-chairs, and sometimes street-organs.

3. India. The beasts used for either purpose are the ass, the pony, the ox, and the camel.

(*a*) The ass. Used by brickmakers for carrying bundles of bricks, and by washermen for carrying bundles of clothes. Not used for draught.

(*b*) The pony. Used by tradesmen for carrying merchandise from place to place, as rice, wheat, firewood, etc. Goods placed in pack-saddles. Not used for draught.

(*c*) The ox. Universally used for ploughing the fields and drawing carts. Indians use the ox, where Englishmen use the cart-horse. Not used for burdens.

(*d*) The camel. For carrying very heavy goods or large quantities of goods. Sits down to be loaded, and if the load is too heavy, refuses to rise. Much used in India, as in Arabia and Egypt, and coming into use in Australia. Not used for any kind of draught, except for drawing a camel-cart crowded with passengers above and below.

19. *Falsehood.*

1. By word. Saying what is directly contrary to fact; disguising or distorting fact by false colouring or false construc-

tion; keeping back a portion of the facts and thus creating a false impression of the whole.

2. By silence. Concealing something which ought to be made known, and thus indirectly deceiving a person.

3. By looks or gesture. Misleading a person by the expression of the face or gesture of the body.

4. A liar injures himself. Even when he speaks the truth, he is not trusted. One who makes a constant habit of lying deceives himself at last and believes his own lies.

20. *Advantages and Disadvantages of Competition in Trade.*

1. Competition means that any one can compete against any one else, that no one has a monopoly, *i.e.* an exclusive right to produce or sell a certain article or set of articles. Where the field is not open to all, or where favouritism is shown to some, there is no fair competition.

2. Competition may take two different forms. One man may try to undersell another, *i.e.* to produce and sell an equally good article at a lower price. Or one man may try to surpass another, *i.e.* to produce a better article at the same price.

3. Advantages of competition. It compels producers to make better things, if possible, and it prevents traders from charging unfair prices. If there were no competition, there would be no inducement to do either, and the public would be badly served.

4. Disadvantage. When the competition becomes very keen, there is fear of workmen being underpaid, and producers and sellers making less profit than they are entitled to. But this remedies itself in time. Advantages far greater than the disadvantage.

21. *The Power of Words.*

1. Words may be a source of good or of evil. Of good, when they console the afflicted, explain difficulties, enlighten the ignorant, admonish the incautious, appease the angry, etc. Of evil, when they disguise the truth, excite to anger, seduce into vice, speak evil of others, etc. A man must govern his tongue when he is in company, his thoughts when he is alone.

2. A word once spoken can never be recalled. It is repeated again and again. Confidence once betrayed is never given back; it is lost for ever. A calumny once spoken circulates

far and wide. A cutting speech is remembered and cannot be recalled; it is like an arrow shot from a bow.

3. The fable of the Feast of Tongues. Æsop was told by his master to put the best of everything on the table. He put nothing but tongues. Next day he was told to put the worst of everything. Again he put nothing but tongues. When called to account by his master, he had a very good explanation to make.

22. *Cleanliness.*

1. We turn away from uncleanliness with the same disgust as from ungodliness; hence the proverb "cleanliness is next to godliness." "To have clean hands" is said of those who have kept aloof from evil-doing. "To have a clean heart"; see *Psalm* li. 10.

2. Cleanliness in person and dress. A dirty skin unhealthy, because the pores, which act as drains for carrying off bodily waste, must be kept open: disagreeable also to others. But it is useless after washing the skin to put on dirty clothes; clean dress and clean person must go together.

3. Cleanliness in house and surroundings. House must be swept out, because dust carries infection, and foul matter gives bad smells, which are bad for health. But refuse must be carried clear away, and not left to stand anywhere near the house.

23. *Influence of Climate on National Character.*

1. Climate of England. Mild winters and mild summers. Much time can be spent in open air. Hence manly sports, cricket, football, lawn-tennis, cycling, riding, shooting, boating, —all of which have helped to form the national character by stimulating active habits, competition, energy, a sense of fair play, pluck, etc.

2. Great heat. A dry heat not necessarily conducive to inaction. Look at the hardihood and valour of the Arab, the Sikh and other inhabitants of Upper India, the Zulus of South Africa, the Egyptians. But moist heat induces languor of muscle; and in such countries abundance of cheap food weakens the motive to labour.

3. Great cold. Conduces to sluggishness of body and mind. Inhabitants of very cold latitudes always backward, because the difficulty of preserving life against cold and hunger leaves no leisure for anything else. No sports, no cultivation of

mind, no progress in anything. In northern Siberia the natives live by hunting and fishing; in Tartary by pasturing flocks. There is no scope for doing anything better.

24. *The Commonwealth of Australia.*

1. Australia, the continent of the South Pacific. All the colonies are now confederated into one political whole, called a Commonwealth, but still a part of the British Empire. The white inhabitants all of one stock,—English. The Commonwealth includes Tasmania, but not New Zealand.

2. Area about 3,000,000 square miles; length from east to west, 2500 miles; breadth from north to south about 1950 miles—nearly equal in size to United States excluding Alaska. Coast-line, 8000 miles, with hills at the back, at various distances from the sea. Interior consists for the most part of a vast plain with occasional undulations.

3. Agriculture suited to the various climates of the belt of coast-line, and capable of vast extension. In the southern half of Australia wheat, vines, and other fruit-trees of the temperate zone; sugar-cane, rice, cotton, tobacco in the northern half. Rainfall at Adelaide (South Australia) about 20 inches; in Victoria about 30 inches; in New South Wales about 45; in Queensland from 50 to 90, the amount increasing as we go north. Very little of all this rain reaches the great interior plain, which is usually very hot and very dry, but sometimes gets a flood of rain.

4. Climate. Varied, but considering the variations of latitude wonderfully uniform. The southern provinces or states have the climate of Southern Europe: the north is tropical, but much more suited to the health of white settlers than tropical climates elsewhere.

5. Other sources of wealth besides agriculture are mineral, pastoral, and manufacturing. Minerals are gold, iron, copper, tin, lead, antimony, coal. Not yet fully explored. Australia is the greatest wool-exporting country in the world, but the wool-industry, like agriculture, is only beginning.

Note on Essay-writing from "School World."

We append a few extracts on the teaching of essay-writing from an article by Mr. C. J. Battersby, M.A. (Senior English Master in the Bradford Grammar School), which appeared in *School World*, Sept. 1899. These very useful notes are said by the author to be "the outcome of much experience in teaching English composition to large forms," and the writer published them "in the hope that they would prove helpful to the junior members of his profession."

A suitable Subject should be chosen, and due notice given.—Let us suppose that we are dealing with a form of boys aged about fifteen. Our first object is to make them write, not very correctly, not very wisely, but with pleasure to themselves, and at fair length—not less, let us say, than 800 words. It is only by inducing the boys to write a tolerably long essay that we shall inspire them with confidence in their own powers. We must choose a fit subject, one that is well within their mental grasp, and concerning which they already possess, or can easily acquire, plenty of information. . . . Notice of it should be given some days before the essay is to be written, and at the same time the subject should be a little unfolded by the master.

Preparing an Outline.—Our next step will be to exact visible proof that such information has been collected, and not only collected, but arranged in satisfactory order. The boys must be told that we shall expect an outline of the essay to be prepared at home and sent up with the essay itself. . . . Sometimes it will be useful to go to the blackboard and show how we ourselves tackle a subject, first putting down notions just as they suggest themselves, then working related notions with the same number, and last, with the numbers to guide us, writing them out afresh in groups. At a later time, when the boys have grown accustomed to breaking up a subject, the headings, which they have previously sent up on a separate paper, may with advantage be transferred to the margin of the essay. This practice gives their work an attractive look, and checks rambling.

Argumentative Essays.—The boy must be told to take up a definite position, and sum up in favour of it. The fault often found in argumentative essays is that of see-sawing now to this, now to that, side of a question without any indication of one's own preference. We must tell the boys to choose a side and stick to it. They should state their opponent's case and then their own, taking care to put the latter in such forcible terms as to justify a strong conclusion in its favour. From a literary point of view decisiveness, even in a wrong cause, is preferable to shilly-shally.

Correcting the Essays.—Let us now suppose that the essays have been written, and that the time has come for correcting them and giving them back. After many years' experience I am of opinion that minute correction of essays is a game not worth the candle. It will be sufficient to mark just what is wrong; at the same time a fixed code of signs should be employed. Thus a misspelling may be enclosed in a rectangle, a grammatical error noted by a marginal star, and a misused word by a marginal query. At the end of the essay a succinct criticism should be put—for example, "handwriting good, arrangement confused, facts sometimes incorrect, expression fluent and clear."

Giving back the Essays.—With our boys before us in regular form-order, we begin by making a few general remarks on the success or failure with which the subject has been treated by the form as a whole. If any boy has done particularly well, we bestow public praise on him. Then, taking up the topmost essay from our bundle, we tell the writer our opinion of it, and after that bombard him with his errors. If he cannot correct them then and there, we pass them down the form for others to correct, and he loses his place. We deal with every essay in the same way. This method has several advantages. It saves school-time, puts the boys on their mettle to correct the mistakes they have made, and by continued repetition drives some of the principles of essay-writing into their heads.

A Caution.—One caution, however, must be given. If a boy, in the simplicity of his heart, has expressed some sentiment, a little foolish perhaps, which he does not intend for the ears of the whole form, we must not raise a laugh by reading it with sarcastic voice and comment. Should we do so, we shall forfeit the confidence, not only of the individual boy, but of all his fellows. They will shrink before the possibility of ridicule, and cease to be free and natural in their writing. On the other hand, if they find that we can keep secrets, they will tell us secrets, and enjoy the exercise of that instinct which has produced our finest literature,—the instinct of self-revelation.

Summary.—I will now conclude by summarising the chief points of the method here rapidly sketched :—

(1) Subjects should be chosen of so easy and interesting a nature that even the dullest boys can write largely on them.

(2) The Master should talk over the subjects with his boys.

(3) Some days should be given for preparation of material, and an outline should be required.

(4) In the interests of style, boys should be forbidden the use of certain colourless words, as "nice," "nasty," "funny," "silly," "good," "bad," and of initial "ands."

(5) Errors should be marked, but not necessarily corrected, by the Master.

(6) A brief criticism in broad lines should be appended to each essay.

(7) Errors should be corrected by the boys themselves in class.

C. J. BATTERSBY.

Subjects set for Essays in the Cambridge Local Examinations.

December 1891. (Senior. None set in Junior.)

(*a*) A backward spring.
(*b*) Free education in elementary schools.
(*c*) Sympathy.
(*d*) "The heights by great men reached and kept
Were not attained by sudden flight."

December 1893. (Senior. None set in Junior.)

(*a*) Punctuality
(*b*) A strike.
(*c*) Sunrise.
(*d*) Free libraries.
(*e*) "A bird in the hand is worth two in the bush."
(*f*) "Evil is wrought by want of thought
As well as want of heart."

December 1894. (Senior. None set in Junior.)

(1) Some ancient building which you have visited.
(2) European disarmament.
(3) Camping out.
(4) Wasps.
(5) A summer night.
(6) "There is no new thing under the sun."
(7) "I am never less lonely than when I am alone."

December 1896. (Junior.)

Butterflies.	Egypt.	Money.	Telescopes.
Cycling.	Heroism.	Novel-reading.	

December 1896. (Senior.)

(*a*) Clouds.
(*b*) One of Sir Walter Scott's novels.
(*c*) South Africa.
(*d*) "The fairy tales of Science."
(*e*) Duty, "Stern daughter of the voice of God."
(*f*) "We live in deeds, not years."
(*g*) "The old order changeth, yielding place to new."

December 1897. (Junior.)

The morning newspaper.
Collecting postage-stamps.
School punishments.
The bully.
Sir John Franklin.
Johannesburg.
Early rising.
More haste, less speed.

December 1897. (Senior.)

(*a*) The Sun.
(*b*) Sir Walter Scott's *Ivanhoe* or *Kenilworth*.
(*c*) Greater Britain.
(*d*) A ruined abbey.
(*e*) Nelson.
(*f*) England in 1837 and in 1897.
(*g*) "He is the free man whom the truth makes free,
And all are slaves beside."

December 1898. (Junior.)

Private theatricals.
Holiday tasks.
Bores.
Compulsory games.
Tennyson.
"A lie which is half a truth is ever the blackest of lies."

December 1898. (Senior.)

(*a*) Arctic exploration.
(*b*) Alfred the Great.
(*c*) Wild flowers.
(*d*) The river Nile.
(*e*) Knowledge is power.
(*f*) "He prayeth well, who loveth well,
Both man and bird and beast."

December 1899. (Junior.)

(*a*) Rustic sports.
(*b*) A town or parish council election.

(*c*) Popular superstitions.
(*d*) Rudyard Kipling.
(*e*) Khartoum.
(*f*) Prevention is better than cure.

December 1899. (Senior.)

(*a*) A storm at sea.
(*b*) Westminster Abbey.
(*c*) A flower-garden.
(*d*) The English lakes.
(*e*) Music.
(*f*) "Take up the White Man's burden."
(*g*) "The stately homes of England,
How beautiful they stand,
Amid their tall ancestral trees,
Through all this pleasant land."

December 1900. (Junior.)

(*a*) The value of indoor amusements.
(*b*) Hobbies.
(*c*) Ladysmith.
(*d*) Is war an unmixed evil?
(*e*) Every man is the architect of his own fortune.
(*f*) Sweet are the uses of adversity.

December 1900. (Senior.)

(*a*) Moorland scenery.
(*b*) Vesuvius.
(*c*) John Ruskin.
(*d*) The force of example.
(*e*) Wit and Humour.
(*f*) Our colonies and the mother country.

Subjects set for Essays in Matriculation Examinations in India.

Calcutta Matriculation.

(*a*) The late Calcutta International Exhibition.
(*b*) The manner in which you spent the last long vacation. (1885.)

Any outdoor game that you have seen or taken part in. (1886.)

(*a*) The last cold-weather holidays.
(*b*) The cow.
(*c*) A river.
(*d*) Punctuality.
(*e*) Truthfulness. (1887.)

(*a*) The Jubilee celebration in your town or district.
(*b*) Bodily exercise.
(*c*) Friendship.
(*d*) Snakes.
(*e*) The rainy season. (1888.)

(*a*) The hot season of 1888.
(*b*) The best time for holding university examinations in India.
(*c*) Learning to swim.
(*d*) "Be it ever so humble, there's no place like home."
(*e*) The electric telegraph. (1889.)

(*a*) Snake-charmers.
(*b*) Self-denial. (1890.)

(*a*) Manliness.
(*b*) Deafness.
(*c*) The use and abuse of speech. (1895.)

Madras Matriculation.

(*a*) Benefits arising from gymnastics. (1889.)
(*b*) Rivers and their uses. (1890.)
(*c*) A bazaar in an Indian town or village. (1891.)
(*d*) The uses of rain. (1892.)
(*e*) An Indian village at sunrise. (1893.)
(*f*) The importance of good handwriting. (1893.)
(*g*) Coal and iron. (1893.)
(*h*) Some animal useful to man, and the way in which it is useful. (1895.)

Bombay Matriculation.

(*a*) Every man is the architect of his own fortune. (1889.)
(*b*) Advantages to a Hindu student of a knowledge of English. (1890.)
(*c*) The occupations in which you take most pleasure. (1892.)

(*d*) The benefit that a man derives from having to work for his living. (1893.)

(*e*) Contrast the blessings of peace with the honours of war. (1894.)

(*f*) Hot and cold weather in India. (1895.)

Allahabad Matriculation.

(*a*) The advantages of books; using the materials suggested by the following hints :—

Books record what others have seen, thought, discovered, known. One tells a thing and goes away; we wish to hear it again, but cannot: books preserve it; we can pause and ponder. Man's life short; knowledge of men stored in books helps others. Printed books easily read. Results, if we had no books. (1892.)

(*b*) Magna Charta :—outline.

The tyranny and rapacity of John—the Barons determine to vindicate their rights—Magna Charta drawn up—its chief provisions—John refuses to sign it—London is seized by the nobles—he reluctantly signs the document—persuades the Pope to amend the Charta—traverses the kingdom with hired mercenaries—his sudden death relieves the nation. (1893.)

(*c*) The seasons of the Indian year. (1896.)

Punjab Matriculation.

(*a*) Gymnastics. (*b*) Habit. (*c*) Steam. (*d*) The rainy season. (1890.)

(*a*) Cashmir. (*b*) Punctuality (*c*) Child-marriage. (*d*) The advantages of physical exercise. (1891.)

(*a*) Lord Clive. (*b*) The horse. (*c*) The Diwali. (*d*) Home. (1892.)

(*a*) Town and country life. (*b*) How to spend a holiday. (*c*) Object lessons. (*d*) Improvement of Vernacular literature. (*e*) Education of women. (1893.)

(*a*) The advantage of a liberal education. (*b*) The tramway. (*c*) The city of Lahore. (*d*) True bravery. (*e*) The value of a good name. (*f*) Our country. (1894.)

CHAPTER V.—LETTER-WRITING, PRIVATE, COMMERCIAL, AND OFFICIAL.

SECTION 1.—PRELIMINARY REMARKS.

43. General Precautions.—Letters may be written in various forms and for various purposes. But of whatever kind the letter may be, there are certain general rules that are applicable to all.

Penmanship.—Avoid scribbling or bad penmanship under any circumstances. Make a habit of writing legibly even to your most intimate friends. Half the pleasure that your friend might have in reading your letter will be destroyed, if he is puzzled to make out your writing. In letters of business illegibility may lead to a misreading of what you write, and this may have serious consequences. If the pen does not suit you, get another. If the ink is too thick, change it. Make no idle remarks at the end of your letter:—"Excuse this daub, I was in a hurry"; "excuse this scrawl; I had a bad pen"; "the ink wouldn't run; it was too thick." Among examples of bad penmanship we include the careless habit of omitting to cross the *t* or dot the *i*. If in writing the word *repeat* you omit to cross the last letter, the word that you leave on the paper is *repeal*, which gives a sense almost the opposite to what you intended.

Spelling.—Good spelling is as important as good penmanship; and should not be neglected even in the most familiar forms of correspondence. A word misspelt creates a bad impression, whoever the reader may be; and there is no certainty that the letter you have written may not go beyond the person to whom it was addressed. If you have any doubt about the spelling of a word, look it out in the dictionary. One who is habitually careless about his spelling incurs the risk of being considered careless about other matters, or of being looked upon as ignorant and badly educated.

Division of Syllables.—Avoid such division altogether

if you can. But if it is necessary, as may sometimes happen, to break a long word into two, let the breaking be properly done (as shown in Chap. III. §§ 35, 36). You will get no credit for giving the right spelling to such a word as *fatigued*, if you end a line with *fatig-* and begin the next line with *ued*. The word in question consists of only two syllables, and these, if they are to be written apart, must be shown as *fa-tigued*. If there is not room enough to write the whole word "fatigued" at the end of the line, it would be better to write the whole word at the beginning of the next line than to end the former line with such a short syllable as *fa-* or to begin the next line with such a false syllable as *ued*.

Punctuation.—Much obscurity is sometimes caused by not putting the stops in places where they are wanted, or by putting them in wrong ones. Bad punctuation indicates either carelessness or ignorance on the part of the writer. It annoys some readers to receive a letter so written, and there is always a risk that the sense may be obscured, if not reversed, by faulty punctuation. Among examples of this error we include the omission or the misuse of the apostrophe that accompanies the Possessive case. The writer must bear in mind that, when the noun is Singular, the apostrophe is placed between the last letter of the Singular noun and the *s*, as in *father's;* that when the noun is Plural, the apostrophe is placed after the last letter of the Plural noun without any *s* being added, as in *fathers';* and that in *hers*, *ours*, *yours*, *theirs* the apostrophe is not used at all. Hence in closing a letter to a friend, no such mistake as *your's sincerely* should be made.

Postscripts.—Avoid postscripts as much as possible. Say all that you have to say before you finish the letter. If you collect and arrange your thoughts well before you begin to write, no postscript will be necessary. But if something turns up unexpectedly after you have signed your name to the letter, and you find it necessary to mention this new fact in reference to what has gone before, then to save the trouble of writing a fresh letter you may add a postscript in some such form as the following :—

Since the above was written I have learnt from a letter (or telegram) just received (or from a friend who has just come in) that, etc., etc.

Revision.—Make a point of reading over your letter before you put it into its envelope. You may have left out a word, and the omitted word might happen to be the most telling word in the sentence: the omission (for example) of such a little word as *not* would make a marvellous difference in the sense. You may have made a misspelling, or used a wrong preposition or a wrong stop, or committed a false concord or some other error in grammar, into which persons are as apt to fall in writing as in talking. Many persons (who would know better, if they stopped to think) write *who* for *whom*, *him* for *he*, *I* for *me*, etc., through inadvertence. All such oversights can be detected by reading the letter over with some care, before you put it up. If the corrections are numerous, the letter should be rewritten. It is against good manners to send out a letter full of scratches and corrections. A correction made by putting your pen through a word and writing the proper word above it looks better than a scratch or erasure, which when the pen is applied to it ends in a daub.

44. **The Direction or Outside Address.**—Before describing the letter itself, we offer a few remarks about the outside address, the direction to be written on the envelope. Every one is aware of the necessity of *clearly* writing down in separate lines, one line under another in the order here given—(1) the name and designation of the addressee; (2) the name of his house (if it has a name); (3) the name of the village, or the name of the street together with the number of the house; (4) the name of the post-town nearest to the village, or the name of the town in which the street is situated; (5) the name of the county, if the name of the town is not very widely known; (6) the name of the country, state, colony,

or province, if the addressee is living or sojourning abroad.

If the addressee is a visitor staying at another person's house, the letter should be addressed to the care of (c/o) that person in such form as the following:—

W. Cookson, Esq.
c/o Mrs. Evans
4 London Road
Kingston
Surrey

The only point about which anything more need be said is the first, "the name and designation of the addressee." This matter calls for a good deal of care. However familiar may be the terms of the letter itself, there must be no familiarity on the outside of it, no want of formality on the envelope. If a person is not addressed externally in terms suitable to his rank or position, he may take it as an intentional slight, or regard the writer as ignorant of good manners. Those to whom letters are likely to be addressed fall mainly into three classes—(*a*) ministers of religion, (*b*) commoners below the rank of knight,[1] (*c*) men in the military or the naval service.

(*a*) *Ministers of Religion.*

Write *Rev.* for all denominations alike. Between *Rev.* and the surname of the addressee write his Christian name, or the first letter of it, or (if these are unknown) write *Mr.*—

Rev. Charles Paley; Rev. C. Paley; Rev. Mr. Paley.

---

[1] In an elementary book like the present we have not considered it necessary to discuss higher titles. It may be pointed out, however, (1) that a commoner of the rank of knight (which is not hereditary) is addressed as *Sir* followed by his Christian name and then by his surname, as *Sir Ashley Eden;* (2) that a commoner of the rank of Baronet (which is hereditary) is addressed in the same way as a knight up to the end of his surname, and that *Baronet* or *Bart.* is written after his surname, as *Sir Walter Scott, Bart.;* (3) that all above the rank of Baronet are nobles or peers of the realm, and have a seat in the House of Lords, and that the gradations of rank are Baron, Viscount, Earl, Marquis, Duke, the last being immediately below the rank of king or queen.

It is better to write *Rev. Mr. Paley* than *Rev. — Paley*, or *Rev. Paley*.

In the Church of England a clergyman holding the rank of archdeacon is addressed as—

The Venerable Archdeacon Paley; The Ven. Archdeacon Paley.

Observe, no Christian name or initials are given before the surname in such a case.[1]

(b) *Commoners below the rank of Knight.*

All married women, whose husbands are of the above class, and this from the highest down to the very lowest grade, are addressed as *Mrs.* It would be much more convenient if commoners of all grades below that of knight could be similarly addressed as *Mr.* This would save the difficulty that is often felt in attempting to distinguish between those who are and those who are not in the rank of "gentleman." Those who are or who wish to be considered in this rank expect to be addressed as *Esqre.* (the short for *Esquire*, Old French *escuyer*, Latin *scutarius*),—a title which has come down from the Middle Ages, and meant originally a "shield-bearer," whose duty it was to attend on a knight, and whose rank was therefore below that of a knight. When the office of esquire or shield-bearer died out, it would have been better if the title had been dropped also. *Mr.*, not *Esquire*, is the title printed on a gentleman's visiting-card, and in speaking of or to a gentleman we call him *Mr.* It is only in writing his address on an envelope that we have to call him *Esquire*.

Three facts should be noted. (1) The title *Esquire*, if it has to be written at all, is always written after the surname. (2) If any other title, such as *Rev.*, *Dr.*, *Sir*, or *Mr.* has been already placed before a name, the title *Esquire* is never put after it; thus we cannot say "Sir Henry Jones Esquire," "Dr. Scott Esquire," or "Rev.

[1] A dean is addressed as *The Very Rev.*; a bishop as *The Right Rev.*; an archbishop as *The Most Rev.*

Wilson Esquire." Similarly in the inside of a letter we never use such a form of address as *Dear Jones Esquire.* (3) The title *Esquire* can be given without hesitation to medical men, solicitors, barristers, merchants or wholesale dealers, bankers, certificated engineers, artists, musicians, architects, stockbrokers, authors, publishers, editors of newspapers, journalists, public officers, directors of companies, partners in firms, large employers of labour, teachers of higher class schools (when they are laymen). We cannot enumerate all the positions or callings to which the title of *Esquire* is appropriate. Much depends on the style in which a man lives, the company that he keeps, and the degree of refinement that he displays in manner, habits, and appearance.

The word *Mr.* (always placed before the name, never after it) is used in writing to shopkeepers, artisans, and all kinds of labourers, skilled or unskilled. But we cannot draw a precise line as to where *Esquire* ends and *Mr.* begins.

Firms of *all* kinds, without any exception, are addressed as *Messrs.* —— and Co. Even if the director or head partner is a man of title, no allusion to such title is made in addressing the firm. Thus the founder of the great engineering firm at Newcastle acquired the title of Lord Armstrong; yet the firm itself during his lifetime never ceased to be addressed as Messrs. Armstrong, Whitworth, and Co. Observe, too, that *Co.* is written, not *Company.*

(c) *Men in the Military or the Naval Service.*

Commissioned officers in the army, from the highest rank down to captain (inclusive) are addressed as Field-marshal, General, Colonel, Major, or Captain according to the rank that the individual holds for the time being; and the title is placed before the name. One whose rank is below that of captain is always addressed as *Esq.* This title he can justly claim, since, as we have already explained, it was originally a military title, and should not have been given to civilians at all.

A non-commissioned officer is addressed as Sergeant or Corporal according to the rank he holds. An ordinary soldier of the line is addressed as Private; a cavalryman as Trooper; an artilleryman as Gunner.

In the navy the gradations of rank are Admiral (the highest rank), Vice-admiral, Rear-admiral, Commodore, Captain, Lieutenant.

How women are addressed.—All married women whose husbands are of the class (*a*), (*b*), or (*c*) are addressed as *Mrs.*, and all unmarried as *Miss.* No distinction of any kind is made according to the rank of the husband. An archbishop is addressed as "The Most Rev. the Archbishop of Canterbury," but his wife is merely "Mrs." The wife of a General and that of a Private are equally addressed as "Mrs."

When several brothers are married, their wives are distinguished from one another by the Christian name of the husband; as, "Mrs. John Davis," "Mrs. Charles Davis," etc. If the mother is alive, she is addressed as "Mrs. Davis," no Christian name being inserted. If the mother is dead, the wife of the eldest brother takes her place, and she is addressed as "Mrs. Davis," the Christian name being dropped.

It remains to say something about the use to be made of academical degrees and other personal distinctions.

Academical Degrees.—In official letters addressed to professors, schoolmasters, lecturers, or any similar class of men, the academical degree, such as B.A., M.A., Ph.D., B.Sc., etc., may be written after *Esquire;* as, "John Conington Esq., M.A." In official letters addressed to clergymen or other ministers of religion, the academical degree of B.A. or M.A. may be written after the surname; as "Rev. S. Dyson, B.A." In private letters, however, between friends and relatives the academical degree is seldom or never mentioned.

Professional Degrees and Titles.—These should not be omitted either in official or in private letters. Thus, if a clergyman has taken the degree of D.D. (Doctor of Divinity), he should be addressed as—

Rev. Charles Paley, D.D.; Rev. C. Paley, D.D.; Rev. Dr. Paley.

Similarly, in the medical profession, a physician who has taken the degree of M.D. (Doctor of Medicine) should be addressed as "J. Vincent Esq., M.D." (It is more formal and rather more deferential to address him in this way than to say "Dr. J. Vincent.") A surgeon who has taken the degree of F.R.C.S. (Fellow of the Royal College of Surgeons), but has not taken the degree of M.D., should be addressed as—

J. Vincent Esq., F.R.C.S.

But if he has also taken the degree of M.D., then both degrees should be named, the *M.D.* being given first.

One who holds the office of Justice of the Peace or Honorary Magistrate has J.P. written after his surname.

Honorary Titles.—Honorary titles, such as D.C.L. or C.B. in England, and C.S.I. or C.I.E. in India are added after *Esquire.* In India Members of Council and Judges of the High Court are addressed as *The Honourable,* or *The Hon'ble,* or *The Hon.*

45. Classification of Letters.—The most convenient classification of letters is into :—

I. Private correspondence ;
II. Business correspondence.

The former class consists mainly of letters written for the sake of keeping up an interchange of kind feelings and civilities between friends or relatives, who live at some distance apart and cannot meet, or whom it may be more convenient for any other reason to address through the post-office.

The latter class consists of letters written on any kind of business either private or public.

SECTION 2.—PRIVATE CORRESPONDENCE.

46. Four Parts of a Private Letter.—A private letter consists of four different parts :—

(1) The heading. This gives the writer's place of residence and the date of writing the letter.

(2) The salutation ; *i.e.* the terms in which the writer greets the addressee.

(3) The body of the letter. This is of course the main part, all other parts being mere accessories.

(4) The ending; *i.e.* the words in which the writer brings his letter to a close before signing his name.

In a postcard the salutation (part 2) is often omitted; and for the ending (part 4) nothing need be given but the signature of the writer. The postcard is a very short form of letter, and should not be used, unless there is good reason to believe that the recipient will not object to it.

47. The Heading.—This consists of (*a*) the place where the letter is written, (*b*) the date of writing it. The heading is written at the top of the first page on the right-hand side, and might run as follows:—

Elgin House
16 Grove Place
Bruton
Somersetshire
4 July, 1901

In the above specimen we have given the heading in full, viz. the name of the house, the number of the house with the name of the street, the name of the town, and the name of the county. This shows the recipient how he is to direct the envelope in sending his reply. In writing to an intimate friend it may not be necessary to give more than the top line. But it is a good thing to make a habit of always writing the heading in full, firstly because the recipient may not happen to remember all the particulars, and secondly because, if the letter should miscarry, the post-office authorities on opening it will know how to send it back to the writer.

Note 1.—A practice is springing up, by which the heading, instead of being put at the top of the letter on the right-hand side, is written at the bottom on the left. This practice is not so common as the other, and is not recommended. Business firms always put the heading at the top, because (as will be explained below) the space at the bottom of the left-hand side is sometimes used for another purpose. In private correspondence it is more convenient to the reader to put it at the top, as in most cases he can tell who the writer is from the name of the place without having the trouble of turning over the page to look at the signature.

Note 2.—There are other ways of writing the date of a letter. Thus for 4 July, 1901 (as given above), we might write July 4, 1901, or more briefly 4/7/01, the day of the month being placed first, then the number of the month, and lastly the last two figures of the century.

48. The Salutation.—The form in which the salutation or greeting is worded depends upon the degree of relationship or intimacy subsisting between the writer and the addressee.

(1) A parent addressing a son or daughter, and brothers or sisters addressing each other, write *My dear* or *My dearest*, followed by the Christian name or by some more familiar form of it. A son or daughter addressing a parent writes *Father* or *Mother* in lieu of the Christian name: (*Papa* and *Mamma* are childish).

(2) An uncle or aunt addressing a nephew or niece writes *My dear nephew* (or *niece*); or "nephew" and "niece" may be dropped and the Christian name substituted. Cousins, if they are sufficiently intimate, may address each other by the Christian name, as brothers and sisters do; or by the more formal salutation, *My dear cousin.* This mode of greeting, though rather more formal, is not by any means distant.

(3) In correspondence between friends and equals of the male sex, the form of salutation depends upon the degree of intimacy. (*a*) The most intimate form is by using the Christian name only, as *My dear Edward.* (*b*) The next is by using the surname only, as *My dear Dalton.* Or, if we are writing to a military officer, we may say, *My dear Captain, My dear Major*, etc. (*c*) The next mode of address, rather more formal than the preceding, is by inserting *Mr.*, or *Captain*, or *Dr.*, or *Professor* (as the case may be) between *My dear* and the surname; as *My dear Mr. Dalton, My dear Dr. Blades, My dear Professor Skeat*, or *My dear Major Harris.* Even if the

addressee is a clergyman, we never say *My dear Rev. Dalton*, but *My dear Mr. Dalton*. (*d*) The least intimate and the most formal mode of addressing a friend or acquaintance is by dropping the *My*, as *Dear Mr. Dalton*, *Dear Captain Jones*.

(4) A servant writing to his master on some private matter in which both are concerned, or a subordinate writing for some private purpose to an official superior of far higher rank than his own,[1] should address him as *Dear Sir*. On the other hand, a master writing to a servant can call him by his Christian name, if he is in the habit of doing this in talking to him.

(5) In *all* private letters written by a male to a married woman, whatever her rank may be, or whatever the degree of friendship may be, he must address her as *Mrs.*, never by her Christian name; as *Dear Mrs. A.*, or *My dear Mrs. A*. The former is rather more distant than the latter. The most formal mode of addressing a lady friend is by saying *Dear Madam*; and this is suitable where there is a great disparity of rank or position.

(6) An unmarried lady, who is not a sister of the writer, or is not nearly related by blood in any other way, is never addressed by her Christian name alone, but as *Miss A*. The Christian name may, however, be inserted between *Miss* and the surname, if it is necessary to distinguish one sister from another. The word *Dear* or *My dear* is prefixed according to the degree of intimacy.

49. The Body of the Letter.—The body of a letter is of course the substance or main part of it. A few specimens will be given below, but in the meantime we may remind the reader of the general precepts as to penmanship, spelling, punctuation, etc., given in § 43, and offer a few other remarks in addition. Because a letter is private,—an exchange of ideas and feelings between relatives or friends,—it does not follow that the writer

---

[1] There is no occasion to write *Honoured Sir* or *Respected Sir*. Whatever honour or respect is due to the addressee can be expressed by the tone in which the body of the letter is written.

should set aside as unnecessary or as unworthy his attention the rules of neatness, accuracy, legibility, good composition, and, above all, good grammar. In the choice of words, the quality of matter, and the general tone of the composition more freedom is allowed in a private letter than in a formal essay or narrative. What passes between friends by letter is not intended to be formal (unless the acquaintanceship happens to be very recent and therefore still distant), but to express in an easy and natural style the kind of talk that would pass between them if they met. At the same time, a young student who has not acquired facility in writing correctly impromptu, had better err, if error it can be called, on the side of carefulness in arranging his ideas before he begins, and in considering how he is to express them.

Colloquialisms, though unsuitable in an essay, are not out of place in friendly correspondence; but slang words, which do not sound well in conversation, look a good deal worse in a written letter. In writing to a relation or to an intimate friend one is naturally inclined, and, under certain circumstances, one may be compelled, to say a good deal about oneself. But the frequent use of "*I*" has a bad effect and looks egotistical. This can often be avoided by giving a fresh turn to the sentence or by dispensing with the pronoun altogether in some sentences. Thus, for "I think," etc., you can say "It strikes me" (*me* being a more modest form of the pronoun than *I*), or simply "It appears, etc." Instead of saying "I look forward to your coming, etc.," you can say "It will give us great pleasure if you can come, etc.," or "We are looking forward to your coming"; this can always be done in cases where the writer himself is not the only person in the house concerned.

50. The First Sentence of a Letter.—As in a paragraph the opening sentence is usually so framed as to give some indication of what is to follow (§ 13), so in a letter the first sentence should as a general rule be so worded as to give some indication of the writer's feelings or of his reasons for writing the letter. If he is the first to begin the correspondence, or if he has received no answer to a letter written some time ago, he might commence in some such way as the following:—

I am writing to tell you of my safe arrival here last night.

I have been so busy of late, that I could not find time to write to you before.

I have some good news to tell you, and I am sure it will come as a surprise.

After my long silence you will, I fear, have begun to think that I was never going to write to you again. There could not have been a greater mistake.

You will be very sorry to hear that, etc.

The result of the examination is out, and though it is disappointing in one respect, it might have been a great deal worse.

I heard incidentally that you had suffered from overwork and needed rest and change of air. If this is so, I hope you will come to us for a few days, etc.

I wrote to you about a month ago, but as I have heard nothing since, I begin to fear my letter may have miscarried.

I heard that you had left —— about a month ago; and as I have now discovered your address, I take the first opportunity of breaking the silence.

I am going to ask you if you will do a little job for me in the place where you are, as I am unable to go there and do it myself.

As I know you will be anxious to hear how my mother is, I send a line to say, etc.

I was obliged to wait till the vacation commenced, before I could write to you again.

We have had a great shock since you last heard from me.

I promised to give you my impressions of this place, as soon as we had lived here long enough for me to form an opinion.

Do not be surprised at hearing from me again so soon. The matter about which I wrote has suddenly entered upon a new phase.

If the writer is replying to some letter, it is usual to make some reference to the date and its contents. We give a few specimens of the manner in which the opening sentence might be worded:—

Many thanks for the congratulations contained in your letter of the 3rd.

My delay in answering your letter of the 14th has not been intentional. I mislaid your address.

I gladly avail myself of the kind offer contained in the letter received from you this morning.

Your letter of the 7th, inquiring after the health of my son, gave the wrong number to the house, and therefore did not reach me till this morning.

I was much pained by the sad intelligence conveyed to me by your letter of yesterday's date.

I hope you will excuse me for having put off answering your last letter so long.

I have done what you asked me to do in your letter of the 25th ultimo, and hope the result that I am now going to report will be satisfactory.

We were all extremely glad to learn from your letter of the 10th inst. that your son had made such a good start in life.

I sat down to answer your letter of the 4th inst., when your reminder suddenly turned up. So this letter must be an answer to both.

You will see from the heading given above that I have changed my house.

I do not lose a mail in answering the very important letter that I received from you this morning.

I have much pleasure in accepting your very kind invitation to spend part of the ensuing vacation at your house.

The news contained in your letter of the 12th inst. caused me much astonishment and still more regret.

51. The Ending.—The signature of the writer is given last of all in a line by itself. But except in a postcard (§ 46) a writer does not sign his name to the letter without taking leave, as it were, in terms expressive of the degree of friendship or relationship existing between himself and his correspondent. The form of ending should always be in keeping with that of the salutation: it may even repeat the salutation in such words as the following:—

I am, my dear Charles,
Y^{r} affect^{ate} father

I remain, my dear Dalton,
Y^{rs} sincerely

If the salutation is repeated, as above, in the ending, it must be introduced by *I am*, or *I remain*, or *Believe me, my dear ——, to be*, etc. But there is no necessity to repeat the salutation, or even to use the words *I am*, *I remain*, *Believe me to be.*

For blood-relations such forms as the following are suitable :—

I am (or I remain), yours affectionately,
Your affect[ate] (or loving) son, father, nephew, etc.

If for any reason cousins have seldom or never met, and hence the acquaintanceship is either slight or non-existent, it would be affectation to make professions of an affection or love that has had no chance of being established. In such a case it is correct to say :—

I am, my dear Cousin,
Y[rs] sincerely

For friends, who are not related by blood, the words used at the close of the letter will depend upon the degree of intimacy or upon the impression that the writer desires to leave on the mind of the addressee. If he wishes to be very cordial, he can end his letter with *yours ever*, *yours always*, *yours affectionately*, *yours very sincerely*, *ever yours sincerely.* The words *yours sincerely* (sometimes in inverted order, as *sincerely yours*), though less effusive, are suitable for any degree of friendship that is well established.

If the salutation has the more distant form of *Dear Mr. A.* or *My dear Mr. A.*, the corresponding ending should be *Yours truly*, or at most *Yours very truly.* After such a salutation as *Dear Sir*, the ending might be *yours respectfully*, or whatever will best express the feelings of the writer without making him appear to be too familiar.

Examples of Private Letters.

1. *From Lord Chesterfield to his Son* (A.D. 1742).

I am very well pleased with the substance of your letter. As for the inaccuracies with regard to style and grammar, you could have corrected them all yourself, if you had taken time. I return it to you here corrected, and desire that you will attend to the difference, which is the way to avoid the same faults for the future.

I should like your next letter to be in English, and let it be written as accurately as you are able; I mean with respect to the language, grammar, and stops; for as to the matter of it, the less trouble you give yourself, the better will it be. Letters should be easy and natural, and convey to the persons to whom we send them just what we would say to these persons if we were with them. You may as well write it on the Wednesday at your leisure, and leave it to be given to my man when he comes for it on Thursday.

As I know you do not love to stay long in the same place, I flatter myself that you will take care not to remain long in that you have got, in the middle of the third form. It is in your power to be soon out of it, if you please; and I hope the love of variety will tempt you.

Pray be very attentive and obedient to Mr. Fitzgerald. I am particularly obliged to him for undertaking the care of you; and if you are diligent and mind your business when with him, you will rise very fast in the school. Every remove (you know) is to be attended by a reward from me, besides the credit you will gain for yourself. I know very well you will not be easy till you have got above Master Onslow. As he learns very well, I fear you will never be able to do it, at least not without taking more pains than I believe you will care to take. But should that ever happen, there will be a very considerable reward for you besides Fame.

Let me know in your next what books you read in your place at school, and what you do with Mr. Fitzgerald. Adieu.

2. *From Sir Walter Scott to his son Charles.* (*Not quoted in full.*)

I cannot too much impress upon you that *labour* is the condition which God has imposed upon us in every station of life. There is nothing worth having that can be had without it, from the bread which the peasant wins with the sweat of his brow to the sports by which the rich man must get rid of his languor.

As for knowledge, it can no more be planted in the human

mind without labour than a field of wheat can be produced without the previous use of the plough. There is indeed this great difference, that chance or circumstances may so cause it that another shall reap what the farmer sows. But no man can be deprived, whether by accident or by misfortune, of the fruits of his own studies; and the liberal and extended acquisitions of knowledge which he makes are all for his own use.

Labour, therefore, my dear boy, and improve the time. In youth our steps are light, our minds are ductile, and knowledge is easily laid up. But if we neglect our spring, our summer will be useless and contemptible, our harvest will be chaff, and the winter of our old age unrespected and desolate.

Your affectionate father,

WALTER SCOTT.

3. *From Macaulay at the age of twelve to his Father.*

SHELFORD,
22*nd Feb.* 1813.

MY DEAR PAPA,

As this is a whole holiday, I cannot find a better time for answering your letter. With respect to my health, I am very well, and tolerably cheerful, as Blundell, the best and most clever of all the scholars, is very kind and talks to me and takes my part. He is quite a friend of Mr. Preston's. The other boys, especially Lyon, a Scotch boy, and Wilberforce, are very good-natured, and we might have gone on very well, had not one, a Bristol fellow, come here. He is unanimously allowed to be a queer fellow, and is generally characterised as a foolish boy, and by most of us an ill-natured one. In my learning I do Xenophon every day, and twice a week the *Odyssey*, in which I am classed with Wilberforce, whom all the boys allow to be very clever, very droll, and very impudent. We do Latin verses twice a week, and I have not yet been laughed at, as Wilberforce is the only one who hears them, being in my class. We are exercised also once a week in English composition, and once in Latin composition, and letters of persons renowned in history to each other. We get by heart Greek grammar or Virgil every evening. We had the first meeting of our debating society the other day. A vote of censure was moved for upon Wilberforce, but he getting up said, "Mr. President, I beg to second the motion." By this means he escaped. The kindness which Mr. Preston shows me is very great. He always assists me in what I cannot do, and takes me to walk out with him every now and then. My room is a delightful snug little chamber, which nobody can enter, as there is a trick about opening the door. I sit like a king with my writing-desk before me; for (would you believe it?) there is a writing-desk in my chest of drawers; my books are on one side, my box of papers on the other, with my arm-chair and my candle; for every boy has a candlestick, snuffers, and extinguisher of his own. Being pressed for room I will conclude what I have to say to-morrow, and ever remain

Your affectionate son,

THOMAS B. MACAULAY.

4. *From Cowper (the poet) to his cousin, Lady Hesketh.*

HUNTINGDON,
Sept. 14, 1765.

MY DEAR COUSIN,

The longer I live here, the better I like the place and the people who belong to it. I am upon very good terms with no less than five families, besides two or three odd scrambling fellows like myself.

The last acquaintance I made here is with the race of the Unwins, consisting of father and mother, son and daughter, the most comfortable social[1] folks you ever knew. The son is about twenty-one years of age, one of the most unreserved and amiable young men I ever conversed with. He has not yet arrived at that time of life, when suspicion recommends itself to us in the form of wisdom, and sets everything but our own dear selves at an immeasurable distance from our esteem and confidence. Consequently he is almost known as soon as seen, and, having nothing in his heart that makes it necessary for him to keep it barred and bolted, opens it to the perusal even of a stranger. The father is a clergyman, and the son is designed for orders. The design, however, is quite his own, proceeding from his being and having always been sincere in his belief and love of the Gospel.

Another acquaintance I have lately made is with a Mr. Nicholson, a north-country divine, very poor, but very good

[1] We should now rather say "genial, sociable" for "comfortable, social."

and very happy. He reads prayers here twice a day all the year round, and travels on foot to serve two churches every Sunday through the year, his journey out and home again being sixteen miles. I supped with him last night. He gave me bread and cheese, and a black jug of ale of his own brewing, and doubtless brewed by his own hands.

Another of my acquaintances is Mr. ——, a thin, tall, old man, and as good as he is thin. He drinks nothing but water and eats no flesh, partly I believe from a religious scruple (for he is very religious), and partly in the spirit of a valetudinarian. He is to be met every morning of his life, at about six o'clock, at a fountain of very fine water about a mile from the town, which is reckoned extremely like the Bristol spring. Being both early risers, and the only early walkers, we soon became acquainted. His great piety can be equalled by nothing but his regularity; for he is the most perfect timepiece in the world.

I have received a visit likewise from Mr. ——. He is very much a gentleman, well read, and sensible. I am persuaded in short that if I had had the choice of all England, where to fix my abode, I could not have chosen better for myself, and most likely I should not have chosen so well. Yours ever,

WILLIAM COWPER.

5. *From an Indian Gentleman to a retired English Official living in England.*

4th April 1900.

DEAR SIR,

Kindly accept my most sincere thanks for your note, from which I was much pleased to hear of your own and your children's welfare. I remember the days when they used to play in my tent while I was out in camp with you. I am also very glad to hear that they have made such good progress in their education, and shall be still more glad if any of them can come out to India in some high post.

I am sorry to hear that for some time past you have been troubled with asthma, which I suppose is on account of your living in a cold climate after having spent so many years in a hot country like this, where your very hard work added to the effects of the heat may have overtaxed your strength.

I have still a few more years to serve, before I can complete the thirty years required for pension. When that time comes,

I shall devote myself to looking after my land and to reading the books that I like best in English and Persian literature. I have bought two village-properties lately out of the savings of my life-time. These, together with the estate that has fallen to me by inheritance, will be enough to occupy my time pleasantly in my old age.

We had good rains in Jan. 1900, which improved the prospects of the spring-harvest. Otherwise we should have had another great famine in this province, as they have in other parts of the country. Bombay, Madras, and the Central Provinces are the greatest sufferers at the present time. It is very kind of the English people that, in spite of the Transvaal War, and the heavy calls on private liberality for the support of the widows and children of soldiers who have fallen in battle, they have been sending out subscriptions towards the relief of their fellow-subjects in India.

Plague is doing havoc in Behar and seems likely to approach this province. Indeed one village in the Allahabad district has already been infected with it. I wish it could be stamped out: but it appears to have taken a firm hold of certain parts of India.

With kind regards to Mrs. —— and yourself,

I am, yours respectfully,

---

6. *Answer to the Above.*

May 6, 1900.

DEAR SIR,

I was much pleased at receiving your letter of April last. I am glad to say that the asthma about which you enquire has left me for the present, or at least has a good deal abated. The best month of spring is now on us. When May is over, there will be at least three months of summer to come. Warm bright weather after the winter fogs and cold is a pleasant change, especially to those who are subject to that troublesome complaint. But I must not throw all the blame on this much abused English climate. Age has something to do with it. Infirmities will and must creep on us, as we advance in years.

It is a sad thing that India should be so subject to visitations of famine. What makes the matter worse is that, when the people have got over one bad season, they often have another year of scarcity to face; for I have noticed that when once the Indian seasons, ordinarily so regular, get out of gear, it takes two or three years before they entirely recover themselves.

The persistent hold that the plague seems to have taken of certain parts of the country is much to be regretted. As the disease has now been some four or five years in India and all attempts to drive it completely out have been unsuccessful, it seems probable that it will become endemic as cholera and malarial fever have become.

I am very glad indeed to hear that you have decided on devoting your time, when you retire on pension, to looking after your estates. Considering how very largely the prosperity of India depends upon agriculture, that country of all others needs good landlords. The experience that you have had as a Government servant in the revenue department will be of the greatest use to you in estate management, and I feel certain that on your estates the interests of the tenants will be identified with your own. A retirement such as you have before you, to be spent among your own people, with a congenial occupation and the agreeable companionship of books, is as happy a prospect as can well be conceived or desired.

With kind remembrances from Mrs. ——, who has not forgotten her camping days in India,

I am, yours sincerely,

———

7. *From a Japanese Gentleman to a Friend residing in England.*

TOKYO,
Sept. 20, 1900.

DEAR MR. ——,

Before saying anything else I have to apologise for my long silence. I got back to Japan about five months ago, after an absence of nearly one year and a half from my own country. I left Southampton on the 7th ——, and arrived in New York on the 15th. From there I visited Boston, Philadelphia, Washington, the Niagara Falls, Chicago, and St. Louis; all this was done in a flying journey of three weeks. Then I took ship at Vancouver for Yokohama: the voyage across the Pacific took two weeks.

After I had reached home I found myself in a constant whirl of cares and troubles. To get rid of these I have been obliged to devote all my time and energy; and I am still very busy. This is the reason why I was compelled to let so much time pass before writing to you. But every now and then a kind of nightmare would come upon me, whenever I thought of my negligence.

Now I heartily thank you for the great kindness you showed me during my stay in your country. I have derived immense benefit from my recent journey abroad. What I saw and experienced is all taken down in my diary, and whenever I look into it, it gives me a great deal of pleasure.

After what I have seen of the world, I do not hesitate to pronounce England the best country. It is full of interesting historical associations, and is the birthplace of many eminent authors. The people are polite and hospitable. I like England best of all countries in the world, except my own native land ; and I should be glad to see it again, if Providence allows me to do so.

Perhaps you would like to know what were my impressions of America. Well, my impressions of the New World were not so favourable as those of the Old. When I first landed in New York, I was rather shocked with the roughness of the people. They are not so polite to strangers as you are. It is very dangerous to cross the streets, as electric cars flying along at a terrible pace are constantly passing and repassing the foot-pavements. The manner of people in hotels is especially rude and provoking. What a contrast with England! They say Boston is more like England than any other American city. This is quite true. It is a literary centre, as you know. I visited Harvard and Yale Universities, each of which has a group of magnificent buildings. Their general appearance is quite different from that of Oxford or Cambridge.

It must be admitted that these American Universities have strong points of their own. But in one respect at least they are not comparable to their English sisters. They have no antiquarian relics in their libraries. I saw in Yale a reproduction or imitation of the Rosetta stone; I say "imitation," because it is not the original stone that we see in the British Museum.

I hope this letter will find you and your family in good health. Please remember me to Mrs. —— and the other members of your family.

I remain, dear Mr. ——,

Yours very faithfully,

——

8. *Reply to the Above.*

DEAR MR. ——,

Many thanks for your long and very interesting letter, which I ought to have answered sooner than I am doing.

I am glad to see that you are satisfied with the tour that you have taken in foreign countries, and especially that you do not regret having spent the greater part of your time in England.

I too found American manners rather rough or (to put it mildly) off-hand, especially among hotel-servants. But the hotel which I visited was not in New York, but in Halifax, British territory; and I was really glad to get away into the quiet country-place for which I was bound. There I found people as neighbourly and courteous as could be wished.

Your countrymen are not more fond of visiting England than mine are of visiting Japan. A friend of mine, who is living not far from this house, but who held an appointment for many years in Burma before his retirement, spent a year's furlough in Japan instead of coming to England. He brought away with him a large number of photographs, some of them coloured, showing the manners and customs of the country and some buildings of interest. The sight of these makes one all the more desirous of going there to see the originals.

Your country has within the short space of half a century made wonderful progress in the arts and sciences of the West. A young man, with whom I am well acquainted, and who has taken part, though a small one, in the building of a huge battle-ship for the Japanese Government, says that the knowledge of shipbuilding and naval engineering that he has seen displayed by your countrymen is quite equal to that possessed by Englishmen. It is my opinion that the regeneration, of which China stands so much in need, and which she will have to get unless she is to be swallowed up by the different European powers, will come from her nearest neighbour, Japan, whose population is kindred to her own.

With every best wish and with kind regards from Mrs. ——,

I am, yours sincerely,

———

9. *From Queen Victoria to Tennyson, late Poet-Laureate.*

DEAR LORD TENNYSON,

I was not unmindful of yesterday's anniversary, and would wish you my warm good wishes on the return of your natal day.

It was also my son Alfred's, and my son-in-law Lorne's, birthday, and there was a gathering at Osborne Cottage of my children, grand-children, and relations.

Your beautiful lines have been greatly admired.

I wish you could have seen the wedding; for all say it was the prettiest they ever saw.

The pretty little village church, all decorated with flowers, the sweet young bride, the handsome young husband, the ten bridesmaids—six of them quite children with flowing fair hair—the brilliant sunshine and the blue sea, all made up pictures not to be forgotten.

Believe me always,

Yours affectionately,

V. R. I.[1]

10. *An invitation to dinner, with the reply.*

DEAR MRS. JONES,

Will you and Mr. Jones give us the pleasure of your company to dinner on Thursday next, the 20th inst., at 8 P.M.

I am,

Yours sincerely,

ADA WHITE.

If the invitation is accepted, the answer would be as follows:—

DEAR MRS. WHITE,

We have much pleasure in accepting your kind invitation to dinner on Thursday next, the 20th inst., at 8 P.M.

I am,

Yours sincerely,

ELLA JONES.

Note.—Let care be taken to avoid the error of saying "We *shall have* much pleasure in accepting," etc. The *acceptance* is a present pleasure, not a future one. It would be correct, however, to say, "It will give us much pleasure to dine with you on Thursday next," etc., because the *dining* is a future pleasure, not a present one. The common error referred to arises from a confusion between these two ideas.

---

[1] Victoria Regina Imperatrix. Victoria Queen Empress.

If the invitation is declined, the answer would be in such terms as the following:—

DEAR MRS. WHITE,

We are sorry that we are unable to accept your kind invitation to dinner (or, We are sorry we shall not be able to dine with you) on Thursday next, the 20th inst., as we shall be away from home on that day (or, owing to a previous engagement, or for any other reason that the writer may think fit to assign).

I am,
Yours sincerely,
ELLA JONES.

OUTLINES OF PRIVATE LETTERS TO BE EXPANDED.

52. Practice in Letter-writing.—The teacher can, of course, set any subjects that he may consider most suitable for the pupils under him. We recommend, however, (1) that the subjects should be such as do not require formal discussion or description, like the subjects of an essay; (2) that the pupils should be encouraged not to restrict the letter to one single subject, but to allude to any other topic or topics, such as usually find a place in private correspondence; (3) that if the pupils seem puzzled to know what to say, some kind of outline be furnished by the teacher. As specimens of outlines we give the following. Each figure (not to be repeated in the letter) is intended to indicate the commencement of a new paragraph.

1. *From son or daughter to parent. Complains of not being promoted.*

1. Has had no promotion, and thinks he deserved it. He has not been idle, and is quite old enough to go into a higher class.

2. Asks parent to address master on the subject, or remove him at end of term.

3. Feels discouraged at seeing others of his own age or of a younger age promoted, and himself left in the same class.

4. May he get a new umbrella? The old one lost. Constant rain; no likelihood of a break.

2. *From parent to son or daughter. Answer to the Above.*

1. Is sorry for his disappointment, but cannot comply with either of his requests.

2. No occasion to be discouraged. Promotion will come in due course, when student is fit. Teacher knows best.

3. New umbrella can be got. But how came the old one to be lost? Umbrellas are expensive, and must not be left about.

4. Weather here has cleared. Mowing has commenced in the fields. Prospects of a good hay-crop this June.

3. *From cousin to cousin. Visit to the Sea-side.*

1. Scenes and amusements on the sands. Crowds of people every day.

2. Sea-view from front window of lodgings.

3. Had a cruise out with friends in a sailing-boat. Began to feel rather ill, but managed to fight against it.

4. Asks cousin whether he cannot join them. An extra bed can be got ready in the same house, if immediate notice is sent. Fresh tourists coming in every day.

4. *From cousin to cousin. Answer to the Above.*

1. The letter had to be forwarded, as they had left home, and are now at a sea-side place themselves.

2. Cannot now change lodgings. But in August next year they might arrange to go to the same place together.

3. Describes a day's fishing on a rather rough sea, and what fish they caught.

4. A deer-park about three miles off, in which they have already had one ramble. Luncheon under a spreading oak. A tame deer came to be fed with bread and biscuits.

5. *From a young man to his mother. On a Cycle Tour with friend.*

1. Has just reached a quaint little village. All the cottages thatched. He and his friend will halt here for a day or two's rest.

2. Expects to reach a certain country-town (to be named) by a certain date (to be named). Can she send him a postal order, which will reach him there on that date?

3. He wants (if she can send it) a certain sum (to be named),

as he has still many interesting places to visit before he returns home; and has to pay his way as he goes on.

4. His friend is making a similar request to his parents.

6. *Mother's answer to the Above.*

1. Will send the postal order, but finds it difficult.
2. Heavy expenses on account of internal repairs of house and outside painting.
3. Weather has been very favourable for spring-sowings. Good supply of flowers and vegetables expected in summer.
4. A martin has just begun to build over the window that looks on the garden. Hopes the same martin will return year after year, as these birds sometimes do.

7. *Son's answer to the Above.*

1. Thanks her for the promise to send the postal order.
2. Has decided, however, on returning home at once, and has still enough money for the purpose.
3. Feels that it would be selfish to put her to further expense on his account.
4. His friend will not object to his leaving him, as he was expecting another friend to join him.
5. Will pass through a village (to be named) on his way home, and will spend the night at his uncle's house.
6. Hopes to reach home by a certain date (to be named).

8. *From boy or girl to aunt. Discomforts of Sea Travelling, etc.*

1. Unpleasant experiences of a sea voyage from one part of the British coast to another (each place to be named). Rough sea, and almost every one ill.
2. Prefers the dry land, and has decided to return by rail.
3. Enjoys looking at the waves from the shore, and is glad not to be on them.
4. Had a picnic party yesterday a few miles inland. Gives a description of it.
5. Hopes to hear that the parrot is learning to talk.

9. *From aunt to nephew or niece. Answer to Above.*

1. Advises a second experiment of a sea voyage. Every one can get used to the sea by perseverance.

2. Much to be seen in foreign countries, but no chance of getting to them from England except by water.

3. Parrot has learnt a good many words. Is very fond of a lump of white sugar.

4. Went to a garden party yesterday. Beautiful lawn. Badminton and croquet.

10. *From father to son, who is about to enter the Navy.*

1. Reminds him that obedience is the first duty in the navy. There must be no questioning and no delay.

2. As he chose this profession himself, he is likely to do well in it.

3. Will have several examinations to pass before he can become anything above a midshipman.

4. Great opportunities of seeing many parts of the world at the expense of the Government.

5. No class of men more popular than sailors, and none more useful to their country.

11. *From son to father. Answer to the Above.*

1. Feels much pleased with his prospects, and hopes to have a prosperous career.

2. Will go on board in three days' time.

3. Has seen some of the officers, and was well received by them.

4. Is sorry, however, to hear that he will have more examinations to pass.

5. Will write from Gibraltar as soon as he gets there.

12. *From schoolboy to friend. A Football Match.*

1. A football match has just been played by his own school against a neighbouring school.

2. Players on the opposite side bigger, but did not play so well together. They made only two goals out of five.

3. Great cheering at the result. Hopes to be in the school team himself next season.

4. Return match will be played a month hence.

5. One of their students has just come out high in the London matriculation.

13. *From boy (or girl) to grandfather. Making a Snow-man.*

1. Have had snow falling for two days and two nights; and have just made a snow man.

2. They fitted him up with an old hat and a long clay-pipe.

3. Expects to win a prize for mathematics at the next examination.

4. Hopes he is keeping well and has less trouble from rheumatism.

14. *From boy to parent. A Brook and Rabbit-Warren.*

1. Description of brook a few fields off the schoolhouse. Banks yellow with primroses, and overhung with willows half standing in water.

2. Description of birds frequenting the brook,—kingfisher and moor-hen.

3. On a sloping bank a little higher up there is a rabbit-warren. Description of the furze in flower about the warren.

4. A rabbit hunted by a spaniel managed to escape into its hole; but only just got into it in time.

5. The brook widens at a certain point; and here the boys are allowed to swim. Not deep enough for any one to be drowned. No fear of accidents.

15. *From girl to aunt. Barn-swallow's Nest.*

1. Two barn-swallows flew into the woodshed belonging to the house.

2. She watched what they were going to do, till she saw them begin building a nest. Much twittering and excitement.

3. Describes how the nest grew, and what it was made of.

4. Eggs laid in the nest and hatched.

5. Young ones fed by both birds.

6. Presently young ones attempt to fly, but one of them is seized by the cat.

7. The cat locked up till the rest are able to fly and take care of themselves.

16. *From boy (or girl) to uncle (or aunt). A ride in a Motor-car.*

1. Movement of motor-car smoother and less noisy than that of a carriage drawn by a horse.

2. Driver knew how to turn the handle for guiding the car, but did not seem to know anything else.

3. Suddenly the car stopped. Driver did not know what

to do to make it go on. So a horse had to be brought to drag the car home.

4. Motor-cars very useful; but drivers must be taught the machinery.

5. Hopes cousin will be able to pay them a visit next vacation.

17. *From girl to girl-friend. Summer Vacation in Country.*

1. Describes the wild-flowers,—the water-lily, the daisy, the buttercup, the cowslip, the convolvulus, the poppy in corn-field, the wild roses.

2. Advises her friend to leave town, if she can, during such a beautiful season, and pay her a visit.

3. Says they have a pony-carriage and can take drives together. Her brother will sometimes accompany them.

4. Has made good progress with her holiday-task, and hopes her friend has done the same.

18. *From friend in Upper India to friend in England. Break of the Monsoon.*

1. The periodical summer rains, called in India the monsoon, broke on 24th June.

2. Dry state of the country previously. Not a blade of grass. Innumerable cracks in the ground.

3. Dead stillness. Suddenly the clouds came up, and rain set in with a violent thunderstorm. Very heavy fall for several days.

4. Frogs of a pale green colour suddenly appear in pools of water. Loud croaking. He does not know where these frogs come from, and cannot find any one to tell him.

5. Cooler days and nights. Grass begins to sprout again.

6. His health continues to be good. Is very careful to have his drinking-water well filtered. Avoids alcohol as much as possible. Goes to bed early and rises early. Takes regular exercise in early morning, unless he is stopped by a drenching shower.

19. *Friend's answer to the above, written some months afterwards.*

1. Is sorry he has been so long in answering his letter, but gives a reason.

2. Much interested in his description of India. Cannot help

paying him back by a description of England in the autumn, which is now coming on.

3. Beech leaves are turning into a deep olive colour; oak leaves into a bronzy brown: ground is scattered with fallen beech-nuts and acorns. Flowers have faded or dropped, and seed-pods are forming in their place.

4. He loves country life, and has just entered the agricultural college at Cirencester. Hopes to take up agriculture as a calling, and see if it cannot be made to give a better return than it has done of late years in England.

20. *From boy to parent. First impressions of Business Life.*

1. Found the lodgings provided for him quite comfortable. His fellow-lodger, who belongs to the same office that he does, is an agreeable companion.

2. Has had about a week's experience of office work. Found it rather difficult at first. Much care necessary in copying and docketing letters. Has not yet been asked to draft a letter, but will have to do this before long. Wishes he had paid more attention to composition, while at school.

3. Office closes at 5 P.M. to outside callers; but there is sometimes much work done inside up to a much later hour.

4. There will be a free week at Christmas time. May he bring his fellow-lodger home with him, if he cares to come?

21. *From friend to friend. A Technical School.*

1. Has just joined a technical school to learn shorthand. Knows type-writing, but did not find it enough.

2. With the help of shorthand one can take down a lecture or speech, as fast as it is delivered.

3. Shorthand may give him an opening as a newspaper reporter.

4. New class has just been formed. Every one eager to begin, and much in earnest.

5. Will be glad to hear how he likes the study of electricity in the City and Guilds of London Institute. Hopes he will not be killed by an electric shock.

SECTION 3.—BUSINESS CORRESPONDENCE, ADVERTISEMENTS, NOTICES, ETC.

53. **Kinds of Business Letters.**—The term "business-letter" is intended to include all kinds of letters not

belonging to the class already described. The business may be either (*a*) private or (*b*) public.

(*a*) A *private* business-letter is one written to or by some man in his business capacity, and not as a private friend,—such as a schoolmaster, a manufacturer, a tradesman or retail dealer, a merchant or wholesale dealer, a banker, a lawyer, a contractor, a broker, an agent, a professional man of any kind; and the letter may be addressed either to an individual or to a company, such as a water company, a gas company, an engineering firm, a publishing firm, a printing firm, etc.

(*b*) A *public* business-letter (more commonly known as an "official" letter) is one written to or by any one in his official capacity. Such a person may be either holding some public office, or representing some important public association, such as a School Board, a Municipal Board, an Urban Council, a County Council, etc.

54. Five Parts of a Business Letter.—In business correspondence, whether private or public, there are five parts to a letter against four in private correspondence between friends and relatives (§ 46).

(1) *The heading.*—Precisely the same as in private correspondence (§ 47).

(2) *The salutation.*—Not the same as in private correspondence. If the business letter is of the class (*a*) (private), the form used in addressing an individual is *Sir* or *Dear Sir*, or (if the addressee is a clergyman) the form can be expanded, (though this is hardly necessary), to *Rev. and Dear Sir*, or simply *Rev. Sir*. The form used in addressing a firm or company is *Sirs*, or *Gentlemen*, or *Dear Sirs* (never *Dear Gentlemen*).

If the business letter is of the class (*b*) (public), the form of salutation is invariably *Sir;* and the body of the letter commences with, "I have the honour to," etc., or "I beg to," etc.

(3) *The name and designation of the addressee.*—In writing the name and designation of the addressee use precisely

the same words as those written on the envelope: see above, § 44.

This is a new item, and is peculiar to a business letter. It is not required in private correspondence between friends and relatives, because in such letters the surname of the addressee is either not necessary or is given in the salutation. In a business letter the surname is always necessary, and as it is not given in the salutation, it must be written somewhere else, so that there may be no doubt as to the name of the person or firm or public body for whom the letter is meant. Such words as *Sir*, *Gentlemen*, *Dear Sir*, might apply to any one.

The name and designation of the addressee can be written either immediately above the salutation, or at the very end of the letter on the left-hand side after the writer has signed his name. In official letters they are always written immediately above the salutation.

Note.—If the correspondents happen to be well acquainted with each other, the writer instead of saying *Dear Sir* may (if he prefers it) address the other person by his surname, as *Dear Jones* or *My Dear Jones.* In this case it is of course not necessary to write the name of the addressee either above the salutation or at the end of the letter. In official correspondence such a letter is called "demi-official."

(4) *The body of the letter.*—The composition of a business letter is different from that of a private one: (*a*) it is more formal and more carefully worded; (*b*) it limits itself strictly to the business in hand, and deals with it in the fewest and plainest terms.

(5) *The ending.*—If the business letter is of a private character, the form of ending is *yours faithfully*, or in the case of a tradesman writing to a customer, *yours obediently*: such adverbs as *truly*, *sincerely*, etc., are not used. If the letter is official, the form of ending is:—

I have the honour to be,
Sir,
Your obedient servant,
N. or M.

The following is a specimen of the parts of a letter that might be addressed to a mill-owner:—

(1) *Heading*

16 Chapel Place,
Bruton,
Somersetshire,
10*th Aug.* 1901.

(2) *Name and designation of addressee*

To A. Jones, Esq.
Manager of Elgin Mills.

(3) *Salutation*

Dear Sir (or Sir),

(4) *Body of letter*

In compliance with your letter of yesterday's date, I shall be happy to meet you at your office on Wednesday next at 12 o'clock (noon), to discuss the terms of the proposed contract for the supply of military tents required for the forth-coming manœuvres on Salisbury Plain.

(5) *Ending*

I am, dear Sir,
Yours faithfully,
N. or M.

55. Use of the Third Person.—Sometimes, to save time, the use of the first and second persons is avoided altogether, and only the third person is used. Thus a tradesman might be addressed as follows:—

Mrs. —— requests Mr. —— to supply the following articles, all of which are required by 4 P.M. on this date.

A. M.

An invitation might be worded as follows:—

The members of the Constitutional Club request the pleasure of Mr. A.'s company to dinner at 8 P.M. on the 10th inst., to meet, etc.

N. or M.,
Secretary.

When an official letter, the purport of which can be expressed in very few words, is written in the third person, it is called a docket:—

Has the honour to inform him that the undersigned cannot consent to the amount allotted for prizes being exceeded. He has no power, in fact, to sanction the proposed additional expenditure.

N. or M.,
Inspector of Schools.

If a letter is commenced in the third person, care must of course be taken that it does not glide into the first or second before its close, as in the following:—

> Has the honour to inform him that the undersigned cannot consent to the amount allotted for prizes being exceeded. I have no power, in fact, to sanction the additional expenditure that you propose.

EXAMPLES OF BUSINESS LETTERS, NOTICES, ETC.

1. Application for employment in the engineering branch of a London Tea Company; with answer. (Both genuine.)

4 ELY PLACE,
LONDON,
W.
18*th Feb.* 1901.

To the Managers
Mazawattee Tea Co., Ltd.

DEAR SIRS,

I beg to offer my services as "Superintending Engineer" in answer to your advertisement which appeared in *Engineering* of Feb. 8, 1901.

I served my apprenticeship at the —— Works, Newcastle, for a space of four years, one of which was spent in the drawing office.

Since leaving these works I have studied electricity under Professor Ayrton at the Technical Institute of the City and Guilds of London, and have had a theoretical and practical training in direct and alternating current machinery. I have also had experience in transformers, secondary batteries, etc.

While at the Works in Newcastle, I had considerable experience in machinery of all kinds, and was for a certain period in charge of the construction of a few boilers, engines, and several other pieces of work.

During my residence in Newcastle, I attended in the evenings the Rutherford College of Science, from which I passed two examinations held by the South Kensington School of Science in Machine Construction and Design.

I shall be twenty-three years of age next October, and would be content with a salary of £80 or £100 a year to start with.

Awaiting the favour of your reply,

I am, dear Sirs,
Yours faithfully,
A. G. M.

MAZAWATTEE TEA CO.,
TOWER HILL,
LONDON,
E.C.

To A. G. M—— Esq. *Feb.* 28, 1901.

DEAR SIR,

In reference to your application of a recent date, we take the earliest opportunity of letting you know that we have made a final selection from the very numerous letters which we received, and regret that we have not been able to offer you the appointment.

We do not wish you to regard this letter in any way as reflecting the idea that we took a negative view of your qualifications, as we could only make a choice of many excellent offers.

Yours faithfully,
THE MAZAWATTEE TEA COMPANY.

2. Application for employment in a Printing firm; with answer.

4 QUEEN STREET,
EDINBURGH,
NORTH BRITAIN,

To Messrs. Bereing Bros. *6th Dec.* 1901.

DEAR SIRS,

I understand there is a vacancy in your office in the book-binding branch on a salary of one hundred pounds a year, and I beg to offer my services for your acceptance.

I have had three years' experience as a printer, and five years' experience as a binder, as the enclosed copy of my testimonials will show. My sole reason for leaving the firm with whom I have worked hitherto is that the climate of Edinburgh for the greater part of the year is trying to my chest; and my medical adviser considers it necessary that I should go farther south, where the east winds are less keen. In one of the accompanying letters it will be seen that my present employer speaks favourably of my work, and is kind enough to express regret at the prospect of my leaving them. Hoping for a favourable answer,

I am, dear Sirs,
Yours faithfully,
R. C——.

14 OXFORD STREET,
LONDON,
W.
10*th Dec.* 1901.

To R. C——, Esq.

DEAR SIR,

I have your letter of the 6th inst., and have shown it to the Managers, who have instructed me to say that they have no vacancy at present, but were favourably impressed with your certificates, and have ordered your application to be placed before them again when the next vacancy occurs.

I am, dear Sir,
Yours faithfully,
J. M——,
Secretary.

3. Application for the office of clerk in a merchant's office, with the reply :—

12 GRACE BANK,
CHISWICK,
W.
3*rd April* 1901.

Messrs. Hicks, Palmer & Co.,
3 Austin Friars.

GENTLEMEN,

Having seen in this morning's *Daily Express* an advertisement for a clerk who is acquainted with book-keeping, I beg to offer myself as a candidate for the vacancy.

After having passed the senior examination in the Oxford Locals, in which I came out in Class II., I received some temporary employment in the office of Messrs. Beg, Dunlop & Co., as one of their book-keepers, and when the period for which I was engaged expired, I took lessons in shorthand and type-writing in the hope that these additional qualifications would be some recommendation for future employment.

During my engagement with Messrs. Beg, Dunlop & Co., which lasted more than two years, I became thoroughly conversant with the methods of book-keeping practised in that office, as most of the Company's books passed through my hands. The enclosed testimonial from the firm named, besides explaining why my services could not be retained, bears witness to the confidence placed in me by my employers, and the satisfaction that I gave them.

Though your advertisement is for a book-keeping clerk only, I should be happy to do any general work in which my services, especially my knowledge of shorthand and type-writing, might be found useful.

I am, gentlemen,.
Your obedient servant,

———

———

3 AUSTIN FRIARS,
LONDON,
E.C.
5th April 1901.

SIR,

We have received your letter of the 3rd applying for the vacant clerkship in our office. If you will call to-morrow at any time after nine o'clock in the forenoon, we will discuss the matter and see whether on further proof being given you appear likely to suit us. It must be understood, however, that, as we have to decide between yourself and several other candidates, we do not in any way commit ourselves to offering you the appointment.

Yours faithfully,
HICKS, PALMER & CO.

4. Correspondence between client and solicitor:—

19 BEACONSFIELD ROAD,
RICHMOND,
LONDON,
S.W.
2nd Feb. 1901.

To M. B——, Esq.,
Solicitor.

DEAR SIR,

I write to ask you to draw up for me a will, the purport of which will be very simple; viz. that I leave all my real and personal estate to my wife absolutely and unreservedly. I also wish to appoint her my residuary legatee, so that at the time of my death there may be no delays or complications of any kind. As two executors will, I presume, have to be appointed, I hereby nominate Mr. J. B. ——, her brother, as one, and perhaps you would not object to being appointed the other. Please let me know what will be the cost of making out this will, including the cost of registration; for I presume it will have to be registered in Somerset House or elsewhere.

I may explain that this will is intended to provide against the possible contingency of my wife being suddenly left a widow; for I understand that if I were to die intestate, she could get only one-third part of my estate, the remainder being divided in equal parts among my children without reference to age, sex, or individual needs. As some of my children are grown up and able to take care of themselves, while others are still at school and require much care and attention, such a devolution of my property would not be at all advantageous to her or just to them. It is against such a contingency as this that I wish to provide by making the very simple kind of will that I have described.

I am,
Yours faithfully,
C. M——.

---

7 Duke Street,
Strand,
London,
W.C.
4th Feb. 1901.

Dear Sir,

My partner (who is confined to his bed from illness) has handed me your letter to him of the 2nd inst., and has asked me to prepare a will in accordance with your instructions. What you have stated as to the devolution of your property, in the event of your dying intestate, is substantially correct. As you propose to leave everything to your wife, there is no occasion to make her a residuary legatee, nor is there any occasion to appoint executors other than your wife, unless you think it would be an assistance to Mrs. M—— in winding up your estate. In that case I should suggest that you appoint one executor (not two) to act with your wife. No registration is required. For a simple will such as you propose to make our fee would be two guineas. If you would like to discuss any point with me, I shall be happy to see you, if you will make an appointment.

Yours faithfully,
G. N——.

C. M——, Esq.,
19 Beaconsfield Road,
Richmond,
S.W.

---

19 Beaconsfield Road,
Richmond,
S.W.
5th Feb. 1901.

G. N——, Esq.,
Solicitor.

Dear Sir,

My wife does not desire that any executor should be named in the will. The will that is required is so simple that it may be drawn up at once for my signature. I will call at your office for this purpose on any day that you may appoint—afternoon preferred to the forenoon, if that will suit you.

Yours faithfully,

C. M——.

5. Correspondence between landlord and tenant regarding tenure of a house:—

13 Albion Place,
Whitby,
Yorkshire,
2nd Feb. 1901.

To A. C——, Esq.,
Occupant of 21 Crescent Avenue,
Scarborough.

Dear Sir,

As I am anxious to sell No. 21 Crescent Avenue and you have declined to avail yourself of the chance of buying it, I am sorry to be obliged to give you notice that the house must be vacated by the end of June next on quarter day, on which date your agreement with me expires. No one is likely to buy the house, if he cannot enter into possession at once. Hence the necessity of this notice.

I am,

Yours faithfully,

P. H——.

---

21 Crescent Avenue,
Scarborough,
15th June 1901.

To P. H——, Esq.

Dear Sir,

As I hear that you have not yet succeeded in selling the house, and only two weeks remain before the notice that you sent me on the 2nd Feb. takes effect, I write to inquire whether you would have any objection to my staying on here for another quarter, viz. until 29th Sept., by which time I hope to be in a position to decide definitely whether I shall remain in Scarborough or whether I shall get occupation which will take me elsewhere.

Yours faithfully,

A. C——.

13 Albion Place,
Whitby,
17*th June* 1901.

To A. C——, Esq.

Dear Sir,

For the last three weeks I have been in treaty with a gentleman, who wishes to settle in Scarborough and seemed inclined to buy the house. He has now written to say that he considers the price too high. Under these circumstances you are at liberty to remain in the house for another quarter.

Yours faithfully,
P. H——.

---

21 Crescent Avenue,
Scarborough,
19*th June* 1901.

To P. H——, Esq.

Dear Sir,

Thanks for your letter. I am sorry for your sake that the matter has gone no further. But for my personal convenience 29th Sept. is best. By that time I shall be prepared to go.

Yours faithfully,
A. C——

6. Correspondence between shipbuilder and coal company:—

Birkenhead,
Cheshire,
10*th March* 1898.

To the Secretary,
Welsh Coal Co.

Dear Sir,

We shall be obliged by your sending to our shipyard twenty tons of Welsh coal, the price of which at the terms last quoted is twenty-five shillings a ton. The coal should be delivered within a fortnight from the present time.

We are, dear Sir,
Yours faithfully,
Layard & Co.

Welsh Coal Co.,
Cardiff,
12*th March* 1898.

Messrs. Layard & Co.

Gentlemen,

We are prepared to comply at once with the order contained in your letter of the 10th. But before doing so I think it necessary to inform you that, owing to the very heavy demands for Welsh coal both from Russia and Germany, the price has risen since the last quotation, and now stands at thirty shillings a ton. I am unable to predict any date by which the price is likely to fall.

I am, dear Sirs,
Yours faithfully,
A. SMITH,
Secretary.

BIRKENHEAD,
CHESHIRE,
13*th March* /98.

To the Secretary,
Welsh Coal Co.

DEAR SIR,

Your letter of the 12th inst. We are ready to pay at the rate named by you, provided the coal reaches us not later than the 24th inst., on which date the vessel must load.

Yours faithfully,
LAYARD & CO.

WELSH COAL CO.,
CARDIFF,
14*th March* /98.

Messrs. Layard & Co.

GENTLEMEN,

I have dispatched the twenty tons of Welsh coal ordered by you, and trust that they will reach Birkenhead in about a week's time, two or three days sooner than the date stipulated by you. I enclose the invoice, and shall be glad to hear of the arrival of the coal.

Yours faithfully,
A. SMITH,
Secretary.

7. Correspondence between tradesman and customer:—

9 GROVE PARK,
HANWELL,
LONDON,
W.,
7*th March* 1901.

Mrs. G—— requests Messrs. Whiteley & Co. to send two lbs. of the wool called Scotch Fingering, according to the enclosed specimen and colour. The wool will be paid for on receipt.

From William Whiteley, Ltd., Universal Providers,
Westbourne Grove, Bayswater.

8/3/01.

MADAM,

Your esteemed order has been received, and the wool shall be procured and forwarded as early as possible. Payment will be taken on delivery.

Yours obediently,

WILLIAM WHITELEY, LTD.

8. Correspondence between householder and water company :—

From Grand Junction Waterworks Company,
65 South Molton Street,
London, W.

To R. F——, Esq.,
14 Acton Green.

10*th July* 1899.

SIR,

I beg to remind you that water supplied for garden use must be paid for in addition to that supplied for the house. I beg to request therefore that you will fill up the enclosed form showing how many taps are fixed to the garden wall of your house, and what are the dimensions of the garden.

I am, Sir,

Your obedient servant,

J. L——,

Secretary.

---

14 ACTON GREEN,
LONDON,
W.

To Secretary,
Grand Junction Waterworks.

15*th July* 1899.

SIR,

I beg to invite your attention to my letter with cheque enclosed d/ 1st April last, from which you will find that I paid the sum of One Pound in advance for the additional water to be supplied for my garden during the summer months.

Yours faithfully,

R. F——.

To R. F——, Esq.,
14 Acton Green.

65 SOUTH MOLTON STREET,
18*th July* 1899.

SIR,

I regret to find from your letter of the 15th inst., that the circular letter respecting the use of water for garden purposes was inadvertently sent to you; and I trust you will accept my apologies on behalf of the Company for the trouble caused by the error.

I am, Sir,
Your obedient servant,
J. L——,
Secretary.

9. Correspondence between schoolmaster and parent:—

18 Tavistock Road,
Hanwell,
Middlesex,
10*th April* 1901.

To the Principal
Kingston Proprietary School.

Dear Sir,

I shall be obliged if you will send me the prospectus of the Kingston Proprietary School. I wish to place my son, who is now ten years of age, as a boarder at some establishment where he can receive a training suitable for commercial life, and I have heard that yours is a school of this description.

I am, dear Sir,
Yours faithfully,
W. F——.

Kingston Proprietary School,
Kingston,
12*th April* 1901.

W. F——, Esq.

Dear Sir,

In compliance with your letter of the 10th, I send a copy of the prospectus of this school, giving details as to the course of study and the terms for day scholars and boarders.

As the system on which the curriculum is based is somewhat different from that prevailing elsewhere, and was drawn up with special reference to the requirements of commercial life, I beg to explain what the main points of the system are, as this can be done more effectively by letter than by a mere prospectus.

In the first place, I wish to point out that what we especially aim at teaching in this school is (*a*) Modern Languages, (*b*) Mathematics, (*c*) Elementary Science. Greek we do not teach at all; Latin is taught only to those whose parents desire it.

In the second place, I trust it will be quite clear from the prospectus and from what I have just said about the subjects taught, that this is not a technical school, and makes no pretensions to being one. Those who wish to have a technical training, *i.e.* one that will place them in direct preparation for some particular branch of industry, such as the mixing of drugs, the surveying of lands, architectural drawing, etc., must either go to one or other of the technical institutes where such specialities are taught, or get themselves apprenticed to some firm which takes young men into training. All that we attempt to do is to prepare boys from an early age up to about eighteen for a commercial career, *i.e.* a career in which the exchange, and not the production, of commodities is the main pursuit.

(*a*) Modern Languages.—Amongst all modern languages we give the first place to the mother-tongue. In the early stages of a boy's education the teaching of English must be the centre; and in this school care is taken that it shall retain the place of honour even in later years when the time devoted to it has to be considerably shortened. Many secondary schools in England do not include English among the "modern languages"; and as it is not a "classical language" either, it is often neglected to a mischievous extent. A thorough knowledge of English grammar (which is a far better mental discipline than many persons imagine) and frequent practice in English composition we consider indispensable as a preparation for commercial life.

Next to the mother-tongue we place German, firstly because the life and ways of a German student are most closely akin to those of an English one; secondly, because the form of the language comes nearest to that of English both in the sound of the vowels and in the vocabulary; and thirdly, because the grammar of German is much more inflectional than that of English, and thus gives the student an insight into grammatical principles almost as complete as what he could get by the study of Latin.

Next to German we place French, which, if the parent prefers it, can be studied side by side with its ancestor, Latin. French is scarcely less useful for commercial life than German, besides being an equally valuable aid to the study of English, on which we have laid so much stress. A knowledge of German and French enables us to understand the two great nations with which we are brought into contact in so many different ways; for a commercial career such knowledge is essential.

Lastly, as to the method in which those languages are taught. I do not employ a Frenchman to teach French, or a

German to teach German. I have secured the services of two young Englishmen, who have lived several years on the Continent and can speak and write German and French as accurately as if they were German or French by blood. I do not find that a French teacher can keep proper order in a class of English boys. In the teaching of French and German we give much time not merely to the grammar and literature of those languages, but also to conversation and composition.

(*b*), (*c*) I have said so much about the study of modern languages that I have no space to describe what we do, or rather aim at doing, in Mathematics and Elementary Science. Nor is this necessary, as the prospectus shows clearly enough what our aims are. Our system in these two branches is much the same as that existing in other commercial schools.

I am, dear Sir,
Yours faithfully,

———

———

18 Tavistock Road,
14*th April* 1901.

Dear Sir,

I am much obliged to you for your very explanatory letter of the 12th, and shall be glad to place my son with you as a boarder from the commencement of next term. I am not quite sure that I can get over my partiality for the early study of Latin. But I am glad to see that you bring German to the front; for the Germans will no doubt be our great commercial rivals of the future. The neglect of German is at the present time the gravest defect of our secondary schools.

I am, dear Sir,
Yours faithfully,

———

10. A letter of introduction from Dr. Johnson to Warren Hastings, Governor-General of India :—

9*th Jan.* 1781.

Sir,

Amidst the importance and multiplicity of affairs in which your great office engages you, I take the liberty of recalling your attention for a moment to literature, and will not prolong the interruption by an apology which your character makes needless.

Mr. Hoole, a gentleman long known and long esteemed in

the India House, after having translated Tasso, has undertaken Ariosto. How well he is qualified for the undertaking he has already shown. He is desirous, Sir, of your favour in promoting his proposals, and flatters me by supposing that my testimony may advance his interest.

It is a new thing for a clerk of the India House to translate poets; it is new for a Governor of Bengal to patronise learning. That he may find his ingenuity rewarded, and that learning may flourish under your protection, is the wish of,

Sir,

Your most humble servant,

SAM. JOHNSON.

11. An address to electors of a municipal ward by a gentleman seeking re-election :—

15*th March* 1901.

LADIES AND GENTLEMEN,

I beg to ask the renewal of your Votes and interest on my behalf at the forthcoming election on the 25th inst.

Since I was elected by you three years ago, it has been my endeavour to fulfil the pledges I then made to you, and I venture to hope I have done so with success. My colleagues elected me to the important position of Chairman of the Finance Committee, a post which has cast on me the odium of providing funds to meet not only the legacy of past inadequate finance, but the growing expenditure of the District at a time when the multiplicity of new schemes necessitated a corresponding augmentation of revenue. I am happy to say we have now turned the corner, and I look forward to the time, I hope in the near future, when I can present a more popular Budget.

The issue of a Yearly Statement of Accounts in detail was initiated by me, as foreshadowed in my last election address, and this is now published in the Council's Year Book.

My energies have not been directed solely to Finance. I have attended every Council Meeting (except one Special Meeting), and I am a Member of the Electric Lighting, Housing, and Tramway Committees, at all of which I am a regular attendant.

Trusting this will commend itself to you,

I am,

Your obedient Servant,

———

12. Application from a gentleman seeking to be appointed a member of a local committee:—

7th March 1901.

To Sec. of Committee.

DEAR SIR,

I am writing to ask if you will do me the favour of seconding me, when I am proposed on Thursday next as a member of the "Cambridge Locals" committee. Mr. P—— will propose me.

Though I have not the pleasure of knowing you personally, I feel confident from what you know of my father that you will do this for me; and hope you will excuse me for asking you.

Yours faithfully,

W. B——.

13. Circular notice of a meeting of members of a swimming club:—

Richmond Swimming Club.

18th March 1901.

DEAR SIR,

I beg to inform you that the annual general meeting of the above club will be held at the Baths on Monday, 25th March, at 8.30 P.M.

The meeting will be followed by a special general meeting for the proposed alteration of rules as per agenda herewith forwarded.

I have the pleasure to send you herewith a copy of the balance-sheet for the past season.

I am, dear Sir,

Yours faithfully,

——

Hon. Sec.

14. Tradesman's annual advertisement—circular for sale of plants and bulbs:—

29 HAMMERSMITH BROADWAY,
LONDON,
W.,
1st Jan. 1901.

DEAR SIR (OR MADAM),

I have much pleasure in submitting my new spring catalogue for 1901, again thoroughly revised and priced.

I have done my utmost to make the prices as low as trade-interests would allow, and customers may rest assured that all bulbs are cultivated by myself, and that all bulbs and plants will be of the first quality and strictly true to name.

I beg to return my thanks to all customers for their patronage and recommendations during the past year.

I shall be pleased to procure for you on short notice and at reasonable prices any kinds of roots or plants not named in this price-list, and would ask you to favour me with your valued orders as early as possible.

January and February are recommended as the best months for ordering.

I am, dear Sir (or Madam),
Yours faithfully,

———

15. Petition for redress of a grievance :—

To His Grace the Duke of Buckingham and Chandos,
His Majesty's Principal Secretary of State for the Colonies.

SINGAPORE,
30th June 1868.

May it please your Grace! We, the undersigned inhabitants of Singapore, have learnt with great concern and alarm that the power possessed by the Governor of the colony to suspend public officers extends to the judges of our Supreme Court.

Ever since the establishment of that Court, over sixty years ago, the Straits Settlement have enjoyed the inestimable advantage of having justice administered by Judges entirely independent, not only of the local governors, but even of the Governors-General of India; and that position of dignified independence secured to the Judges the entire respect and confidence of the various communities, both Native and European.

We deem it essential to the pure administration of justice that this independence should be preserved intact, and that the Judges should never be in a position in which they might be suspected of being under the influence of the Executive; any change in this respect we should consider deeply injurious to the best interests of the Colony.

We therefore pray that your Grace will take such measures

as may be fitting to restore that complete judicial independence which we enjoyed under the Government of India.

And your Petitioners will ever pray.

Signed THOS. SCOTT,
R. LITTLE, M.A.,
and by 200 others.

OUTLINES OF BUSINESS LETTERS TO BE EXPANDED.

For a List of Trade Terms in Common Use see Appendix.

1. (*a*) A youth having left school and seeking employment as Traffic-manager's clerk on a railway, applies to his late teacher for a testimonial.

(*b*) Teacher in reply sends a testimonial, giving particulars of the position that the applicant held on leaving school and of the opinion that he (the teacher) had formed of his character.

(*c*) Youth receiving the testimonial writes a letter of thanks to the teacher.

(*d*) Youth applies for the post of railway clerk and encloses copy of the testimonial, together with copy of the certificate of having passed the Junior Cambridge Local.

2. (*a*) Tenant gives notice to landlord of his intention to give up the house, on ground of the rent being too high and the situation having proved unhealthy.

(*b*) Landlord offers to reduce the rent, and suggests withdrawal of notice.

(*c*) Tenant thanks landlord for his offer, but on grounds of health declines to withdraw notice.

3. (*a*) Parent gives notice to teacher of removal of pupil on account of change of residence, but expresses regret at the necessity having arisen.

(*b*) Teacher thanks parent for his kind appreciation of his services, and wishes pupil every success in his new school.

4. (*a*) Gentleman, desirous of purchasing a house in a London suburb, writes to landlord with reference to landlord's advertisement, and proposes a day for him to call and see the house.

(*b*) Landlord accepts the day proposed for the meeting, and will be at the house to receive him and show him over it.

(*c*) Applicant (after seeing over the house) informs the landlord that he is favourably impressed, but inquires whether the house is freehold or leasehold, and whether with the price asked the landlord will put the house in thorough repair.

(*d*) Landlord answers that the house is freehold and that he does not undertake any repairs.

(*e*) Applicant declines to purchase.

5. (*a*) A customer writes to draper, enclosing a list of articles required and asking for early despatch.

(*b*) Draper sends the invoice by post and informs customer that the articles have been despatched by parcel post.

(*c*) Customer acknowledges receipt of parcel and sends cheque for payment.

6. (*a*) Gentleman applies to Messrs. Bickers & Son, 1 Leicester Square, London, W.C., for a copy of Breen's *Modern English Literature*, published in 1857.

(*b*) Bookseller replies that the book named has long been out of print, but he will depute his agent to search for it among old and second-hand bookshops in London.

(*c*) Gentleman (some time after) inquires whether book has been found.

(*d*) Answer in the negative.

7. Boy applies for a situation in a Railway Parcels Office. He addresses his application to the Manager of the Railway. States his age, names the school that he attended, and gives the name and address of the headmaster, to whom reference can be made as to his character and attainments. Promises to do his best to give satisfaction, if he is allowed a trial.

Letters to be Written in Reply to the Following Advertisements.

Clerks, Managers, Assistants.

1. A correspondent clerk wanted, who can write shorthand, in an office of a North-west auctioneer. Salary 25 sh. weekly. Address A. A. at Horncastle's, Cheapside, E.C.

2. Three first-class mechanical draughtsmen wanted; none but men who have had shop experience need apply; electrical knowledge not essential. Apply, with full particulars as to experience and salary received up to date, and as to salary now required, to E. G., care of S. L. Ferrar & Co., Hollinwood.

3. A young man wanted, in printing department of large manufacturing stationers in N.W. district. Must be a good time-keeper [1] and able to keep accurate costs of orders. Address

[1] One who keeps a record of the time spent by workmen at their work.

M. B., Box 5005, Postal Department, *Daily Telegraph*, Fleet Street, E.C.

4. Assistant clerk wanted, able to correspond in French and German. Reply by letter, stating age and salary required, to Box 62, Deacon's Advertising Offices, Leadenhall Street, E.C.

5. Clerk required in engineer's office, for posting and invoicing. Must be good writer and quick at figures. Aged about 19 or 20. Salary to start with 20 sh. per week. Address R. W. T., Box 5083, Postal Department, *Daily Telegraph*, Fleet Street, E.C.

6. Clerk wanted, aged 25 to 30, with thorough knowledge of book-keeping, to keep the accounts of a public charity and assist generally in the clerical work of the office. Salary £80 to £100. Apply, stating qualifications and experience, with copies of not more than three testimonials, to Institution, care of Messrs. Wills and Co., Ltd., 151 Cannon Street, E.C.

7. Wanted a youth as beginner in drawing office; three years' college, three years' shop experience; good references. P. O., Box 200, Manchester.

8. Clerk wanted in City office, between the age of 16 and 20. Preference given to those with knowledge of shipping and Custom House work. Apply, stating salary required, to L. C., care of Abbots', Eastcheap.

9. Junior clerk wanted, English, aged 18-20, with slight knowledge of French preferred. Good prospects. Address, stating full particulars and wages required, Alpha, Box 4957, Postal Department, *Daily Telegraph*, Fleet Street, E.C.

10. Engineering assistant wanted for District Engineer's office. Must be good leveller and surveyor, with good general experience and knowledge of sewerage. Salary £100 per annum. Apply, with copies of testimonials and statement of age and experience, to

J. B. FERGUSON
District Clerk
County Buildings, Hamilton.

11. Wanted, storekeeper for engineers' works employing about 500 hands; under-storekeeper in large works preferred. Address, stating age, experience, and wages expected, G5, offices of *Engineering*, 36 Bedford Street, Strand, W.C.

12. A vacancy for young gentlemen (aged 15 to 25) in

several engineering and electrical works, as pupils. Premiums £30 upwards. Address Box D, 78 Temple Chambers, City.

13. Mining engineering.—Vacancies for two pupils at colliery in Staffordshire; modern plant; small premium. For further information apply to "Mining Engineer," care of J. W. Vickers, 5 Nicolas Lane, E.C.

14. Wanted immediately a clerk for a large London firm; must have a knowledge of the details of pumping machinery and up-to-date methods of keeping costs. Address G. 42, offices of *Engineering*, London.

15. Junior clerk wanted, in wholesale office. Boy leaving school preferred. Address, stating age and salary expected, Box 5026, Postal Department, *Daily Telegraph*, Fleet Street.

16. Junior clerk wanted.—Young lady typist and shorthand writer, as clerk and correspondent in a ladies' outfitters establishment. Apply by letter to 8 Wardour Street, London, W.

17. Junior clerk or office-boy wanted, for solicitor's office. Apply by letter in own handwriting, stating salary required, Nelson, 145 Cannon Street, E.C.

18. Office boy wanted, in an accountant's office. One fresh from school preferred. Apply, in own handwriting, to X, 11 Queen Victoria Street, E.C.

19. Office boy wanted, in architect's office. Intelligent, good penman, with knowledge of shorthand preferred. Address, Walsingham House, Piccadilly, W.

20. Lady clerk.—Wanted a young lady, one just left school preferred, as cashier clerk. Apply in person at 160 New Bond Street, W.

Teachers and Private Tutors.

1. An English lady desires to learn German by correspondence with German lady. Apply, with statement of terms, etc., to G., Box 14, Hanwell office of this paper.

2. Wanted a Cambridge graduate, who can prepare senior boys in English subjects and mathematics for the Cambridge Senior Local by visits or by correspondence. Apply with statement of references to A., 20 Acton Green, London, W.

3. Wanted an experienced daily governess, who will be disengaged after Easter, and can produce good references. Apply, with statement of qualifications, to Beta, 24 Bedford Row, Bedford Park, Chiswick.

4. Wanted a gentleman who can give private tuition in

Italian on moderate terms. Address Asti, Box 28, Richmond office of this paper.

5. Wanted a private tutor for mathematics and science for a youth in preparation for London matriculation. Address A. D., Box 31, Acton office of this paper.

6. Wanted a youth as pupil-teacher in a school preparing for the Oxford Locals. Will be required to teach only the lower classes, and only in the forenoon. Can receive instruction in higher classes in the afternoon. Reply, with particulars as to age, qualifications, and salary expected, to M., 14 Fairfax Road, Willesden, N.

7. Wanted an assistant master in a school preparing for the examinations held by the College of Preceptors. Will be required to assist in the evening preparation as well as to teach during the hours of session. Salary, with board and lodgings, £80 a year. Apply, with all particulars as to certificates held, qualifications, and previous experience, if any. Address M., Box 14, Oxbridge, Middlesex.

8. Northern Polytechnic Institution, Holloway, London, N.—The governors are prepared to appoint an assistant demonstrator in electric machinery. Applications must be made before 30th March, on forms, which, together with detailed information on any point that the applicant may inquire about, may be had on application to the undersigned. Personal canvassing of the governors will be regarded as a disqualification. W. M. Macminn, *Clerk to the Governors.* 6th March 1901.

APPENDIX.—TRADE TERMS IN MORE OR LESS COMMON USE.

Abatement.—An amount deducted or cancelled from a bill of costs. Sometimes called a rebate.

(To) **accept a bill.**—To make oneself responsible for the payment of a Bill of exchange on its becoming due. (This is done by writing the word "accepted" across the bill and signing one's name under the word. For **Bill of exchange** see below.) One who accepts a bill of exchange is called an acceptor.

Account current.—An account that is not closed, but is still running on. ("Current" means literally "running.")

Accumulative.—A share in a commercial concern is said

to be accumulative, when the interest promised for each year accumulates, so that if the full amount is not paid in one year, the unpaid balance is added to the amount due in the following year or years.

Acquittance.—A written acknowledgment that acquits (releases) any one from debt or other liability: a receipt in full, that bars further demand.

Actuals.—Realised amounts, *i.e.* amounts actually received, as distinct from estimated ones.

Actuary.—One whose profession it is to calculate the risks incurred by an Insurance Company on account of fire, men's lives, etc.

Ad valorem.—Literally, "according to the value." This phrase (a bad coinage from Latin) is used to denote a duty or charge laid upon certain goods, at a certain rate per cent upon their value, as stated in their invoice; as an *ad valorem* charge or duty of 20 per cent.

Advance.—Money given before it is due; as an advance to a workman before the work is finished or before the right date of payment.

Agio (ā-ji-o).—The charge made by money-changers for exchanging one currency for another. The kind of money given in exchange is considered to be of more value than that which is received in exchange.

Alias.—Literally, "otherwise" (a Latin word). An assumed name.

Apprentice.—One who is bound by indentures or legal agreement to serve some company or individual for a certain time, with a view to learn the art or trade, in which the firm or individual is bound to instruct him.

Arrear, arrears (generally plural).—A balance which remains due to some one after a portion of the debt has been paid; as arrears of rent, arrears of wages, arrears of taxes, etc.

Asset, assets (generally plural).—The entire property of all kinds, belonging to a person, a company, or estate of some deceased person, is called the assets. When the word is applied to the estate of a bankrupt, his debts are called his liabilities; and what he can pay towards these are called his assets.

Assignee.—A person to whom some duty, business, or power is assigned. The word is generally applied to some person appointed, under a commission of bankruptcy, to manage the estate of a bankrupt for the benefit of his creditors.

Attorney.—One who is deputed or authorised by another to transact business for him, as to sell shares, take rents, etc. A private person (not being an attorney at law or solicitor) can receive such authority by what is called a Power of Attorney.

Audit (Lat. *auditus*, a hearing).—The examination of an account, with the hearing of the parties concerned, by persons appointed for that purpose, who compare the charges with the vouchers, examine the parties and witnesses, allow or reject the charges, and state the balance. A person appointed for such a purpose is called an **auditor.** (The examination, however, is often done without any "hearing" of witnesses.)

Balance. — The sum or amount necessary to balance (equalise) the two sides of an account; it may be either a debit balance or a credit balance. To strike a balance is to find out the difference between the debit and the credit side of an account.

Barter.—To take one kind of goods for another instead of taking money.

Bequest.—What is bequeathed by will, especially personal property: a legacy.

Bill.—Any written statement of particulars may be called a bill; as "a bill of fare," "a bill of mortality." In trade it usually means a statement (in gross or by items) of what is due from customer to dealer.

Bill of exchange.—A written order or request from one person or house to another, desiring the latter to pay within a specified time to some person (designated in the order) a certain sum of money therein named, and charge it to the account of the drawer. The person or house that draws or writes the bill is called the *drawer*. The person on whom it is drawn is called the *drawee*. The person to whom the money is to be paid is called the *payee*.

Bill of lading.—A written account of goods shipped by any person, signed by the agent of the owner of the vessel, or by the master of the vessel, acknowledging the receipt of the goods, and promising to deliver them safe at the place directed, dangers of the sea excepted.

Bill of parcels.—An account given by the seller to the buyer of the several articles purchased, with the price of each.

Bogus.—Anything that is false or not genuine; as a "bogus contract."

Bonâ fide.—In good faith; with no dishonest intention.

Bonded goods.—Imported merchandise of any kind, on which Custom House duties have to be paid. Such merchandise, until the duty is paid, is said to be "in bond." After the duty has been paid, the merchandise is said to be "out of bond."

Bonus.—(1) A gift to the shareholders of a joint-stock company, paid out of accumulated profits. (2) A premium paid for a charter or other privilege granted to a company. (3) Extra salary paid to employés on completion of a profitable year's trading.

Broker.—An agent employed as a middleman or negotiator to effect bargains or contracts between two other persons. He contracts in the names of those who employ him, and not in his own. The remuneration which he receives is called *brokerage.* There are many different classes of brokers, as bill-broker (one who buys or sells bills of exchange), insurance-broker, stock-broker, etc.

Bullion.—Uncoined gold or silver. The name is also given to coined gold or silver, when the coins are not counted and the amount is reckoned by weight in the mass.

Capital.—The sum invested or lent as distinct from the income or interest that it yields.

Cargo.—Any kind of merchandise carried in a boat or vessel.

Carriage.—The charge made for carrying goods.

Cash.—Ready-money; generally applied to coin or specie, but also applied to bank-notes, drafts, bonds, Government notes, and any other form of paper easily convertible into coin.

Cash account.—An account of money received, disbursed, and on hand. (A word used in book-keeping.)

Cash-book.—A book in which is kept a register of money received or paid out.

Cashier.—Cash-keeper: the officer who has charge of the payments and receipts of a bank or a mercantile company.

Charter.—The contract or instrument by which a ship is hired or let for a certain time, or by which some special privilege is conferred. "To charter a ship" means to hire it for a season.

Cheque.—A written order on a banker or broker to pay money in his keeping which belongs to the signer.

Cheque-book.—A book containing a collection of blank forms of cheques.

Commission.—The brokerage or allowance made to an

agent for transacting business for another; as a commission of ten per cent on sales. Commission is generally reckoned by a percentage.

Consignment.—The goods or commodities sent or addressed to any one at the same time and by the same conveyance. The person to whom they are sent or addressed is called the *consignee*.

Contraband.—Goods or merchandise, the importation or exportation of which is forbidden.

Contract.—A formal writing, which contains an agreement between two parties with a statement of the terms and conditions, and which serves as a proof of the obligation.

Counterfoil.—That part of a leaf left in a cheque-book, on which are noted the number, amount, and destination of the corresponding cheque; copy of invoice retained by tradesman, and anything of a similar nature.

Coupon.—A printed certificate or ticket to be presented for payment of interest due. Usually many tickets are printed together in a series on the same sheet. At each time of payment one of these tickets is cut off.

Credit.—This word is used in two senses for trade-purposes: (1) expectation of future payment for property transferred, or of fulfilment of promises given; as "to buy goods on credit," *i.e.* on trust. (2) A term used in book-keeping. The credit side of an account (as distinct from the debit side) is that on which are entered all items reckoned as values received from the party named at the head of the account.

Cumulative.—The same as *accumulative*, explained above.

Currency.—That which is in current circulation as having or representing a money-value. There may be a paper currency in the form of notes, or a specie currency in the form of coins.

Customer.—A person with whom a shop or business-house has dealings.

Customs.—Duties or tolls imposed by law on imports or exports.

Days of grace.—Those days (generally three) allowed to a debtor beyond the last day when payment of a bill or note became due. No legal action is taken against a debtor till after the days of grace, *i.e.* of favour or mercy, are completed.

Debenture.—A written document acknowledging a debt, entitling the lender to regular payment of interest for a certain period, and giving him a prior claim to shareholders.

Debit.—An entry on the debtor side of an account, the opposite to *credit* (2). See above.

Deficit.—Literally "it falls short"; Latin. The sum or amount by which loss exceeds gain or expenditure exceeds income.

(On) **Delivery.**—At the time when the package, parcel, or goods are delivered (handed over) to the person for whom they were intended; as "the goods must be paid for on delivery." "An undelivered order" is an order for goods which are still in transit or have not yet been delivered at their proper destination.

(On) **Demand.**—When the words "On Demand" are written on a document, it signifies that the amount named in the document is payable whenever payment is asked for.

Demurrage.—If a ship is detained in port beyond the time fixed for loading or unloading, the master or owner of the ship is entitled to some compensation from the owner of the merchandise for such delay or detention. This compensation is called demurrage. The same word is used for the compensation to be paid for delay in clearing goods from a railway.

Depositor.—One who makes a deposit of money in a bank.

Discount.—A deduction made for interest in advancing money before it is due. *True* discount is the interest, which, added to a principal, will equal the face-value of a note when the note becomes due. (The face-value of a note means the exact amount written on it without any addition for interest or reduction for discount.) *Bank* discount is a sum equal to the interest that is charged from the time of discounting the note until the note becomes due.

Discounting a bill. — Paying the amount stated in an account at some date before payment is due, after deducting the discount.

(To) **Dishonour.**—To refuse payment of a cheque or bill of exchange when it is presented.

Dividend.—A sum of money to be divided and distributed among the shareholders of a solvent company or among those entitled to share in a bankrupt estate.

Draft.—An order from one person to another, directing the payment of money.

Drawer, drawee.—See these words explained above under **Bill of exchange.**

Duty.—Lit. "that which is due." Any sum of money

required by Government to be paid on the importation, exportation, or consumption of goods. All such goods are said to be dutiable.

Endorse, indorse.—To write one's name on the back of a cheque to secure its being paid.

Exchange.—The process of settling accounts or debts between parties residing at a distance from each other, without the intervention of money, by exchanging orders or drafts. These are called Bills of Exchange. Such bills may be drawn (written) in one country and payable in another, in which case they are called *foreign bills*. Or they may be drawn and made payable in the same country, in which case they are called *inland bills*. The term "bill of exchange" is often abbreviated into "exchange"; as to buy or sell exchange.

Example.—A. in London is creditor to B. in New York; and C. in London owes D. in New York a like sum. A. in London draws a bill of exchange on B. in New York. C. in London purchases the bill from A., by which A. receives his debt due from B. in New York. C. transmits the bill to D. in New York, who receives the amount from B.

Excise.—A tax on articles produced and consumed in a country; an internal duty or impost, as distinct from "customs," which are a tax on merchandise imported or exported. The word "duty" covers both. An excise can also be levied on licenses to pursue certain trades and deal in certain commodities.

Execute.—To complete what is necessary to give validity to a document, as by signing, and perhaps sealing and delivering.

Face-value.—The exact amount expressed on a bill, note, bond, or other mercantile paper, no addition being made for interest and no deduction for discount.

Fee.—Not the same thing as commission. A commission is so much per cent on the value of a transaction, as "a commission of ten per cent on sales." A fee is of optional amount or of an amount agreed to beforehand between the parties or regulated by custom. A commission is what is paid to an agent or broker: a fee is what is paid for professional services, as "a doctor's fee," "a dentist's fee," a "solicitor's fee," etc.

Firm.—A commercial or manufacturing company.

Flotsam.—Goods which float, when cast into the sea intentionally or by shipwreck.

Foreclose.—To "foreclose" a mortgage is to obtain a judgment of court for the payment of an overdue mortgage, and in default of payment to take possession of the mortgaged property or expose it to sale to meet the mortgage-debt.

Freight.—A sum paid for the carriage of goods. Sometimes, but not often, used as a synonym of "cargo."

Freighter.—The man for whom the goods are carried and who pays the freight.

Goodwill.—The goodwill of a trade is the probability that the old customers will keep up their connection with the old place, after it has changed hands. So when a man sells his business, he sells the assumed goodwill of his customers with it. The price paid for "goodwill" (apart from the stock, the plant, or the premises) is often the equivalent of one year's average custom.

(To) **Honour.**—To honour a cheque or bill of exchange is to give cash for it as soon as it is presented.

Hypothecate.—To pledge, without delivery of possession or transfer of title, any kind of property as security for a debt or loan.

Indenture.—A mutual agreement in writing between two parties, each of whom has a counterpart or duplicate. A contract by which a youth binds himself as apprentice to a master is called Indentures of Apprenticeship.

Insolvent.—A man is insolvent, when he is not able to pay his debts as they fall due in the ordinary course of trade or business, and the actual or cash value of his assets is not equal to his liabilities.

Instrument.—A written document which binds any one to the performance of some act, contract, etc.

Insurance.—A contract whereby one party undertakes to indemnify another up to a certain specified amount against loss by fire, death, burglary, or other unavoidable accident.

The person who undertakes to pay in case of loss is called the *insurer.* The person protected is called the *insured.* The danger against which the insurer undertakes to protect the insured is called the *risk.* The sum which the insured pays for the protection is called the *premium.* The contract itself, when reduced to form, is called the *policy.*

Invoice. — A written account of the particulars of merchandise shipped or otherwise sent to a purchaser, with the prices stated.

Jetsam.—Goods which do not float, but sink, when they are cast into the sea. (Observe the difference between flotsam and jetsam.)

Lease, leasehold.—A lease is a contract for the tenure of property granted to any one by a landlord for a certain period and under certain conditions. The tenure itself is called a *leasehold.* The person to whom the lease is granted is called a *lessee.*

Legacy.—A gift of property, especially personal property, by will; a bequest. The person to whom the gift is made is called the *legatee.*

Legal tender.—That currency or money, which the law authorises a debtor to tender and requires a creditor to accept. The law varies in different countries. Thus in India silver money is legal tender up to any amount, while in England it is legal tender up to a very small sum.

License.—Formal permission granted to any one by the recognised authorities to perform certain acts or carry on a certain business, which without such permission would be illegal; as a license to keep a public-house, a license to sell gunpowder, a license to keep firearms, a license to practise medicine, etc. A person who has acquired such license is a *licentiate,* but this term is limited to callings of a higher class, such as medicine.

Lien.—A right possessed by any one to hold another's property until some claim is paid or satisfied.

Life annuity.—An annual payment, which will continue to be made to the end of one's life.

Life insurance.—An insurance against death; a contract by which the insurer undertakes, in consideration of his receiving a premium at stated intervals, to pay down a stipulated sum on the death of the insured person to his heirs.

Life-interest.—An interest or estate which lasts during a certain person's life, but does not pass to his heirs by inheritance.

Limitation.—There is a certain period prescribed by law, after which a claim for payment of debt is barred by the Statute of Limitation.

Limited company.—Called also a limited liability company. A company in which the liability of each shareholder is limited by the number of shares that he has taken, so that he cannot be called upon to contribute beyond the amount of his shares.

Liquidation.—To go into liquidation is to turn over the

assets and accounts of an individual or of a company to a trustee, in order that the several amounts of indebtedness may be ascertained and the assets applied towards their discharge.

Locum tenens.—Lit. "holding the place" of another: a temporary substitute.

Monopoly.—The exclusive power, right, or privilege (legally granted) of dealing in some article or of trading in some market. Thus the proprietor of a patented article has the sole power of arranging for the sale of that article.

Mortgage.—A conveyance of property as security for the payment of a debt or the performance of a duty, to become invalid as soon as the debt is paid or the duty performed. He who thus mortgages or pledges his property is called the *mortgager.* The man to whom the property is mortgaged or pledged is called the *mortgagee.* To *redeem* a mortgage is to take the mortgaged property out of the hands of the mortgagee by paying him down in full the sum that he lent on the security of that property. For the meaning of "*foreclose* a mortgage" see **Foreclose.**

Negotiable.—A draft, cheque, bill of exchange, or any other kind of commercial paper is said to be negotiable, when it can be bought or sold or transferred to another by endorsement.

Notary.—Generally called a "notary public." A public officer who attests deeds and other writings or copies of them, usually under his official seal, to make them authentic.

Note of hand.—See below under **Promissory Note.**

Paper currency.—See above under **Currency.**

Par.—Literally "equal." This word is used in three phrases. *At par,* at the original price, neither higher nor lower; as when shares are sold at exactly the same price at which they were bought. *Above par,* above the original price, at a premium. *Below par,* below the original price, at a discount.

Par value.—Face value. (See above under **Face-value.**)

Patent.—A written document, which secures to an inventor, for a term of years, the exclusive right to his invention.

Payee.—The person named in a bill or note, to whom or to whose order the amount is promised or directed to be paid.

Percentage.—The allowance, duty, rate of interest, discount, or commission on a hundred.

Permit.—A written permission given by some one who has authority to grant it; as, a permit to land goods subject to duty.

Personalty.—Personal as distinct from real property: property in cash, shares, etc.

Plant.—The whole of the machinery and apparatus employed in carrying on a trade or mechanical business.

Policy.—The writing or instrument on which an insurance is embodied. (See above under **Insurance.**)

Preference shares.—Those shares in a commercial concern, the owners of which can claim their dividend, and sometimes their capital, should the concern become bankrupt, in preference to ordinary shareholders. Preference shares are at a fixed rate, while ordinary shares may rise or fall. A dividend paid on preference shares is called a preferential dividend.

Premium.—Literally, a "reward" or "prize"; Latin. For trade purposes this word is used in four different senses. (1) A sum of money paid in advance to any one for teaching a trade or art to one who is apprenticed to him for that purpose. (2) A sum in advance of or in addition to the nominal or par value of an investment; as, "he sold his stock at a premium," *i.e.* for more than the original price. (3) The sum paid to an insurer for a policy: see above under **Insurance.** (4) A synonym of *bonus* (2): see above under **Bonus.**

Presentment (of a bill of exchange).—The offering of a bill to the drawee for acceptance or to the acceptor for payment.

Promissory note.—Sometimes called a Note of Hand. A written promise to pay to some person named, and at a time specified therein, or on demand, or at sight, a certain sum of money.

Pro ratâ.—Written in full this is *pro ratâ parte;* Latin, "according to estimated part or proportion." *Pro ratâ* thus means "proportionately"; according to the share, interest, or liability of each person concerned.

Pro tempore.—Often contracted to *pro tem.*, "for the time being," until something is permanently settled.

Proximo.—Often contracted to *prox.*; in the next month after the present; in the coming month.

Proxy.—One who is officially deputed to act or vote as the substitute for another.

Re.—Latin word, "in the matter," *i.e.* concerning. At the head of a business letter it is a common practice to name the subject, as "*Re* Sale of Coal."

Realty.—Real as distinct from personal estate; property in houses or land.

Rebate.—A deduction made from the original price: see above under **Abatement.**

Redeemable.—Capable of being repurchased; held under conditions permitting or compelling repurchase; as, "bonds redeemable four months after date," "bonds redeemable in gold."

Reference.—A person to be referred to. Before closing a bargain or contract with a stranger, it is usual to ask him for references, *i.e.* the names of persons to whom reference can be made as a guarantee to his integrity, capacity, or other kind of fitness.

Reimburse.—To pay back an equivalent to what has been taken, lost, or expended.

Remittance.—Money sent, transmitted, or remitted to a distant place in satisfaction of a demand or in discharge of an obligation.

Retainer.—Called also a "retaining fee." A fee paid to engage a lawyer to maintain a cause or prevent his being employed by the opposite party in the case.

Royalty.—A duty paid by a manufacturer to the owner of a patent, or by a publisher to the author of a book, for each article or each copy that is sold. Also a percentage paid to the owner of an article by one who hires the use of it.

Salvage.—The compensation allowed to persons who voluntarily assist in saving a ship or her cargo from loss at sea.

Schedule.—A written or printed scroll of paper; especially a formal list or inventory attached to a larger document, as to a will, a lease, a statute, etc.

Security.—Something given, deposited, or pledged to make certain the fulfilment of an obligation, the performance of a contract, the payment of a debt, or the like. The word is sometimes applied to a person who becomes security or makes himself responsible for another.

Share.—One of a certain number of equal portions, into which any property or invested capital is divided.

Sinecure.—An office or position requiring little or no work of the holder, but giving him a regular salary.

Sine die.—Lit. "without day," no day being mentioned. An engagement is said to be postponed *sine die*, when no day is named or hinted at for resuming it.

Sleeping partner.—A partner who takes no part in the active business of a company or partnership, but is entitled to a portion of the profits or subject to a portion of the losses. He is sometimes called a dormant or silent partner.

Tariff.—A schedule or system of rates, charges, etc.; as, a tariff of fees, railway fares, etc.

Tender.—An offer or proposal made for acceptance; as, a tender of a loan, of service, of a contract, of a commodity, etc.

Testator.—One who makes a will or testament, which will come into force at his death. Feminine form, *testatrix.*

Ultimo.—" In the last month"; Latin: the month preceding the present month, as distinct from *proximo*, or the month following.

Underwriter.—One who writes his name under an insurance policy, especially a marine policy: an insurer.

Usufruct.—The right of using and enjoying the profits of an estate, without impairing the substance.

Wind up.—To wind up a company is to arrange and adjust its affairs for a final settlement of all existing claims.

THE END